Few skiers realise the great beauty and vast variety of
dendrites photographed by Wilson Bentley.

THE GUINNESS BOOK OF

In memory of Antoinette

THE GUINNESS
BOOK OF
SKIING

PETER LUNN

1931–7
Competitor in seven World Championships
(1934 9th slalom, 1935 10th downhill, 1936 9th downhill)

1936
Captain British Olympic Ski Team
(15th downhill, 13th slalom, 12th combined)

1972
Jumped 66ft (20m) Princes Water Ski Club Championships

1982
2nd Butser Grass Ski Club Men's Championship

1978–83
Competitor the Inferno Downhill Race
(1981 810th out of 1381)

GUINNESS SUPERLATIVES LIMITED
2 CECIL COURT LONDON ROAD ENFIELD

Editor: Josie A. Holtom
Design and layout: Print-Ability
Line diagrams: Jan Holtom
First published 1983
© Peter Lunn and Guinness Superlatives Limited
1983

Typeset in 10/11½pt Plantin and 9/10pt Univers by
Fakenham Photosetting Ltd., Fakenham, Norfolk.
Printed and bound in Spain by Mateu Cromo Artes
Graficas, S.A. Pinto (Madrid)

Guinness is a registered trademark of Guinness
Superlatives Ltd.

ISBN 0–85112–219–1

British Library CIP Data
Lunn, Peter
Guinness Book of Skiing
1. Skis and skiing
I. Title
796.93   GV854

+--------------------------------+
| *Also by Peter Lunn* |
| HIGH-SPEED SKIING |
| EVIL IN HIGH PLACES |
| A SKIING PRIMER |
+--------------------------------+

Picture Acknowledgments

Jakob Vaage, Holmenkollen Ski Museum,
Norway 10, Popperfoto 11, 40, 46–7, 53, 54,
58–9, 61, 63, 65, 66, 81, 82, 85, 98, 109 left, 113,
116 top, 122, 140, Mürren Tourist Office 30, 86,
142, Austrian Tourist Association 21, 34, 77 top,
104, 130 bottom, Lunn Poly 23, Hotel Eiger,
Mürren, Switzerland 25, Max Amstutz 29; this
photograph was kindly sent to the author by Air
Vice-Marshal Howard Ford, Central Press 42–3,
49, 64, Keystone Press 57, 62, 88 top, Yugoslav
National Tourist Office 68, 69, Swedish Tourist
Office 73, Swiss National Tourist Office 75, 77
bottom, 126, 130 top, 164, 167, Harper & Row
92, Wilson Bentley 94 and endpapers,
Kurverwaltung Oberstdorf 74, 169, Alta Tourist
Office, USA 99, 163, German National Tourist
Office 70, 124, National Council of Tourism in
Lebanon 108, George Konig 76, 78 top left and
right, 129, The Photographers' Library 111,
Gerry Cranham 78 bottom left, All-Sport 78
bottom right, 112 bottom, Wengen Tourist Office
96, *Snow Structures & Ski Fields* by G. Seligman
(1936) 101, 102, 109 right, 115, 116 bottom, 118,
119, French Tourist Office 112 top, Librairie
Delgrave (from Samivel) 114, Hart Ski Mfg. Co.
USA 136, Ski Club of Gt. Britain 171.

Jacket design from an idea by Peter Holtom.

Frontispiece Skiing on the piste above
Garmisch-Partenkirchen, West Germany. (*German
Tourist Office*)

Contents

Acknowledgements

Throughout my researches for this book I have received invaluable assistance from Elisabeth Hussey, Editor of *Ski Survey*. Sigge Bergman delved into his unique archive of racing records to help me with the Results Appendix; in this area I also received assistance from S. Theisen of the International Ski Federation and from Heinz Single of the German Grass Ski Technical Committee. I am indebted to Arnold Kaech, editor of *FIS Bulletin*, for many enlightening conversations about the skiing world. Roland Huntford, author of *Scott and Amundsen*, provided me with information about the use of skis in Polar exploration. Jakob Vaage, Director of the Holmenkollen Ski Museum, did the same about the history of Norwegian skiing. Emili Miura, in her excellent English, answered questions on behalf of her father, Yuichiro Miura. I am indebted for many helpful comments to my step-mother, Phyllis Lunn, who read my manuscript as I wrote it. Finally, I would like to say how much this book owes in clarity of presentation to the Guinness Superlatives editor, Josie Holtom.

PETER LUNN

Abbreviations

Andorra	AND	Israel	ISR
Argentina	ARG	Italy	ITA
Australia	AUS	Japan	JPN
Austria	AUT	Jugoslavia	JUG
Belgium	BEL	Korea	KOR
Bolivia	BOL	D.P.R. Korea	PRK
Brazil	BRA	Lebanon	LIB
Bulgaria	BUL	Liechtenstein	LIE
Canada	CAN	Luxembourg	LUX
Chile	CHI	Monaco	MON
China	CHN	Mongolia	MGL
China/Taiwan	CTA	Morocco	MAR
Costa Rica	CRC	Netherlands	NED
Czechoslovakia	TCH	New Zealand	NZE
Cyprus	CYP	Norway	NOR
Denmark	DAN	Poland	POL
Finland	FIN	Portugal	POR
France	FRA	Rep. di San Marino	RSM
Germany	GER	Roumania	RUM
Federal Republic of Germany	BRD	Senegal	SEN
German Democratic Republic	DDR	Soviet Union	SOV
Great Britain	GBR	Spain	SPA
Greece	GRE	Sweden	SWE
Hungary	HUN	Switzerland	SUI
Iceland	ISL	Turkey	TUR
Iran	IRA	United States of America	USA
Ireland	IRE		

PART I

HISTORY

▲ Three skiers carved on rock in north-west Russia about 1000 BC.

▼A line of six skiers carved on rock in north-west Russia about 1000 BC.

1 Prehistoric Skiers

The oldest sports are those that have their roots in man's natural needs, in his struggle to survive and improve his living conditions. These sports were practised out of necessity long before they were practised for pleasure. They include running, various forms of combat, riding, boating, and also skiing.

Finds of Prehistoric Skis

Wood exposed to the air rots quickly, but wood that has fallen into a bog, and thus become protected from the atmosphere, can last for thousands of years. A number of prehistoric skis have been found in Sweden, Norway and Finland.

The Hoting Ski

The oldest find, about two-thirds of a single ski, was at Hoting, Sweden, in 1921. It is estimated to be about 4500 years old, so it was in use around 2500 BC. It is the world's oldest ski and indeed, it seems improbable that any other sport can claim a piece of equipment which is older.

The Hoting ski is complete in its length but about a third of its breadth has disappeared. It is made of pine and is 111cm (3ft 8in) long. It is calculated to have been 9.5cm (3¾in) broad at the upturn, 10.4cm (4in) at the foot space and 10cm (4in) at the rear. So it was broadest at the centre, the opposite to modern skis which are narrowest at the centre.

The front end narrows to a rounded tip which rises 2.4cm (1in) above the ground. The ski is thin for its breadth, about 1cm (½in) at each end. The thickness gradually increases towards the centre, where it is 2cm (¾in).

The foot space was made by scooping out the wood. There is a hole through which a retaining strap could be threaded.

Altogether a pretty sophisticated piece of equipment for 2500 BC.

The Kalvträsk Skis and Ski Stick

The skis found at Kalvträsk in Sweden in 1924, though 500 years less old than the Hoting ski, are remarkable because they consisted of two complete skis and a ski pole. The wood of one ski, however, was in such a crumbly state that it came to pieces during transportation from the finding place.

The complete skis are 204cm (6ft 8in) long, considerably longer than the Hoting ski. At the centre of each ski are four holes, placed in pairs one behind the other, for the binding. This would have been a single cord, running in a loop above the skis front and back, where it would have gone over the toe and over the heel. Under the ski the cord would have run lengthwise and so would not have impeded movement.

The pole is 156cm (5ft 1½in) long, which includes a 50cm (1ft 8in) scoop at the bottom, which could have been used for the shovelling of snow.

The Rödöy Rock Carvings

Two rock carvings of skiers, one of them very incomplete, have been found at Rödöy, a Norwegian island just north of the Arctic Circle. The complete carving shows a figure standing on skis which are very long in comparison with his height. He is wearing a headdress with hare-like ears, which may have represented some sort of hunting magic. In his hands he carries a pole with a right-angled hook at the bottom, which may have made it useful as a hunting weapon. He is in a good skiing stance with his knees forward over the toes.

The Rödöy rock carvings are thought to have been made about 2500 BC, the same time as the Hoting ski.

The Lake Onega and White Sea Rock Carvings

About 24 rock carvings that depict skiers have been found around Lake Onega and the White Sea in north-west Russia. The rocks, on which two of the most remarkable were carved, have been detached from their original site near the White Sea and transported to the Hermitage Museum in Leningrad.

One rock carving shows three figures on skis, each holding a long single pole. The figures are in profile, so that each is shown as having only one leg and one ski. They are obviously naked. As winter temperatures around the White Sea can drop to below −40 °C

($-40\,°F$), anybody who went skiing naked around there would not last very long. W. J. Raudonikas published a two volume work on the Lake Onega and White Sea rock carvings (Moscow 1936 and 1938), which is written partly in Russian and partly in French; he has described them as *Trois figures humaines phalliques en skis*. But even being phallic does not keep one warm in those sort of temperatures. Perhaps the three figures were gods and impervious to the cold.

The other rock carving depicts a line of six skiers, again in profile. They are far less robust than the three phallic figures. Some of the skiers seem to be standing on one ski and waving the other in the air. It is probable that what seems to be a leg is in reality a piece of clothing streaming out in the wind.

As with the phallic figures, each skier carries a long pole. In both carvings these poles are shown as having a bulbous thickening at the end. This could have been to prevent the pole sinking deeply into the snow, as does the ring on a modern ski pole or perhaps it was intended for use as some sort of weapon.

These rock carvings cannot be accurately dated. Soviet experts think they were made some time between 2000 and 1000 BC, but the opinion has been expressed that they are as recent as 500 BC. In any case they are later than the Rödöy rock carvings.

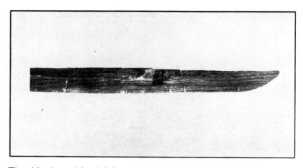

The Hoting ski which was in use about 2500 BC.

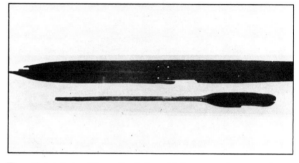

The Kalvträsk ski and stick which were in use about 2000 BC.

The Rödöy rock carving thought to have been made about 2500 BC. ▼

2 The Ski in History, Literature and Myth

It is difficult to appreciate the age of skiing. 2500 BC is further in time from Christ than we are AD. The person who, about 2500 BC used what we now call the Hoting ski, and the person who, about the same time, scratched on Rödöy island the rock picture of a man skiing, were some 300km (186 miles) apart, which shows that the practice of skiing was not an isolated event.

Although skiing is several thousand years old, it has been an organised sport for only just over 100 years, a tiny fraction of its total history. But only of this last 100 years can one write a meaningful history of skiing, that is a history recording development with one event leading to another. Before that there is isolated evidence of skiing in the scanty records that remain. We are inclined to think of the Hoting and Kalvträsk skis as contemporary but the difference in time between them is about the same as that between the fifteenth century and our own day. From our earliest evidence of skiing to the time when it became an organised sport cannot be a continuous story. It can only be a collection of isolated facts, strung out in date order, and that is the inevitable nature of this chapter.

The Scrithiphini

'But among the barbarians who are settled in Thule, one nation only, who are called Scrithiphini, live a kind of life akin to that of beasts.'

The quotation is from Book 2, Chapter 15, of *The Gothic War* by the Byzantine historian Procopius, whose book, written in Greek, was completed about the year AD 552. In the few lines that Procopius devotes to the Scrithiphini and their curious habits there is absolutely nothing that could suggest skiing, but it is assumed that Procopius's Scrithiphini are the people whom later writers called the Skridfinns. Skrid is an old German word for to glide. It is argued that Procopius was referring to Finns who glided. On this somewhat tenuous basis he is mentioned in histories of skiing as the author of the first surviving reference to skiing.

It is in fact doubtful whether Procopius's Scrithiphini is even the oldest surviving reference to the Skridfinns.

As for more than half a century Procopius has figured in both German and British histories of skiing, he has by now perhaps earned his place there by a sort of squatter's rights. But his relevance is not clear.

Early Chinese References to Skiing

On the other hand, early Chinese references to skiing show a direct knowledge of the sport. They are significant because they tell us things we would not otherwise know about the ancient use of skis in the Far East. As the German ski historian, Carl Luther, wrote, the Chinese were ahead of the European centres of civilisation in learning about the use of skis by the peoples to the north of them.

According to Vol 4 of Dr Joseph Needham's *Science and Civilisation in China*, Chinese texts 'indicate conclusively that the knowledge the Chinese had of ski and snowshoes came from their contact with the northern Turkic peoples early in the seventh century AD'.

Dr Needham quotes from the texts a reference to a branch of the Thieh-lo tribe which first brought tribute in AD 629 and who 'riding on pieces of wood, hunt deer over the ice'. He also quotes a reference to a tribe of Turkic nomads from north of Lake Baikal, who sent representatives to the Chinese court in AD 640. 'As their country is so soon covered with frost and snow, they used wooden boards . . . with which to glide over the piled up ice.' The dimensions of the wooden boards are given; they correspond to 15cm (6in) wide and 2.10m (6ft 11in) long.

Carl Luther in his *1952 British Ski Year Book* article, quotes a reference to skiers from the official history of the Tang dynasty (AD 618–907): 'The wooden-horse Turks are accustomed to skim over the ice on so-called wooden horses, that is, on sledges (or runners) which they bind to their feet to run over the ice. And they take poles as supports, and push themselves rapidly forward.'

Ull and Skadi

When we move from the Mediterranean and China to Scandinavia, we move to an area where even the myths are based on practical experience of skiing.

Late in the twelfth and early in the thirteenth century, two scholars set out to collect and record the old stories about the pagan gods and goddesses. One of them was a Dane, Saxo, who was later given the second name Grammaticus. His *Gesta Danorum* is a history of Denmark from the earliest times to his own age. The other was Snorri Sturluson; about AD 1220 he wrote in his native Icelandic a book, known as the *Prose Edda*, which contains accounts of the old myths.

In addition to these two sources, there is the *Elder* or *Poetic Edda*, a collection of anonymous poems discovered in an Icelandic farm house. These poems were not put into writing till after 1100, most of them probably between 1150 and 1250.

There is not much in any of these three written records about Ull, whom Saxo calls Ollerus. But Ull has survived in many place names, so he may have had a wider following than the written record would suggest. He seems to have been skilled with the bow and with his skis. He is referred to as a god of hunting. Snorri Sturluson also refers to him as Onduras, the god of skiing.

The Elder Edda refers to Skadi as Ondurdis, the goddess of skiing. She came from the snow covered mountains, but she married Njord, who came from the warm sea coast. At first they agreed to divide their time between a mountain home and one on the sea coast, spending nine nights consecutively in each. But after a time Skadi went back alone to permanent residence in the mountains, where she hunted on skis armed with a bow. This has been described as the first divorce brought about by love of skiing!

Some skiers wear little medals depicting Ull or Skadi. Others prefer a medal of Saint Bernard, founder of the famous hospices on the passes that bear his name; he is the patron saint of skiers and mountaineers.

The Böksta Memorial Stone

A memorial stone at Böksta near Uppsala in Sweden shows a hunting scene with a skier holding a bow and arrow. The surrounding inscription states that the memorial is to one Aist or Est, and that it was erected by his parents and brothers.

It is estimated that the memorial was made about AD 1050. The stone is 2.60m (8ft 6in) high and 2.25m (7ft 4½in) wide. In the seventeenth century it was smashed into five or six pieces. It was restored in the nineteenth century but the picture had been badly damaged.

A 19th century painting showing the future King Håkon being carried to safety across the Dovre mountains in 1206.

The Sagas

The sagas were the outgrowth of a long oral tradition. They were recorded in writing at various dates between the middle of the twelfth century and the beginning of the fifteenth. This was done primarily in Iceland, where settlers began to arrive from Norway in the ninth century. The sagas have the outward form of history and biography, but are often largely fictitious.

The sagas describe a number of skiing episodes. The earliest concerns King Harald Fairhair, who ruled in Norway at the end of the ninth and the beginning of the tenth century. He is described as being with his court near a mountain:

'What is that,' he asks, 'that comes down the mountain like a whirlwind? Could that be a man on skis?'

It was indeed a skier, a man called Vighard from north Norway. He stopped before the king to greet him, and the king accepted his greeting with pleasure, because he saw that this must be a man of formidable qualities.

The Rescue of Håkon Håkonson

King Håkon, who ruled in Norway from 1217 to 1263, is generally regarded as one of Norway's greatest kings, and skis played a role in saving him for the throne. The saga of King Håkon, written about 1270, describes how in 1206, when he was a two-year-old child, he was in danger from rival claimants to his father's throne. Two skiers, who were loyal to the reigning family, rescued the young Håkon Håkonson,

as he was then called, by carrying him in a snowstorm across the Dovre mountains to safety.

Gustav Vasa

In sixteenth century Sweden skis again played a decisive historical role. The Danes had defeated the Swedes in 1520 and executed 82 leading Swedes in Stockholm; this became known as the Stockholm blood bath. At Mora, to the north-west of Stockholm, Gustav Vasa tried to rally the people for a war of liberation. His appeal was refused. Without support, he had no option but to flee the Danes; he left Mora on snowshoes for the Norwegian border.

After he had gone, the people changed their minds; they sent two skiers to pursue Gustav Vasa and tell him that they were now prepared to throw themselves into the support of his cause. On New Year's Day 1522, the two skiers caught up with Gustav Vasa at Sälen, and he returned with them to Mora. From there he launched his successful struggle against the Danes. In 1523 he became King of Sweden, founding the Vasa dynasty.

The Vasa race was founded in 1922 to celebrate the 400th anniversary of this event. For practical reasons, it is held from Sälen to Mora, that is in the opposite direction to that taken by the two skiers. The distance is 85.8km (53 miles), and this is now the most famous and prestigious cross-country course in the world. Among the famous ski races, the Vasa is unique; it is longer than any of the others and it has also attracted record entries of over 10,000 competitors.

Hunting on skis. Olaus Magnus.

Olaus Magnus

Olaus Magnus was a Swedish Catholic priest, who was born in 1490. While still in his twenties he was sent north on an ecclesiastical mission, during which he learnt something about skiing. In 1523 he went into exile; he died at Rome in 1557.

In 1539 he produced in Venice his *Carta Marina*, a map of the north on which a skier is shown. In his *Opera Breve*, the explanatory notes accompanying the map, there is a picture of two men and a woman hunting on skis with the following text: 'The picture below shows how the people who live under the Pole, men as well as women, go out on the hunt with a certain type of wooden pieces under their feet, these wooden pieces being as long as the persons are tall; they enable them to travel so fast that they can on occasions overtake the wild animals.'

The illustration shows the hunters on pieces of wood which have some resemblance to skis. They are long, though shoulder rather than head height; they are sharply pointed. But they differ totally from skis in one very important respect. They are shown as being cut off immediately behind the heel, so that the skier is shown as standing on the very back of the skis, with no running surface behind him. The skis in Olaus Magnus's illustrations have been described as beaked shoes.

In 1555 Olaus Magnus produced in Rome his history of the northern peoples, *Historia de gentibus sep-* *tentrionalibus*, in which he writes about the Skrikfinns (often referred to as the Skridfinns): who instead of shoes, wear under their feet pieces of wood which are pointed at the front. Each carries a pole to guide himself and on these pieces of wood he 'swiftly traverses hill and vale, taking his headlong course as he curves to his will.'

The pictures in the book again show skis as beaked shoes. It was these illustrations which had an abiding effect on the way in which people imagined skis. They were frequently reproduced, and other artists took their concept of skis from them.

The effect of Olaus Magnus's illustrations lasted for 400 years; and this despite the existence of other, more accurate, pictures of skis.

The Skiers of Carniola

So far all the evidence of European skiing has been confined to the far north. In 1689 we get the first evidence of skis actually being used – as opposed to described, or depicted – south of Norway, Sweden, Finland and northern Russia. That year *Die Ehre des Herzogtums Krain* by Johann Valvasor was published in Laibach, now known as Ljubljana. *Krain* is the German for Carniola, which is part of Slovenia, one of the republics making up Yugoslavia. It was at one time a distinct district within the Austro-Hungarian empire; Carniola was centred around Ljubljana.

Baron Sigmund von Herberstein, Ambassador of the Holy Roman Empire, on his way to Moscow. From his *Rerum Moscoviticarum commentarii* published in Vienna 1549.

Valvasor writes that in certain parts of Carniola the peasants have a remarkable invention, such as he had never seen anywhere else, which enables them to come down high mountains with unbelievable speed.

He describes how the peasants 'take two wooden boards' about 1.50m (4ft 11in) long. 'Such wooden boards are turned up at the front, and have at the middle a leather strap into which one puts one's foot. On each foot one puts one of these wooden boards.'

The peasant, Valvasor continues, takes in his hands a stout stick, on which he leans back and which he uses for steering himself. In this way he is able to come down the steepest mountains, twisting and turning to avoid trees and other obstacles on the slope.

The peasants of Carniola knew how to make skis; they also knew how to do turns when skiing downhill, a technique which Mathias Zdarsky would laboriously rediscover at the end of the nineteenth century, when enthusiasm for skiing eventually spread from Norway to the Alps. Very quickly after that skiing became a sport with a mass following wherever people had, or could get, access to snow covered mountains.

Why, over the long centuries, did skiing never spread from Carniola to the rest of the Alps? For centuries the skiers of Carniola kept alive a tradition which never spread beyond the tiny confines of their land. They had no effect on history, and yet this long and isolated tradition of skiing is one of history's most fascinating curiosities.

Snowshoe Thompson

Snowshoe Thompson was born Jon Thorsteinson in the Telemark district of Norway in 1827. At the age of 10 he came to America with his parents and his name was changed to John Thompson, sometimes spelt Thomson.

In 1851 the gold rush brought him to California, but he soon gave up mining for work on a cattle farm. In those days there was no mail in winter across the Sierra Nevada, a range of mountains rich in snow and some

500km (310 miles) in length. John Thompson remembered the skis he had seen in Norway as a child and made himself a pair out of oak. They were about 3m (9ft 10in) long and weighed about 11kg (24lb), he used a single pole which was about 2m (6ft 7in) long.

He volunteered to carry the mail across the Sierra Nevada and began doing so in 1856. The trip each way took him two or three days and he had to sleep out en route. He carried loads of up to 45kg (99lb).

John Thompson carried the mail backwards and forwards across the Sierra Nevada till his death in 1876, that is for 20 years. There was a special stamp for the mail he carried, **the first stamp** by some 50 years to show a figure on skis. The stamp bears the superscription 'Snow-shoe Express', and he became known as Snowshoe Thompson.

In the history of skiing there are few figures more remarkable than John Thompson. He made his own skis with nothing to guide him except childhood memory. They were too long and too heavy, but he taught himself how to use them. With this primitive equipment, and a technique which must have been equally primitive, he became a ski mountaineer long before the history of ski mountaineering is generally thought to have begun, which was in the early 1890s when skiers tentatively began to cross the Alpine passes. Preceding all later ski mountaineers by decades stands the giant figure of John Thompson.

Lorna Doone

If a classic is defined as a book that has remained in print for over 100 years, then *Lorna Doone* by R. D. Blackmore is a classic. It was first published in 1869. As it is the only classic to contain a description of skiing, it rates a mention here.

Lorna Doone is of course no sort of evidence for the periodically repeated, but totally undocumented, statement that skis were used in south-west England some 300 years ago.

The first skier on a postage stamp. John Thompson carries the mail across the Sierra Nevada, USA.

9

3 Skiing Becomes a Sport

Sondre Norheim 1825–97

There were, of course, isolated competitions in the early history of skiing. But Sondre Norheim is rightly revered as the father of competitive skiing. The flame for the 1952 and 1960 Winter Games was lit, not at Olympia, but in the simple cottage where Norheim was born. No other sportsman of any sort has become associated in such a way with the Olympic flame.

Norheim was born of poor parents in Morgedal, a village in the Telemark district of Norway in 1825. A man of very little education he quickly displayed a genius for all aspects of skiing. In particular, he discovered the essential and basic principle of modern jumping. About 1840, while he was still in his teens, he started to jump, not on to a flat surface as hitherto, but, more daringly, on to a slope. This discovery, of course, made it possible to cover much greater distances. According to Fridtjof Nansen's *Paa Ski Over Grönland*, Norheim is reputed to have jumped 96 Norwegian feet, which is just over 30m (98ft 5in). Even allowing that this figure may be an exaggeration, it was certainly many years before anybody else was jumping such distances. The first world record recognised as such was 23.5m (77ft 1in) by Torjus Hemmestveit, a pupil of Norheim's, in 1879. And this record stood till 1900 when Olaf Tandberg jumped 35.5m (116ft 5in).

Norheim fashioned equipment to match his skills.

Sondre Auersen Norheim, the Norwegian who is revered as the father of competitive skiing.

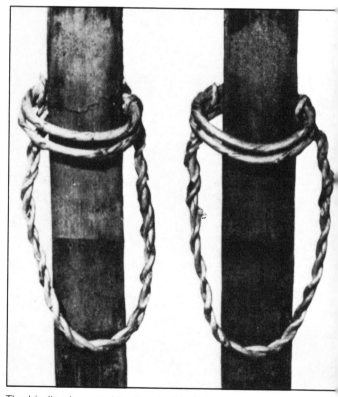

The binding invented by Sondre Norheim: a reconstruction by Jakob Vaage, Director of the Holmenkollen Ski Museum, Norway.

The old fashioned telemark turn invented by Sondre Norheim. It fell into disuse in the 1930s but was revived in the 1970s by cross-country skiers.

He was the first person to make a binding with a heel strap and thus gain some measure of control over his skis. His binding was at the time a very great improvement on anything else available, but the binding of today bears no resemblance whatever to it. By contrast, Norheim produced an innovation in the shape of the actual ski itself, which has ever since been central to all ski design, whether the skis are for downhill or cross-country. He was the first person to give the ski its waisted shape.

In 1868 Sondre Norheim left the Telemark district in order to compete in the Christiania ski competitions, (Christiania is the old name for Oslo). Thus this very simple man carried his skills from the narrow confines of his native district into the wider world.

The Christiania Ski Competitions

In the first year, 1866, this had been a demonstration rather than a formal competition. A peasant, Elling Baekken, arrived from Hönefoss, some 80km (50 miles) away, having issued a challenge that the skiers of Christiania should match their skills against his. He skied downhill, making a few small jumps, and he also demonstrated a little cross-country skiing. A number of Christiania skiers tried to imitate him but none could achieve his standard. He was declared the winner, and a collection was made for him.

This strange event was destined to go into history, because it was the first of a series that would develop into the oldest ski competition in the world, and also the most prestigious apart from the Olympics and the World Championships.

Elling Baekken was invited to return the next year, 1867, when a proper competition was organised. The course, which had to be covered three times, was about 550m (601yds) in length. It included cross-country skiing and downhill; during the latter the competitors had to go over a jump. Marks were awarded, not only for speed, but also for steadiness, style, and what was described as 'sportingly correct use of the stick'. The Christiania skiers had obviously put in some intensive practise during the preceding year because Elling Baekken only finished fourth.

But standards were still very low. A contemporary account describes how competitors of this period relied on their single long, thick pole, not only to reduce speed, but also for support, leaning their weight right back against the pole dragging in the snow. He also describes how frightened competitors looked as they approached the jump, how frantically they tried to reduce speed with the pole, and how they did not try to leap, but simply plopped over the jump, covering a bare 4 to 5m (13–16ft).

These were the conditions when Norheim arrived in 1868 with his skills, with his revolutionary equipment, and carrying one small pole, which he used for balance downhill, to help him along when on the level or going uphill, but never to brake or support himself on the descent.

Norheim, of course, won the competition. But it was not just that. This man of 42 years amazed the Oslo skiers by the standard of his skills, his skills in jumping, across country and also on the descent. His superb technique, his waisted skis, his bindings with a heel strap, all meant that he could manoeuvre his skis in ways hitherto quite unimagined. To one of his turns they gave the name of his district, Telemark. To the other they gave the name of their own city, Christiania, something which a later Norwegian writer criticised: the Christiania skiers had no idea of the christiania turn, any more than they had of the telemark, till they saw Norheim perform it; they had no right to give the turn a name that could be taken to mean that it had originated with the Christiania skiers instead of having been introduced to them by Norheim.

Norheim's performance was all the more remarkable in that he was so much older than the other competitors. He competed again in 1871, when he finished second, and then, for a third and last time, in 1875. He was by then 49; the other competitors were between 20 and 25. On this occasion Norheim finished sixteenth. In 1884 he emigrated to the USA, where he died in 1897.

The Development of the Christiania Ski Competitions

Norheim's example gave an incalculable impulse to skiing as a sport and this was reinforced by a number of his pupils from Telemark who competed at Christiania in later years.

After 20 years there was a radical change in the standards for technique and equipment set by Norheim. The Finns discovered that two poles were an advantage for cross-country skiing. In 1887 for the first time in the Christiania competitions, a competitor, Ernst Bjerknaes, used two poles. This, a reporter at the time boldly prophesied, 'has a future'.

Iverslökka, where the first Christiania ski competitions were held, has long been absorbed into Oslo. In 1879 the competitions were transferred to the Huseby Hill, and the King's Cup, now over 100 years old, was first initiated. The jump and the cross-country race were still one single event. Competitors went over the jump in the course of their cross-country race and marks were given for style as well as for speed. In 1883 the event was separated into a jumping competition and a cross-country race, but the two were regarded as merely parts of one single event. For 50 years until 1933 it would not be possible to compete in the one unless one also competed in the other. The King's Cup continued to be awarded to the skier who did best in the two events combined and had, for a long time, far more prestige than victory in either the jumping or the cross-country.

Holmenkollen

In 1892 the events were transferred to Holmenkollen, where they have remained ever since. There was a cross-country race over 17km (10½ miles) and a jumping competition. A long distance race was introduced in 1900 and was held over a distance of 30km (18½ miles). In 1902 this was lengthened to 50km (31 miles), which has remained the classic distance for the really long event.

From their foundation in 1892 till the first Winter Olympics in 1924, the Holmenkollen events were accepted as the most important competitions in the skiing world. Merely to have competed at Holmenkollen was a title to recognition, but to state this still does not give any idea just what has been the position of Holmenkollen in Norway, a position with which Wimbledon in tennis, Henley in rowing and Bisley in shooting cannot compare. The Holmenkollen jump is only used once a year, on Holmenkollen Day. Between 1940 and 1945, while Norway was occupied, the jump was never used. Anyone who was present at the first Holmenkollen Day after the war, and could feel the charged emotion of the vast crowd as the King made his traditional appearance, will know beyond all doubt that the position of Holmenkollen in Norwegian national feeling is something quite unique. No other sporting occasion can compare with it as a symbol of national identity.

4 Fridtjof Nansen 1861-1930

Fridtjof Nansen is a man who achieved fame in many fields. Several biographies of him have been written, but I have failed to find one which mentioned the profound impact he had on skiing. For it was due to him, and in particular his book *Paa Ski Over Grönland*, which was first published in 1890, that skiing spread from Scandinavia to the rest of the world.

Nansen was born near Oslo on 10 October 1861, and learnt to ski as a child. His mother was a keen skier when skiing was regarded as unfeminine, and even as slightly improper. In 1881 and 1884 Nansen competed on Huseby Hill, the predecessor of Holmenkollen, winning minor prizes on each occasion. At the time of the 1884 event, he was working as curator of the museum in Bergen, and he made the long journey to and from Christiania (Oslo) on ski.

Unexplored Greenland

In the early 1880s the interior of Greenland was a blank on the map. Indeed a legend persisted of an ice-free interior, fertile oases amid the surrounding ice. This mysterious interior of Greenland became a goal for explorers.

In 1867 Edward Whymper, famous as the conqueror of the Matterhorn, was leader of a British expedition. He was quickly forced to retreat, as a flu epidemic deprived him of manpower. Moreover, the thawing snow and ice he met near the Greenland coast in midsummer were very different from the conditions he had known in the Alps.

In 1870, the Swedish explorer, Adolf Nordenskiöld, penetrated about 60km (37 miles) into the ice cap and reached a height of 670m (2198 ft). Ahead of them they could see nothing but an endless ice field sloping evenly upwards to the east, a smooth expanse that was bounded by a horizon almost as unbroken as that of the sea. Despite this view, Nordenskiöld remained firmly convinced as to the existence of inland oases.

Nordenskiöld returned in 1883 with a party that included two Lapps. They came to a halt after covering some 120km (74½ miles) on the ice cap. The two Lapps were skiers and Nordenskiöld sent them on to see if they could find any oases and, if so, to bring back botanical samples. The Lapps returned after 57 hours and reported they had skied on a further 230km (143 miles) and reached a height of 1950m (6398 ft) but had not sighted anything except ice.

The claim by the Lapps to have covered on ski 460km (286 miles) in 57 hours, which is two days and nine hours, was widely disbelieved. As a result, Nordenskiöld organised the following year, 1884, a ski race at Jokkmokk, the home of the two Lapps. The course was over 110km (68 miles) and it had to be covered twice, so the total race was over 220km (136 miles). The substantial money prizes Nordenskiöld offered attracted 15 entries. The winner was Lars Tuorda, one of the Lapps who had accompanied Nordenskiöld on the Greenland expedition. He covered the 220km in 21 hours 23 minutes.

As a comparison, in 1977 Ahti Nevala of Finland set a record by covering 280km (174 miles) in 24 hours. He did this at Rovaniemi in Finland, which, like Jokkmokk in Sweden, is on the Arctic circle.

Nansen on skis. An illustration from his book.

Nansen's party on the journey across Greenland.

Using a sail on the journey across Greenland.

Nansen's Crossing of Greenland

In his book Nansen described how, one evening in 1883, he was listening indifferently as the day's paper was read, and was suddenly electrified by the news about how Nordenskiöld had returned safely from the interior of Greenland. He had found no oasis, 'but only endless snowfields on which his Lapps were said to have covered, on their "ski", an extraordinary long distance in an astonishingly short time'.

Throughout the English translation of his book the words ski, skilöber (skier) and skilöbning (skiing) are in quotation marks, presumably because they were Norwegian and not English words. Indeed, when the word *ski* was first used, it was thought necessary to add a footnote explaining that *ski* 'is the Norwegian name for the form of snowshoe in general use among the northern nations of the Old World ... The only reason why the established English term "snowshoe" should not have been used throughout is that this would have led to inevitable confusion with the very dissimilar Indian snowshoe, of which also frequent mention is made.'

When Nansen heard the news item about Nordenskiöld's Lapps, it immediately occurred to him that a party of expert skiers must be able to get across Greenland, provided they were properly equipped, and provided they started from the east coast.

All previous attempts to cross Greenland had started from the inhabited west coast, which meant that any successful expedition would, after reaching the east coast, have to make the return journey back across Greenland. Nansen's idea was to land on the desolate and ice-bound east coast and thence cross over to the inhabited west coast. There could be then no incentive to turn back and every incentive to press forward. 'The order would be: "Death or the west coast of Greenland."'

In Norway Nansen's plan was criticised as foolhardy. And when in 1888 he actually sailed from Norway a Bergen newspaper commented: 'In June Curator Nansen will give a skiing display with long jumps on the inland ice of Greenland. Reserved seats in the crevasses. Return ticket unnecessary.'

Outside Scandinavia there was incomprehension, so little then being known about the sport of skiing. Indeed one German newspaper came out with an excitable article to the effect that Nansen was going to cross Greenland on skates.

Nansen was accompanied by three fellow Norwegians, all expert skiers, and by two Lapps, who had been attracted by the wages and had very little idea as to what they were letting themselves in for.

Their approach to the east coast of Greenland was seriously delayed by drifting ice, and they did not land till 10 August. As was to be expected, they had hard work at first dragging their sledges up from the coast. Initially Nansen used snowshoes, but they were all on skis from 2 September. Henceforth, they all used their skis invariably till they reached the western edge of the ice.

On 5 September they passed the highest point of the crossing, at just over 2700m (8858 ft). On 11 September they recorded the unusually low temperature of −40 °C (−40 °F) inside the tent.

As they descended they had the wind behind them. They rigged up sails on their sledges, one going ahead of each sledge on skis in order to steer. Nansen describes how the skis 'flew on from the crest of one snow-wave to another'. Once when he was leading the party in this way, and it was already dusk, he saw something dark lying in his path. He thought it was just an irregularity in the snow. Only when close to it did he realise it was a broad crevasse. He was just able to turn his skis sharply enough to bring his sledge up to the wind in time.

After they reached the west coast they had to improvise a boat in order to reach Godthaab. There they spent the winter. The following year, 1889, Nansen returned to Norway, to a tumultuous reception and immediate fame. The first of the Nansen biographies appeared when he was only 35 years old.

A steep descent in the forest. (*From Nansen's book.*)

Paa Ski Over Greenland

From 2 September, they had used their skis continuously for 19 days, from early morning till late in the evening. And in this period they covered a distance not much short of 400km (248 miles).

Nansen made it clear that the success of the expedition was due to their skis. He stated categorically 'that they were an absolute necessity, that without their help we should have advanced very little way, and even then died miserably or have been compelled to return'.

Nansen devoted a whole chapter of the book to skiing. He was writing for a public that knew absolutely nothing about skiing and he judged it necessary to explain the most basic facts.

'"Ski", then, are long narrow strips of wood ... In front they are curved upwards and pointed.

'On flat ground they are driven forward by a peculiar stride ... They are not lifted, and the tendency which the beginner feels to tramp away with them as if he were on mud boards in the middle of a marsh must be strenuously resisted.'

Some of the chapter certainly is basic, and what little it contains on technique, snow conditions and equipment is now almost entirely out of date. Nevertheless, the modern reader cannot but be struck by the maturity and the balance of the advice given by a young man still in his twenties.

The chapter was not meant to provide a manual of instruction, though it inevitably came to be regarded as such, when the book spread enthusiasm for skiing from Scandinavia to the Alps. The aim was primarily descriptive and it gave an account of skiing in many forms: cross-country, jumping and hunting on ski.

The conditions which Nansen knew were very different from those of our day. But in his expression of love for skiing, one finds across the intervening century an immediate rapport with a writer who was not only a great man, who did great things on ski, but who was quite simply a fellow enthusiast:

'I know no form of sport which so evenly develops the muscles, which renders the body so strong and elastic, which teaches so well the qualities of dexterity and resource, which in an equal degree calls for decision and resolution ... Where will one find more freedom and excitement than when one glides swiftly down the hillside through the trees, one's cheek brushed by the sharp cold air and frosted pine branches, and one's eye, brain and muscles alert and prepared to meet every unknown obstacle and danger which the next instant may throw in one's path? Civilisation is, as it were, washed clean from the mind and left far behind with the city atmosphere and city life; one's whole being is, so to say, wrapped in one's "ski" and the surrounding nature. There is something in the whole which develops soul and not body alone.'

Jump from a boulder. (*From Nansen's book.*)

Skis and Polar Exploration

Skis are of debatable value on the rough, broken surface of the Arctic pack ice. Fridtjof Nansen and Hjalmar Johansen, who were Norwegians and both accomplished skiers, did use skis on the journey that took them in April 1895, to 420km (261 miles) from the North Pole, some 300km (186 miles) further north than anybody had ever been before. On the other hand, the American Robert Peary did not use skis when he reached the North Pole in April 1909.

But in the Antarctic skis have certainly proved of value. The Briton Ernest Shackleton did not use skis when, in January 1909, he and his companions got within 180km (112 miles) of the South Pole. This was 670km (416 miles) beyond the previous furthest south and the greatest single advance ever made in Polar exploration. Shackleton said afterwards that if only his party had used skis, they would have reached the Pole. The Norwegian party led by Roald Amundsen, which arrived at the South Pole in December 1911, and the British party led by Robert Scott, which got there one month later, in January 1912, both used skis. It was easily the most famous ski race in history; also much the longest, and by far the most tragic in its consequences.

17 December 1911 Roald Amundsen having won the race to the South Pole.

5 Mathias Zdapsky 1856-1940

Mathias Zdarsky, skiing with his one long pole, now seems to us a figure of fun but he is in fact the father of Alpine skiing. It was his textbook – and this is the measure of his achievement – that has had the most long lasting sales in the history of our sport. Zdarsky could not find an Austrian publisher for his *Lilienfelder Skilauftechnik*, so he sent it to the firm in Hamburg, which had published the German translation of Nansen's *Paa Ski Over Grönland*. They accepted it and the first edition was published in November 1896, though bearing the imprint 1897. For the fourth edition, published in 1908, the name was changed to *Alpine (Lilienfelder) Skifahr-Technik*. The seventeenth edition was published in 1925, so it continued to be reprinted for 29 years.

To understand the great role which Zdarsky played, one must visualise the background against which he played it. Nansen's book spread enthusiasm for skiing. It gave people a thrilling concept of what could be achieved on skis. But it provided no guidance whatever as to how one should ski in steep Alpine country. And skiers really had no idea how to do this. In his *A History of Skiing*, my father, Arnold Lunn, described the Swiss ski teacher whom my grandfather, Henry Lunn, had brought to Chamonix, France, to instruct the clients of his travel business, in the winter of 1898–9. 'Somebody asked him if it was possible to turn. He replied in the negative, but added that a long gradual turn was just possible if one dragged oneself around on the pole. He claimed to have seen an expert perform this difficult manoeuvre, but modestly added that he was unable to demonstrate it himself.'

Stickriding

In those days the vast majority of skiers were like Zdarsky in that they carried one long pole. They were unlike Zdarsky in that they were incapable of turning and depended entirely upon braking with the pole to control speed. My father skied for three winters (1889–91) before he saw anybody do a turn. 'We rode downhill on vast poles.' That is, they sat astride their pole, like a witch on her broomstick, so that their weight on the pole exerted a braking effect. Some skiers did not actually bestride their pole, but leant back against it, with the same result that the pole acted as a brake. Both methods were called stickriding.

Those who could not stickride (perhaps because they belonged to the minority that used two poles as we do today which makes stickriding more difficult), could only ski downhill where there was space to stop. This very much limited the use of skis away from practice slopes. Josef Müller, one of the founders of the Austrian Ski Association in the winter of 1892–3, has described how he carried out a number of pioneer ski ascents, climbing uphill on his skis, and then walking downhill with his skis on his shoulder.

Printed advice on ski technique was unhelpful. The first German paper devoted to skiing stated in one article, 'The runners let the ski carry them where it will until the air acts as a natural brake and brings them to rest.'

And in case that should be regarded as an isolated incidence of idiocy, the following may be quoted from the journal of the Austrian Ski Association:

'On the descent the ski-runner leans back on his stick, and shuts his eyes. Then he darts downward straight as an arrow, and continues till he can no longer breathe. He then throws himself sideways on the snow, and waits until he regains his breath, and then once again hurls himself downwards till he once more loses his breath and throws himself on the snow.'

Zdarsky was born on 25 February 1856. In the preface to his book he tells the reader that he 'enjoyed a comprehensive and many-sided scientific, artistic and physical education'. He had ambitions as a sculptor and a painter. By 1889 he had achieved some distinction as a gymnast. In that year he retired to an isolated house at Habernreith near Lilienfeld in eastern Austria. His aim in withdrawing to this solitary retreat was, as he put it, to be quite free to live in accordance with his 'scientific-artistic ideas'. He had private means and he never married.

It was pure chance that the home Zdarsky had selected was surrounded by steep hills. The first winter was rich in snow but, as Zdarsky said: 'at that time nobody in Central Europe thought of skiing. Then came the fame of Nansen, this northern hero who had crossed Greenland on skis.' He described how he too was 'seized with the Nansen fever'. In 1890 he ordered a pair of skis; he put them on near the post office and proceeded to climb back into his valley. The skis were 294cm (9ft 6in) long, that is about 1m (3ft 3½in) longer than the skis used by the average recreational skier today. They had the then usual cane bindings with no toe irons. The heel could move sideways on the ski, so that the binding provided very little lateral support.

At the point where Zdarsky first put on his skis the uphill gradient was slight. All went well and he was able to congratulate himself on the progress he was making. But then the route steepened. Not surprisingly his skis suddenly slipped backwards from under him and he fell forwards on to his face.

He could not sidestep up the hill because his bindings gave him insufficient lateral support. He tried to zig-zag upwards but had no idea how to turn at the end of each traverse. He dug his pole deep into the snow and swung around on it. It was a very inelegant manoeuvre which distressed his gymnastic soul.

The Austrian Mathias Zdarsky, who was the first person to develop a technique for skiing in steep country.

For the next six winters Zdarsky skied alone without ever even seeing another skier. He had no book to help him. Entirely on his own he had to work out how to use skis on steep Alpine hills.

On that first day, as he walked back home with his new skis, he was already thinking how he must have some binding which, like the attachment of the skate to the boot, would provide lateral stability. After some 200 experiments he eventually produced a binding with a rigid metal toe-piece which satisfied him. The binding was rigid only in the horizontal plane; it allowed him to lift his heel freely from his ski. He reduced the length of his skis from 294 (9ft 6in) to 220cm (7ft 2in); today 210cm (6ft 11in) is regarded as a long ski for recreational skiing. The only piece of equipment he kept unchanged was the long pole.

Zdarsky also worked out for himself how to do stem turns. He had noticed when traversing that, if he pushed his lower heel down so that the ski was in a stemming position, his skis automatically turned uphill. It struck him that, if he put the upper ski into a stemming position, it should be possible to do a downhill turn. The first two times he attempted this he was successful, but after that he kept falling. Zdarsky took off his skis and climbed back up the hill to examine his tracks. He noticed that, whenever he fell, the inner ski had been held on its outside edge, whereas on the two successful occasions it had been flat on the snow. He had discovered the principle of the stem turn: the outer ski is held at an angle and edged so that it exerts a braking effect while the inner ski skids round.

Eventually Zdarsky felt he could ski without falling wherever snow would lie. He particularly enjoyed placing his turns accurately through trees. And he naturally became curious about how he compared with other followers of the sport. Then, by chance, he read in the *Wiener Fremdenblatt* an article describing how, if a Norwegian was skiing downhill and saw some obstacle like a fallen tree lying across his path, he could, by pressing down on his ski tips, take off into the air and clear even very large obstacles.

Zdarsky had built himself a ski jump and had cleared up to 22m (72ft), which was a very good distance for those days. But the idea was new to him that one could, in the middle of an ordinary downhill run, leap high into the air by pressing down on one's ski tips. He had no way of knowing for certain that this belonged to the world of fantasy, and he wondered if he had mastered skiing as well as he thought.

On 2 February 1896, he went to watch a ski competition on the Semmering and was amazed by what he saw: skiers descending a gentle slope leaning back on their pole so as to brake hard. Only on the gentle practice slope were there ski tracks; there were none elsewhere on the broad open slopes of the Semmering.

Zdarsky was not a man to keep to himself either his opinions or his contempt for others. But when he indicated to the leader of the local ski group that it was possible to ski, not only on the gentle practice slope, but also on the steeper slopes around, the leader tapped his forehead to indicate lunacy. As Zdarsky had not got his skis with him, he could not prove his point. He went back to Habernreith and wrote his book, which came out that November.

The book ended for Zdarsky the life of an isolated hermit which he had chosen for himself in Habernreith. People came to him for ski instruction, and he gave it, always free of charge. At first the pupils stayed with him in his Habernreith home. Then, as the numbers increased, they stayed in Lilienfeld. Later the railways were running special ski trains from Vienna to Lilienfeld on Sundays and holidays in the skiing season.

Zdarsky soon had a growing number of trained skiers to help with the instruction, but he himself taught, alone and single-handed, classes of unparalleled size. He frequently taught classes of 200 people, and once when a military instructor in World War I, a class of 1600. Whether his pupils were soldiers under command or Sunday skiers from Vienna, Zdarsky demanded and got a rigid conformity to discipline, a willingness to be drilled in the movements that had to be learnt. As his fame spread he was asked to give ski courses in other Alpine resorts, but it must not be imagined that he was everywhere accepted as the unquestioned authority on skiing in steep mountainous country. On the contrary, he aroused opposition which was every bit as intense as the loyalty he inspired among his followers.

The Austrian Ski Association were enraged that somebody of whom they had never heard, who had never won a prize in a ski competition, who had never published an account of a ski expedition he had undertaken, should have the temerity to tell them that all was wrong with what they had learnt from their Norwegian masters. In Norway itself they were not pleased to hear that a foreigner thought he had a contribution to make to a sport of which they regarded themselves as the universally acknowledged experts.

The opposition was fierce and Zdarsky was not a man willingly to accept that his views should be questioned. 'It is the most primitive rule of conduct,' he has written, 'that of two people who have dealings with one another, one must be the speaker and the other the listener.' He would not have taken kindly to the modern enthusiasm for dialogue, for it did not occur to him that the role of listener might ever be his. Downhill skiing has inspired some semi-mystical controversies. Zdarsky was an appropriate first prophet for an activity which has often been described as not so much a sport as a way of life.

Controversial acerbity went at times to considerable lengths. One of Zdarsky's opponents, Colonel Georg Bilgeri, had in his description of a skiing turn carelessly referred to the 'hind leg', which led Zdarsky to comment that there seemed to be an officer of the Imperial Army who had four legs. Bilgeri's reaction was to challenge Zdarsky to a duel, perhaps the only occasion in history that such a challenge has arisen out of a difference on sporting technique.

What is surprising about this controversy is that the two sides never arranged to meet on the snows and to put their theories to the test while skiing together. Zdarsky did challenge his opponents to a ski race, but on terms that were unlikely to invite acceptance. But in 1905 the Norwegian National Association did send one of their leading skiers, Hassa Horn, to Lilienfeld, not for a race against Zdarsky, but to ski with him and make a first hand report. Where the ground was easy, Hassa Horn had no difficulty in leaving behind Zdarsky and his companions, but on really steep terrain it was a very different story. Hassa Horn stated in his report that he had never before seen anybody who could ski as well as Zdarsky in these conditions. And he added the prophetic warning that the Norwegians must watch this adaptation of skiing to Alpine conditions, or they would find themselves surpassed.

Later that year, on 19 March, Zdarsky organised on the Muckenkogel near Lilienfeld what we would now call a giant slalom. There were 85 gates over a height difference of 489m (1604ft). Though similar events were organised in the Lilienfeld area over the ensuing years, no such races were held in any other area of Austria till 1927, when my father set a slalom at St Anton. The Zdarsky races eventually died out, even in the Lilienfeld area, but the 1905 event did have one significant, if belated, impact. On 19 March 1935, that is 30 years later to the day, the South Tyrolese, Dr Gunther Langes, set the first race to be called a giant slalom on the Marmolata in Italy. It was considerably longer than the modern giant slalom. The start was on the Cabana Marmolata (3250m) (10,663ft) and the finish on the Fedajasattel (2000m) (6562ft), a vertical drop of 1200m (3937ft) compared with the circa 400m (1312ft) of a modern giant slalom.

Zdarsky was not interested in racing. His object with his gate races was really to organise a test of skiing on steep terrain. When he organised a gate race in 1906, he laid down that everybody would be declared a winner who could complete the course in a given time. And this is the form of event which he advocated in his writings.

Zdarsky laid down as a cardinal principle that skiers should always control their speed so that they never fell. It was the 'safety first' aspect that he stressed, which is obviously sensible if skiing is seen simply as an aid to touring and mountaineering, but it is the antithesis of the racing mentality.

Zdarsky gained his imperishable place in skiing history by being the first person to realise that skiing in the mountainous Alps, as opposed to the undulating terrain of Scandinavia, would require a totally new approach to equipment and technique, which he then provided.

In the Lilienfeld area that Zdarsky made famous there is a monument to his memory. After his name and the dates of his life there is the following quotation by Arnold Lunn:

> ZDARSKY WILL NEVER BE DETHRONED
>
> FROM HIS POSITION AS
>
> THE FATHER OF ALPINE SKIING

Zdarsky must be the only person in the world whose monument in his own home country bears an inscription in a foreign language.

A view from the Muckenkogel, near Lilienfeld, Austria.

The monument to Zdarsky at Lilienfeld.

6 The Public Schools Alpine Sports Club

The Foundation of a Winter Sports Travel Business

It must have been about 1875 that a grocer's assistant in his mid teens was travelling by train from Warwick to Birmingham and was joined in his carriage by three men, who at first studiously ignored him and then suggested a game of cards. The young grocer's assistant lost £3 to them, and the three men presumably felt that their time in his company had not been wasted. These unknown benefactors of the human race had, on that short journey, launched the boom in winter sports holidays and the present era of downhill and slalom racing.

The boy they had impoverished did not wish to tell his father, who was a Methodist lay preacher and the owner of the shop in which he worked, that he had been gambling. So to recover his losses, he tried to make extra money in various ways, one of which was the sale of equipment for a new sport *sphairistike* in which he foresaw a considerable future. He was right, *sphairistike* is now known as lawn tennis. The young grocer's assistant, who was my grandfather, Henry Lunn, was on his way to making a fortune when he had a dream which made him decide to abandon commerce and become a missionary. He was not yet 21.

With the money he had already made for himself, he paid for his own university education at Trinity College, Dublin, taking degrees in medicine and theology. Always a radical in politics he became a supporter of Irish independence and was offered a safe seat in Parliament by Charles Stewart Parnell. This he refused, so convinced was he of his call to be a missionary.

He went as a missionary to India, but his health broke down and he came back to England. When he was 32 years of age, this unknown Methodist Minister organised an ecumenical conference to take place in January 1892. As the venue he selected Grindelwald in Switzerland, a country he had never seen. Encouraged by the success of this meeting, he called a second conference to Grindelwald in the summer. He invited the entire Anglican bench of bishops and the leading Free Churchmen as his guests, hoping that there would be enough paying participants to save him from bankruptcy, for he had no private means and no sponsor for his activities. He charged the paying participants £10.50 for the return fare from London and two weeks full pension in the best hotels. 'At the end of the conference,' he wrote, in the tone of one announcing a lamentable mishap, 'I found myself £500 in pocket.'

My grandfather had seen his own ability to organise other people's travel and end up in pocket. He founded Lunn's tours. At first he organised summer travel. Then, wishing to keep his staff occupied throughout the year, and having seen at Grindelwald the potential appeal of winter sports, he tried the experiment of taking a party to Chamonix in the winter of 1898–9. He ordered six pairs of skis from Switzerland and engaged the services of a Swiss guide, who was alleged to know something of the sport.

In his order for skis, he included one short pair, which he gave as a Christmas present to my father, Arnold Lunn, who was then 10 years old. My father described his first experiments on ski, in his book *Skiing*, published 1913.

'A few of us, a very few, armed ourselves with ski and repaired to a neighbouring slope. A little group of men with toboggans halted on a path near by and watched with curiosity. Our instructor, a guide, led off. He slid down the slope, leaning heavily on a vast pole, and when he got to the bottom without falling, we all cheered ... The few visitors who bothered to ski in Chamonix were regarded as reckless faddists. I was a small boy, and I voted skiing a poor sport. You fell about so. Tobogganing was much simpler and quite as much fun. I don't remember skiing much in the next season, and certainly none of the visitors ever dreamt of going on an expedition. Things were rather livelier in Grindelwald in 1900–1901 ... In 1902–1903 I went to Adelboden, and went up my first mountain on ski.'

In 1937 my father returned to Chamonix for the World Championships that were held there that year. He visited the local museum and was surprised to discover that Dr Payot, the pioneer of skiing in

The first winter sports package tour. Henry Lunn, seated on toboggan centre front row, with the party he took to Chamonix, France, in the winter of 1898–9.

Chamonix, and whose portrait hangs in the museum, had made his first tentative experiments on ski only one year before my grandfather took his party there. Payot was the doctor, and he imported a pair of skis in the hope they would be useful for visiting his patients.

In those early days skiing was the despised winter sport. Skaters were greatly admired and tobogganing was widely practised and taken very seriously. Skiers, on the other hand, were regarded as figures of fun; spectators, especially small boys, delighted to mock them as they fell around.

The Indignity of Travelling with Lunn's

My grandfather was seeking to attract in winter rather wealthier clients than his summer tourists. He quickly discovered that the British upper classes regarded it as beneath their dignity to travel under the auspices of a travel agent. It was equally not done to carry a camera or a guide book, because such appurtenances 'make one look like a tripper'. And, of course, nothing made one look more like a tripper than Lunn's labels on one's luggage. My grandfather got round this by founding the Public Schools Alpine

Sports Club, membership of which was limited to those who had attended a British public school and their immediate female relatives; other women and children could accompany them on club tours as their guests. The problem of being a tripper without appearing to be a tripper had been solved. Moreover, the club used to book whole hotels for the exclusive use of its members, so that people could venture abroad serene in the confidence that they would not have to mix socially with foreigners or with British people who were not from the same social background as themselves.

This blatantly snobbish club, with its outlook so bewilderingly foreign to our present way of thinking, would be a subject for the social historian rather than the writer on sport, were it not for the fact that it played a more important role in the early development of downhill and slalom racing than any other club.

Not the least bizarre aspect of the club was that it should have been founded by my grandfather, who had of course himself never been to a public school. But, so that he would not have to blackball himself, he had inserted a weasel clause which made membership also open to University graduates.

The First Kandahar Ski Race

In January 1903, my grandfather organised the first ski race for a challenge cup open to British racers. The Public Schools Winter Sports Challenge Cup (later named the Public Schools Alpine Sports Club Challenge Cup) was awarded on the combined result of three events: skiing, skating and tobogganing.

In 1911 the Public Schools Alpine Sports Club Challenge Cup was abandoned and separate trophies were instituted for the different sports. The Earl of Lytton gave his name to the skating trophy. How Field Marshal Earl Roberts of Kandahar came to give his name to the cup for ski racing is now not known, as he never visited the Alps in winter. It is probable that Lord Lytton acted as an intermediary and asked Lord Roberts to give his name to the cup. It was at that time a most prestigious name. Roberts is the only person ever to have been awarded the VC, the KG and the OM. He was born in 1832. In August 1880 he led a forced march from Kabul to Kandahar to relieve the British forces besieged in that town. When Roberts was made a peer in 1885, he called himself of Kandahar. Roberts held the appointments of Commander in Chief, India, Commander of our forces in the Boer War, and finally Commander in Chief of the British Army.

The 1911 Roberts of Kandahar ski race was held at Montana, Switzerland. The race was not simply a more serious business than the scramble round a flat field in 1903. It was, by any standards, an extremely arduous event.

The ten competitors left Montana (1470m) (4823ft) on 6 January 1911 and took some seven hours to reach the Wildstrubel Hut, where they spent a moderately comfortable night. The next morning there was a mass start from the hut, all the competitors going off together. A short descent took them to the great flat expanse of the Plaine Morte Glacier, which is at a height of 2700m (8858ft). Five kilometres across the Plaine Morte was followed by a short climb to the Col de Thierry. Racing along the level and uphill is of course a far greater strain at 2700m (8858ft) than it is at even 1500m (4921ft).

From the Col de Thierry the course went down the Sinièse Valley to some little distance below Montana. For some 450m (1476ft) below the Col de Thierry the ground was steep, and the snow windswept crust. It is not surprising that most of the competitors fell repeatedly. It was here that my uncle, Brian Lunn, cracked a collar bone, though this did not prevent him finishing the race.

It was on these very difficult slopes that the eventual winner, Cecil Hopkinson, established a commanding lead. They constituted about half of the course, the lower half being through a wood to the finish.

Isolated downhill races had been held before 1911, but the Roberts of Kandahar is the first downhill race with a continuing history. When my father founded the first club to promote downhill and slalom racing, he called it the Kandahar Ski Club, not in memory of Lord Roberts, but after the oldest downhill race in the world. When my father and Hannes Schneider, the founder of the Arlberg Ski School, founded the oldest of all the World Cup races, it was called the Arlberg-Kandahar. Thus came about that association of the word Kandahar with skiing which is such a source of continuing bewilderment to journalists.

Six competitors in the 1911 Kandahar before the climb to the start. Brian Lunn on extreme left.

Mürren Becomes the Main Public Schools Alpine Sports Club Centre

The following year the Roberts of Kandahar race was transferred to Mürren, Switzerland, a centre which my grandfather had opened for winter sports the year before by persuading the railways to run, from Lauterbrunnen in the valley up to Mürren, in winter as well as in summer.

The first train in winter ran on 15 December 1910, taking a group of Public Schools Alpine Sports Club members to Mürren.

The Achievements of the Public Schools Alpine Sports Club

The oldest downhill race in the world, the Roberts of Kandahar, was started by the Public Schools Alpine Sports Club. When my father set the first slalom, at Mürren in 1922, it was for the Alpine Ski Challenge Cup, again a race organised by the Public Schools Alpine Sports Club. The first slalom racing rules to be printed appeared in the Club Year Book, dated 1923, though, in fact published in 1922. (This curious system of dating was because my grandfather thought of the Year Book, not as a record of the past winter but as a vehicle to sell accommodation for the coming winter.)

The first Oxford versus Cambridge ski race was also organised by the Club, at Wengen, Switzerland, in 1922.

The Club played a key role in launching the concept of winter sports holidays. Fifteen Swiss centres were either first opened in winter by the Club, or, in a few cases, popularised by the club after an unsuccessful attempt to open on their own. They were Mürren, Wengen, Adelboden, Klosters, Montana, Pontresina, Kandersteg, Lenzerheide, Maloja, Celerina, Morgins, Beatenberg, Sils-Maria, Campfer, Ballaigues.

The Public Schools Alpine Sports Club was certainly a bizarre organisation, but it played a key role in the development of skiing. A fact which was recognised by an American writer who, after research in past ski publications, wrote a history of our sport. What is not explained in ski publications is that logic, on our side of the Atlantic, demands that very private schools should be known as public schools. And he concluded that the Public Schools Alpine Sports Club represented an aspiration of my Liberal grandfather to make the pleasures of winter sports available to the less privileged members of society.

'It is doubtful,' he wrote, 'if Lord Roberts had ever attended a public school.' (In fact, Lord Roberts was at Eton.) 'But in any event Lord Roberts' alignment with the Club did not harm the image one bit.'

The old railway from Lauterbrunnen to Mürren, Switzerland. (*From the collection in the Hotel Eiger, Mürren.*)

7 The Campaign for Downhill and Slalom Racing

British Racing, the Lonely Furrow

In 1920, my father Arnold Lunn, at the age of 32, was chairman of the Federal Council of British ski clubs. As there was no president, this was then the top job in British skiing. That year the average age of members of the Council was under 30. At his suggestion it was decided that the 1921 British championships should include a downhill race and a style competition as well as a jumping event; there was no cross-country championship. In 1923 a slalom replaced the style competition. At that time all other countries included only cross-country racing and jumping in their championships.

The first countries to follow the British precedent and organise championships in downhill and slalom racing were Australia, New Zealand and Germany in 1932. Austria and Switzerland did the same in 1933. So Britain was several years ahead.

The 1921 British championships were held at Wengen, Switzerland. The style competition took place at Wengernalp on 6 January. Competitors were judged on four linked telemarks, stem turns and jump turns, as well as on four stop christianias to either side.

The downhill race took place the following day. 15 competitors lined up for a simultaneous start some 150m (492ft) below the top of the Lauberhorn. The finish was below Salzegg on the Grindelwald side of the Scheidegg; lack of snow prevented it being lower.

Though the standard of skiing was not uniformly high – some of the competitors used their poles to brake during the race – the event was clearly high in drama. My father described how R. B. McConnell: 'was fouled in the scramble at the start – a piece of bad luck which deprived him of all chance of winning. Still, part of the art of racing consists in getting clear of the crowd and not allowing yourself to be fouled. Needless to say, such fouls are unintentional ... At the Scheidegg Patrick Dobbs and Harper Orr were leading, but they both made the same mistake, took a bad line, ran into some fences and fell heavily.'

Leonard Dobbs won both the downhill race and the style competition. The women competed on equal terms, in exactly the same events as the men. Miss Olga Major, fifth in the downhill and fourth in the style competition, was easily the best woman.

The inclusion of a downhill race and a style competition was challenged at the Federal Council dinner which took place in the spring after the event. As my father wrote: 'The Norwegians, we were told, were the fathers of the sport. They were experts and we were not. It was impertinent of the British, who skied badly, to depart from precedents established by Norwegians, who skied well. All other countries had followed the Norwegian precedent. Who were we to plough a lonely furrow?'

Nevertheless my father published in the *1921 British Ski Year Book* the first downhill racing rules ever to appear in print. They appeared under the heading 'The British Ski Championship Meeting'. The first stated that 'All races during the Championship Meeting shall be downhill races, and shall involve as little uphill or level racing as possible.' This was followed by four rules, the last of which reads quaintly today. It laid down that a competitor 'who wilfully uses his skis as a toboggan shall be disqualified'.

The Invention of the Slalom

My father was dissatisfied with the style competition. He thought it encouraged pretty, rather than fast and accurate skiing.

He was convinced that, if one wished to award the championship to the best all round downhill skier, then one must combine the downhill race with some event which tested turning technique as opposed to courage and the ability to hold high speed. The downhill could never, he thought, test accurate turning because, for reasons of safety, one could never set the course down slopes where the competitor would be forced to turn by trees, rocks and other natural obstacles.

In the early 1920s the Swiss used to organise style competitions that they called by a Norwegian name, slalom. The Norwegian slalom was a downhill event, marked by judges, that used to be held in Norway but it had been discontinued in 1906.

Henry Lunn founder of the travel business seated on right, Arnold Lunn standing, the author seated on the knees of his great grandfather, also called Henry Lunn.

In the Swiss style competitions, which they called slaloms, competitors had to turn round flags or sticks. Sometimes they were asked to do a particular turn, for example a telemark or christiania, at a particular flag.

In 1920 my father organised at Mürren, Switzerland, a competition to test skiing in Alpine country. He called the cup given for this competition the Alpine Ski Challenge Cup. Competitors were taken out on a whole day's tour and were marked by judges, not just on style, but on their overall ability, including an eye for the best line. This was certainly a much more comprehensive test than any style competition, but it had the disadvantage that assessment depended upon the subjective opinions of judges rather than upon the objective measurement of speed.

In 1922, when the Alpine Ski Challenge Cup was held for the third time, my father decided to organise a competition which would certainly test ability to turn, but one in which the criterion would be speed and speed alone. He set flags in pairs down the slope and competitors were timed as they raced through them. There were two runs, the difference then being that instead of both courses being set on hard snow, one was on hard and the other on soft. The winner was John A. Joannides, whose time for the two runs was 2min 1sec.

To this entirely new form of race he gave the name slalom. So the first slalom, as we now understand the term, was set on the Mürren practice slope on 21 January 1922. There has been some confusion as to the date, because in his *The Story of Skiing* (1952) and in his *The Englishman on Ski* (1963) my father gave the date as 6 January. But in his *The Kandahar Story* (1969) he gave the date as 21 January. There is no date given in the accounts written at the time, but in the programme for the winter 1921–2 published in the *Public Schools Alpine Sports Club Year Book*, the proposed date for the race was given as 21 January 1922.

Just as the Roberts of Kandahar is the oldest existing downhill race in the world, so the Alpine Ski is the oldest slalom. And, by a coincidence, the name survives as well in that the downhill/slalom combined event is now known as the Alpine combination.

When my father set this first slalom in Mürren, he had never heard about the similar type of event which Zdarsky had organised in the Lilienfeld district of Austria.

My father's slalom achieved world championship status within nine years. It had this immediate impact because it went beyond the simple concept of a race down a course defined by pairs of flags or gates. Almost at once it began to include not just single gates, but various gate combinations, each of which would present the competitor with a different type of turn, long radius, short radius, and so on. My father stressed that the gates must not be placed where the competitor would find it convenient to turn.

All sport consists in the invention of artificial diffi-

culties for the fun of solving them. With his slaloms my father provided ski racers with a whole new range of exciting demands. To put it another way, he invented a fascinating sport.

The First International Downhill/Slalom Races

Downhill/slalom races began as purely British events. In 1924 my father decided to organise the first international downhill/slalom event, that would be open to amateur skiers of all nationalities. The downhill race was held between Scheidegg and Grindelwald, Switzerland, on 12 January 1924 and the slalom the following day at Mürren. This combined event was won by A. Gertsch of Switzerland. It was purely an individual event, with no team results. But all the competitors were British or Swiss, and it came to be replaced by a five-a-side team event between the British Universities Ski Club and the Swiss Academic Ski Club.

On 30 January 1924 my father founded the Kandahar Ski Club which organised an intensive downhill and slalom racing programme at Mürren and campaigned for the recognition of these new events.

These British initiatives were followed by a young Swiss, Walter Amstutz, whose father owned a hotel in Mürren. Walter was an excellent skier – he won both the downhill and the combined at the 1925 Anglo-Swiss team race – and he was fired by a determination

The start on the Lauberhorn above Wengen, Switzerland, of the downhill race at the British Championships in 1921.

to popularise downhill and slalom racing in Switzerland. He was a student at Bern University and on 26 November 1924 he founded the Swiss Academic Ski Club (Schweizerischer Akademischer Ski-Club – SAS), the aim of which was to join the Kandahar in the development of these new sports. At the time Walter was 22.

On 18 and 19 January 1926 Walter and the SAS organised the first international university ski championships, at St Moritz, Switzerland. The events at this meeting were downhill and slalom races and a jumping competition. There were competitors from five different countries, Austria, Germany and Italy, as well as Switzerland and Britain. The meeting did a great deal to awaken interest in downhill and slalom racing, especially among the Germans.

Hostility to Downhill and Slalom Racing

My father wrote in the *1926 British Ski Year Book*: 'If the downhill and the slalom receive recognition abroad, the credit for this victory will be due, not only to the British, who were the first in the field, but to the SAS, who were broadminded enough to recognise and adopt foreign ideas and who were brave enough to ignore the criticisms of their own compatriots.'

These words make quaint reading today, when it is difficult to visualise the opposition these events once encountered.

In 1926 the Ski Club of Great Britain sent to all other national ski associations a memorandum, which my father had drafted, arguing for the inclusion of downhill and slalom races at international meetings.

At that time the Ski Club of Great Britain was the sole national club and the governing body for skiing in Britain. The memorandum was signed by, among others, the President of the Club. It expressed the hope that those who did not agree with the memorandum would meet the arguments fairly and 'show cause why downhill racing should continue to be excluded'.

In fact, not one single reply of any sort was received to this memorandum, which shows how little interest there was, as late as 1926, for downhill and slalom racing among all the national associations governing the sport, all that is except for the British.

The argument was constantly deployed that downhill and slalom racing were only for those who were too cowardly to jump and too feeble to enter for cross-country races.

Typical of the belief that downhill and slalom racing were unmanly pursuits is the fact that, when in 1928 the Austrians started to include unofficial downhill races at their national championships, they did so for women only.

A group of Kandahar members at Mürren, Switzerland, c. 1924.

Mürren, Switzerland. The first slalom was set on the slope to the right of the railway arches. The high mountain in the background is the Schilthorn where the Inferno race starts.

The 1928 International Ski Federation Congress

The Fédération Internationale de Ski (FIS) Congress that met at St Moritz on the occasion of the 1928 Winter Olympic Games had to consider a British proposal for the international recognition of downhill and slalom racing. My father described their reaction: 'on arrival at St Moritz I was met with much good humoured sympathy. I was told, of course, that it was absurdly sanguine to expect any changes in the International Racing Rules so long as the British were not represented by a team at these International fixtures'.

The situation did seem preposterous. The British had never been represented by competitors at the Olympic Games or any other major international event. My father was English and a citizen of a country with the most limited opportunities for skiing. By contrast the Norwegians at the 1924 Winter Olympic Games had won all the four skiing events; they had also taken all of the four silver medals, and three out of the four bronze.

When my father was introduced to N. R. Oestgaard, the Norwegian Vice-President of the FIS, Oestgaard rather coldly asked him, 'What would you think, Mr Lunn, if I tried to alter the rules of cricket?'

'I wish to heaven you would,' my father answered, 'if you succeeded, we might have fewer draws.'

The FIS appointed a special committee to consider the British proposal. Only one member of the committee, the German, Dr Karl Roesen, gave the British his unqualified support, for which he was later severely taken to task by the German Ski Association.

The Norwegians on the committee said that it was not necessary to have downhill races to test the technique of downhill skiing, because every properly set cross-country race included downhill sections. Nor was it necessary to hold slaloms. In most cross-country races there were sections of wood running, that is natural as opposed to artificial slaloms. The British slalom struck him as a very artificial sort of race.

My father began the defence of his proposal by saying that the British campaign was not inspired by a desire to provide weaklings with gentle exercise. In the end he did not press for the formal recognition of downhill and slalom racing. Instead he put forward a compromise proposal that the national associations represented on the FIS should be invited to try out the British rules for downhill and slalom racing and should report their findings to the FIS Congress due to meet at Oslo in 1930. This compromise proposal was supported by the Swedish President of the FIS, Ivor Holmquist, and was accepted.

Hannes Schneider and the Arlberg-Kandahar

Hannes Schneider was born on 24 June 1890, at Stuben in the Arlberg district of Austria. In 1900 he saw his first skiers and made his own skis out of barrel staves. He was at once fascinated by what was then a strange, new sport; he used to practise by moonlight so as to avoid the taunts of other children. In 1903 he was given his first proper pair of skis and also some elementary instructions; he learnt the telemark and the christiania. Later he saw a skier, a competent one by the standards of those days, do a stem turn and he has recorded how amazed and excited he was. Later Schneider would make the stem turn and the stem christiania the basis of his own instructional system; he would also become the first ski instructor to abandon teaching the telemark.

Hannes Schneider was a most gifted skier and his skill came to more general notice when he attended a ski meeting near Dornbirn, which is in extreme western Austria and close to the frontier with Switzerland. He was offered a job as a ski teacher at Les Avants in Switzerland. But Karl Schuler, who had opened his Hotel Post at St Anton in the winter of 1906, saved Schneider for the Arlberg by offering him a job as a ski teacher. On 7 December 1907, Schneider travelled from Stuben to the other side of the Arlberg Pass and started the career which would make him, and the Arlberg, famous throughout the skiing world.

In his contribution to *Skiing: the International Sport*, edited by Roland Palmedo (New York 1937), Schneider wrote, 'In 1907 I received my call to St Anton-am-Arlberg in the Tyrol as ski teacher. For that time I had probably mastered skiing quite well but actually had not the slightest conception of teaching, and when someone asked me how one made a turn I explained simply that I would now make a turn and that the pupil should watch carefully and then do likewise. That was the whole of instruction.'

In fact, at that time, Schneider was already a wonderful skier. Karl Schuler used to exclaim, 'If only the boy could teach as well as he skis.'

Though Schneider was then inarticulate, he was not a purely instinctive skier. During long solitary runs among the mountains he worked out what seemed to him the ideal way to ski and which he would later make famous as the Arlberg technique.

During World War I, he became a ski instructor and was soon supervising a number of other instructors. He learnt during the war, not only how to teach himself, as opposed to how to demonstrate, but also how to run a large ski school.

Schneider had always been a most talented skier. After the war Arnold Fanck made him and his beautiful technique famous.

Already before the war Fanck had wanted to make a film that would show the beauty of skiing movement. During the war he learnt about slow motion filming, and the film he made, *Das Wunder des Schneeschuhs*, became the first film for public consumption to use this technique.

Slow motion ruthlessly exposes any imperfection in a skier's technique. Fanck knew about Schneider and sent him a telegram asking him to join them. He had already collected around him a group of excellent skiers but he has recorded how staggered they all were by Schneider's skill. He could ski at high speed with great accuracy, master all the turns, and if required, leap from the roofs of chalets or other natural points of take-off encountered in the course of a downhill run. But it was not the spectacular which lived on in the memory of those who saw the film but the rhythmic beauty of Schneider's skiing style, especially when he was doing the stem turn. This, the slowest, least spectacular and simplest of all the turns became, when Schneider did it, a thing of grace and beauty that lives in the memory.

The film was made in 1920. Many of the main film distributors refused to handle what they described as a boring film in which nothing was shown except that four skiers climbed a mountain and then came down again. As a result the film was often shown in lecture halls and other places away from the main cinemas. It was an immediate success, making Fanck as well as Schneider famous, and starting a fashion in skiing films.

In 1926 Fanck and Schneider produced from their film stills a magnificently illustrated book, also called *Das Wunder des Schneeschuhs*. In 1933 an English edition, *The Wonders of Skiing* was published.

As a result of Schneider's influence, and the example of what came to be called the Arlberg School, the Austrian State Ski Examination was established by government decree on 18 December 1928. Only those who had passed the examination were allowed to teach skiing in Austria with the result that a uniform system of instruction was established throughout the country. No other country followed this Austrian example before the war.

In 1927 my father visited St Anton and at the end of his visit set a slalom race for the local skiers. This was the first time that such a race had been held in the Arlberg, indeed anywhere in Austria outside Zdarsky's district of Lilienfeld. The race aroused great interest and my father suggested to Hannes Schneider that the Kandahar should give a cup for a downhill and slalom event to be held annually in the Arlberg. The Arlberg-Kandahar, as the event was named, was held for the first time on 31 March and 1 April 1928 and is the oldest open downhill and slalom event in the world. The next was the Lauberhorn founded by Ernst Gertsch at Wengen in 1930.

The Arlberg-Kandahar quickly achieved great prestige and attracted all the leading racers. It played a significant role in securing universal recognition for downhill and slalom racing.

Hannes Schneider.

The 1930 International Ski Federation Congress

This was held at Oslo in Norway, the country of the great Fridtjof Nansen, mother country of cross-country racing and jumping, heartland of opposition to downhill racing and the slalom.

It is difficult now to realise the reverential awe inspired by Norway throughout the skiing world in the period after Nansen's book had spread enthusiasm for the sport from Norway to other countries.

The English translation of this book had laid down that ski should be pronounced shee, as though the k in ski was a soft h. We all duly talked about shis and shiing. Then I remember my mother telling me one day that the word shi had a nasty meaning in French. It was a long time before I learnt what it was. Shi in French has the same meaning as it has in English when one adds a t on the end.

So we stopped talking about shis and shiing, but the prestige of Norway is well illustrated by the way we pronounced the word ski for some 50 years not as it is written in our own language, but in accordance with instruction laid down in a Norwegian book.

Similarly when my father started putting forward his ideas, British skiers who opposed him gave the impression that no further argument was necessary once they had proved that his views were not accepted by Norwegians.

The 1930 Congress, at which my father was proposing that downhill and slalom racing should be formally recognised as official events on a par with cross-country racing and jumping, took place at the same time as the Holmenkollen events. My father later described his feelings as he watched the events for the first time. 'I looked at that great crowd and my spirits sank. I felt like a pinchbeck Luther up against something more formidable than Papal Bulls. And I knew that if I was a Norwegian I should feel nothing but contempt for this pert heretic from a country where snow falls in fitful showers on muddy roads, a country which had never been represented in the lists at Holmenkollen.'

Norway and the other two Scandinavian countries, while they tended to regard downhill and slalom racing with some contempt, did recognise that these races, especially since the inception of the Arlberg-Kandahar, were increasingly popular in the Alps. They therefore decided not to oppose the British proposals which were carried unanimously at the Congress meeting on 27 February 1930.

It is pleasant to record that also present at the Congress was Walter Amstutz, the first non-British person to support the campaign.

The First World Championships in Downhill and Slalom Racing

To my father's great joy, the Oslo Congress entrusted the organisation of the first World Championships in downhill and slalom racing to the Ski Club of Great Britain. They were first held at Mürren, Switzerland, on 19–22 February 1931, and again in February 1935. My father, on behalf of the Ski Club of Great Britain, organised these events. These must surely be the only occasions in sporting history when a country has organised World Championships on the territory of another country.

There had been annual World Championships in cross-country racing and jumping since 1925. In 1929, when these championships were held at Zakopane, Poland, the organisers had held an unofficial downhill race during the meeting. Apart from the Poles, who were on the spot, and the nine British competitors, all those entered in the downhill race were men who had been sent to Poland as members of their national teams for the cross-country and jumping events. As a result, the Poles and the British did well.

The winner was Polish, Bronislaw Czech, the second being British, Bill R. Bracken. There were two British women racing in this otherwise all male event. They created a sensation by finishing 14th (Doreen Elliott) and 15th (Audrey Sale-Barker) out of 60 competitors. When on their journey home they entered a Warsaw restaurant, all those present stood up and applauded.

In those days these meetings were not officially designated World Championships, because the Norwegians did not wish them to rival in prestige their own Holmenkollen events. They were called FIS (Fédération Internationale de Ski) meetings. 'Don't make a FIS about nothing,' my father used to say to racers who got unduly steamed up about comparatively minor events.

But in fact they were World Championships, and from 1937, on the proposal of my father, they were at last officially designated as such. In 1965 the FIS decided retrospectively to designate as world championships all FIS races back to 1925 for the cross-country and jumping events, and back to 1931 for the downhill and slalom events.

At the 1931 World Championships a British girl, Esmé Mackinnon, won both the downhill and the slalom. Walter Prager of Switzerland won the men's downhill. Quite exceptional snow storms forced the postponement of the men's slalom till the day after the championships had been programmed to finish. The men's slalom was consequently regarded as unofficial and no men's combined result was published.

It had been intended to include as an unofficial event a race over the full Inferno course, top of the Schilthorn (2970m) (9744ft) to Lauterbrunnen station (796m) (2611ft). Owing to the heavy snowfalls, the race could be held only on the bottom section of the course, from Grütsch to Lauterbrunnen. This truncated race produced one bizarre incident.

The finishing posts were immediately outside Lauterbrunnen station. As Esmé Mackinnon came down the road towards the finishing posts, a funeral procession emerged from the station and came up the road to meet her. Esmé stepped politely to one side and waited for the funeral to pass. The time keeper recorded the time she had waited and, by a unanimous decision of the race committee, it was subtracted from her finishing time, with the result that she won that race as well.

The Norwegian, N. R. Oestgaard, had in 1934 succeeded the Swede, Ivor Holmquist, as President of the International Ski Federation. Oestgaard had regarded downhill and slalom racing with derision, but, after attending the World Championships in Mürren, he wrote generously about what he had seen. He stated: 'It is time that the criticism of the Central European downhill and slalom races should cease. To win a really first class downhill race with a large entry is a skiing performance of the same standard as jumping.'

Only those who know with what reverence the Norwegians then regarded jumping can appreciate the full force of this tribute to downhill racing, and also the courage he showed in putting on an equal level with jumping a new competitive event which the Norwegian press had hitherto treated as ludicrous.

The campaign for downhill and slalom racing really ended with these first world championships. The new events were now established and nothing could arrest their growth in popularity and prestige. In 1936 they were included for the first time in the Olympic programme. At that Winter Olympic Games there were 21 nations competing in the men's downhill and slalom races, as opposed to 22 in the 18km (11 miles) cross-country race, which was the most popular of the Nordic (cross-country and jumping) events. At the next Winter Olympic Games in 1948, there were 25 nations in the men's downhill race, 22 in the men's slalom and 15 in the 18km cross-country race.

8 The Olympic Games

The flame from Olympia, Greece, burns at Innsbruck, Austria, for the Winter Olympics.

I Winter Olympic Games
Chamonix, France 1924

The Norwegians, won 11 of the 12 medals available for skiing; that is all of them except for the bronze in the 18km cross-country which went to Finland.

Thorleif Haug won three gold (18km, 50km, Nordic combination) and a bronze for the special jumping. Haug is certainly one of the greatest Nordic skiers of all time. He won the 18km by a margin of 1min 20sec over his fellow Norwegian, the great Johann Grøttumsbraaten, who was to win three gold medals in later Olympics. Haug won the 50km by a margin of 1min 51sec. In the Nordic combination he won the jumping for the event as well as the 18km.

In the special jumping (the jumping for the Nordic combination is a separate event) Anders Haugen, a Norwegian who had emigrated to the USA, and who was competing for that country, jumped 50m (164 ft), which was further than any other competitor. But his style was considered bad and his total marks, calculated on both style and distance, was 17.916. This put him into fourth place, immediately behind Thorleif Haug, who had a total score of 18.

In 1974, 50 years later, it was found that Thorleif Haug's marks had been incorrectly calculated and that his score should have been 17.81, which made him fourth behind Anders Haugen. As a result, Haug's daughter presented her father's bronze medal to the 86-year-old Anders Haugen. It would be 52 years after Haugen's success before the USA would again win an Olympic medal in a Nordic event, and though he indubitably won the bronze medal, this is still shown in the official Olympic results as belonging to Thorleif Haug.

II Winter Olympic Games
Saint Moritz, Switzerland 1928

Drama at the Second Winter Games centred round the special jumping competition.

The majority of the delegates to the International Ski Federation Meeting held at the same time as the Games criticised the St Moritz Olympic jump on the grounds that it was a 'monster jump', designed for the breaking of records and sensationalism; was against the true spirit of sporting endeavour; was designed not for the competitors but for the titillation of the wealthy public who patronise the St Moritz hotels, and all the rest of it. These criticisms seem quaint today. The longest standing jump at the St Moritz Games was 64m (210 ft). In ten years people would be jumping more than 40m (131 ft) further than that. Today the record is about three times the distance being jumped at St Moritz.

A more serious criticism of the St Moritz jump was that it was dangerous, not because of the distances involved, but because a really expert jumper could land beyond the critical point where the gradient begins to flatten. Landing from a big jump is obviously more dangerous if the gradient has eased markedly.

To prevent accidents, the Norwegian starter had put a cord across the top of the inrun and laid down that competitors should start from lower down, from what was known as the Junior Platform. As hardly anybody other than the Norwegians had practised from this point, the decision was most unpopular with the other competitors. They told the Norwegians that, if they thought it dangerous to start from the top platform, then they had the remedy in their own hands; they need not jump flat out. 'It is a point of honour,' was the severe response, 'for a Norwegian to jump flat out.'

Competitors are very highly strung before any dangerous event and the implication they were frightened did nothing to improve Norwegian tempers. Then, when they came up for the second jump, they found a Swiss had cut the cord across the inrun. Eventually it was settled that the jumpers would start not from the top but from between there and the Junior Platform.

Of the Norwegians none was angrier than the great Tullin Thams, who had won the gold medal for jumping in the 1924 Olympics, and the jumping at Holmenkollen during the previous four years. His rage had a personal edge to it. On the first jump he had mistimed and had reached 'only' 56.5m (185.3 ft), whereas the longest jump had been 60m (197 ft).

Now, on his second jump, he put everything into it. It seemed to the spectators that he would never land. When he did it was at 73m (239 ft), well past the critical point. My father wrote that he had 'never seen a more terrifying fall'. The jumping competition was won by Alf Andersen of Norway but it is Tullin Thams who will be remembered.

III Winter Olympic Games
Lake Placid, USA 1932

In the skiing the Norwegians were shocked that, having won all the medals except one (a bronze) for the 18km events in 1924 and 1928, they were in 1932 unable to place anybody in that event. But the hero of the Games was undoubtedly the Norwegian, Johann Gröttumsbraaten, who won the Nordic combination for the second time having been third in 1924. Then, in marked contrast to the present day, the Nordic combination was the skiing event which attracted most prestige.

In the jumping the Norwegian, Birger Ruud, destined to become the greatest jumper of all time, won the first of his gold medals.

In those days Olympic competitors were not subsidised the way they are today and crossing the Atlantic was expensive. There were 306 competitors as opposed to 495 at St Moritz in 1928. They were competing in 14 events. When Lake Placid next organised the Games in 1980, there would be some 1400 competitors and 38 events.

IV Winter Olympic Games
Garmisch-Partenkirchen, Germany 1936

Before the opening ceremony the British contingent were carefully briefed that, as they came before Hitler, they must make it quite clear that they were giving the Olympic salute (arm to the side) and not the Nazi salute (arm to the front). One member of the team did this with such vigour that she hit the nose of the young woman beside her. But all this was lost on the commentator. He announced over the loudspeakers that the British were greeting the German Führer with the German salute.

Once the opening ceremony was over, the organisation of the Games was efficient, which one expects from the Germans, but also fair and unpolitical, which one did not expect on this occasion. The only debatable decision in the slalom was given against a German competitor and there were no complaints from the Germans.

There were 755 competitors at Garmisch, 160 more than ever before. There were 28 nations competing, against a previous 25. But it was in the number of spectators that these Games most exceeded all earlier records. There were 500,000 paying spectators at the various events. The night before the special jumping, trains left Munich station at ten minute intervals from 11pm to 10am. The special jumping attracted the greatest crowd and after that the slalom, making its

Christel Cranz (GER) who won a record 12 World Championships, 1934–9.

Olympic debut. There were 70,000 spectators and it was only fitting that my father, who had invented the slalom 14 years before, should be the referee.

But the Garmisch Games should be remembered, not for the crowds, but for the quality of athletic performance. At any one Games there may be one athlete who goes into history. At Garmisch there were four who, over 40 years later, would still figure in the Guinness Book of Records: Sonja Henie, Norway (figure skating), Ivar Ballangrud, Norway (speed skating), Birger Ruud, Norway (ski jumping), Christel Cranz, Germany (Alpine skiing).

Downhill and slalom racing were included for the first time; there was as yet no giant slalom. At every Games since then there have been medals for the individual events; at Garmisch there were no medals for the downhill or the slalom but only for the combined result. And this, quite illogically, removes some of the glamour from one of the most versatile performances in Olympic history. Birger Ruud won both the downhill race and the jumping, the latter for the second time. He did not do well in the slalom, and was fourth in the combined result, winning no medal. The gold medal was won by Franz Pfnür of Germany. The silver medal went to Guzzi Lantschner, who had raced for Austria in earlier World Championships, but he had become a Nazi and transferred his allegiance to Germany. When he was awarded his medal there were howls of execration from the Austrians in the crowd.

The great favourite for the women's event was Christel Cranz of Germany. She had a bad fall in the downhill, which cost her at least 20 seconds, perhaps as much as 50. By a most memorable performance in the slalom she managed to win the combined and the gold medal. Only one other woman skier rivalled her for the attention of the press photographers, Diana Gordon-Lennox of Canada, 32nd in the downhill and last but one in the slalom. But Diana was skiing with one arm in a sling and, even more exciting, with a monocle.

The most dramatic of the skiing events was the relay race which, like the Alpine events, was included for the first time in the Olympics. My father, who was watching the race with his Norwegian friend, Tor Tangvald, described the event in the British Ski Year Book:

'Each lap of 10km (6 miles 370yd) finished in the Olympic stadium. Iversen, the Norwegian, started for the last lap two minutes ahead of the famous Finn, Jalkanen. Ten minutes later the loudspeakers in the stadium brought us news from the first control. Jalkanen was gaining on the Norwegian. Only a few yards separated them at the third control. Tangvald looked grave and said: "There's some steep downhill running on the last bit, and our man should gain." But the Finn did not fall on the schusses, and overtook the Norwegian just before the finish. Seldom have I seen a racer register more tragic despair than the defeated Iversen. "See him," exclaimed Tangvald rapturously, "he looks as if he had been sentenced to death. That is magnificent. That is the sport."'

V Winter Olympic Games
St Moritz, Switzerland 1948

The 1948 Olympics marked the final ascendancy of downhill and slalom racing. 25 nations had entered teams for the downhill, 24 for the downhill/slalom combined and 22 for the special slalom. The next most popular events were the 18km cross-country and the 500m (547yd) speed skating, both of which attracted 15 nations. And downhill/slalom racing had only been introduced into the Olympic programme at the previous Winter Games, when medals had been awarded only for the combined event. In 1948 medals were awarded for the downhill, slalom and combined event. (There was one downhill race, which also counted for the combined event, but there were two slaloms, one just for the combined event, and a special slalom). Downhill and slalom races were now known as the Alpine ski events, as opposed to the Nordic events, cross-country racing and jumping.

The downhill race proved to be, not only the most popular event, but also easily the most dangerous. The Swiss paper, *Sport*, published a list of the Olympic competitors who had been injured in practice. It was a long list and included three members of the Swiss team. Except for one ski jumper and one ice hockey player, all those on the list had been entered for the Alpine ski events. And, as accidents in the slalom are rare, it must be assumed that the vast majority of those on *Sport*'s list had been injured training for the downhill.

The St Moritz Olympics course was certainly formidable. It had been designed by the Swiss, Rudolf Rominger, who had won the World Championships for downhill and Alpine combination in 1936, and for slalom in 1938 and 1939. Racing down the top slopes, which lasted for something under a minute and a half, was easy. Then there was a short, bumpy traverse, which brought the racer to the top of a big face, which was about 300m (984ft) in vertical descent. Below the face was a series of fast and bumpy wood glades.

While these glades were testing even for the best racers, it was the 300m (984ft) face that was the crux of the course. The face was in three sections, divided by marked changes of gradient. First, there was a long steep slope which ended in a sharp uprise, crowned by some bad bumps. Second, came a short slope which flattened suddenly at the bottom into a shelf about 15ft (4.5m) wide. Third, came an extremely steep slope which ended in a long, flattish, but bumpy track leading to the wood glades.

During practice, I never saw a racer take this slope straight and hold it, though there was one Yugoslav who very nearly succeeded in doing so. He held the bumps at the bottom of the top section, but only just. As he shot into the second section, he had his weight back and looked thoroughly unsteady. Then came the flat shelf from the end of which he was thrown some 12m (39 ft) through the air. He must have been a man of remarkable courage and tenacity because he was still on his feet when he landed. But not for long. In two tremendous bounds he somersaulted to the bottom of the slope. It was an appalling fall and first-aid men rushed towards him, only to see him pick himself up unhurt.

In the race itself, a number of competitors did try to schuss this face but not one of them got further than the bumpy uprise at the bottom of the first section. With one exception, the Italian, Zeno Colo, none of them looked like holding it; self confidence and determination seemed to be lacking.

Zeno Colo is a big man with a strong, somewhat harsh face. He gives the impression that he does not smile easily. He had won the two previous major downhill races: the Arlberg-Kandahar in the latter part of the 1947 season, and the Lauberhorn held in 1948 shortly before the Olympics. He had good reason to expect that he would win the Olympic downhill.

As Colo ran along the traverse leading to the top of the big face, he was obviously travelling faster than any of the others. He came absolutely straight, his skis held on to a hard, clean edge. No spray was flung up with his skis braking against the snow. No other racer ran that traverse so cleanly and determinedly. All the others, sideslipped slightly and thus braked as they ran along the traverse; perhaps the knowledge that they were approaching the top of the big face made them check unconsciously.

At the end of the traverse all the other racers swung out into a wide arc, so as to come into the big face as gently as possible. But Colo, as soon as the traverse brought him to the top of the big face, jerked his ski downhill so that he cut the corner as closely as possible. As a result, he shot over a small bump which the others had missed; from the top of the bump he jumped outwards and downwards, so as to hurl himself into the big face with still greater impetus. At that moment he was already five to ten seconds ahead of any other competitor.

It was his climax. As he landed, one ski caught in the snow and he was thrown forwards in a heavy fall. When he got to his feet again, he moved disconsolately to the side of the course. In those days, before the invention of safety bindings, a racer who had fallen was expected nevertheless to complete the course. Now the crowd shouted at Colo that he should continue. For a moment he stood motionless ignoring their yells. Then, with a sudden quick movement, he lifted up a ski so that all could see that it was broken. A moment later, he reached down, picked up the broken tip and hurled it from him.

It fell in the middle of the course, and the crowd broke into loud booing. Then Karl Molitor, a Swiss who would win a bronze medal in the race, swung into sight at the beginning of the traverse. It looked as though Molitor might trip over the broken ski tip lying in the middle of the course. Colo saw Molitor coming. He jumped round and, stumbling awkwardly over his broken ski, he scrambled on to the course to remove his ski tip. He just succeeded in retrieving it and getting off the course on the other side, when Molitor shot past him. After that Colo disappeared.

Many people will think that Colo's effort was not particularly praiseworthy and indeed he fell higher on the steep face than any other competitor. But despite this, it is his performance, and his alone, that is etched vividly into my memory. Until he fell, the quality of his technique stood out as superior to that of all the others. Even more outstanding was his courage and evident determination, his refusal to compromise with gravity but instead, accepting every risk, to throw himself into the fastest possible line on a slope that nobody had succeeded in schussing. He fell, but his skill and courage produced one of the most memorable moments in the history of ski racing.

After this, it seems almost an anti-climax to state that the race was in fact won by Henri Oreiller of France. The Austrians had the most consistent performance, taking second, fifth and ninth places, and getting all their team of six into the first 20 (102 successfully completed the course out of 111 at the

Henri Oreiller (FRA) who won the downhill race and the Alpine Combination at the 1948 Olympic Games.

start). Certainly in practice the Austrians had shown a lightness of touch and ease of control that the others lacked. Whenever a bump threw them into the air they seemed to come down with the lightness of thistledown. And it was not only their skill that was a pleasure to watch. The happiness that one saw on their faces, gave the impression that they enjoyed skiing more than anybody else.

Oreiller went on to win the gold medal in the Alpine combination and the bronze medal in the special slalom. His total haul therefore was two gold medals and one bronze. He can be described as having been at a quite exceptional personal peak, because it was his only major success in ski racing. He competed again in the 1950 world championships where the best he could manage was fourth place in the giant slalom, an event introduced for the first time into the world championships; it would be included in the 1952 Olympics.

After that, at the age of 25, Oreiller launched himself on a new sporting career as a rally and racing driver. A lot of ski racers try to do this, but none has had the success of Oreiller. In 1958 he won his class in the Tour de France. In 1959 he became French champion in the touring cars category. In 1962 he was killed driving in a race at Montlhéry near Paris.

Despite Oreiller's two gold medals and one bronze, not many people remember his name today. Two other competitors in the 1948 Winter Olympics have won a far more enduring fame. One of them gained only a silver medal at St Moritz. Birger Ruud of Norway had won the gold for jumping at the 1932 and 1936 Olympics. In 1948 he won the silver. As the jumper leaves the platform he is travelling at around 100km (62mph) an hour. Timing his spring to coincide with his take-off requires the reflexes of a very young man. To have won a silver medal, as Birger Ruud did, at the age of 36 must rank as one of the greatest performances in the history of sport.

The other competitor, Nino Bibbia, won Italy's first gold medal in the Winter Olympics, and he did it on the Cresta, the famous skeleton run that has been in existence ever since 1884. Racing on the Cresta was included in the programme in 1928 and 1948 when the Winter Olympics were held in St Moritz. Nino Bibbia was later to become the greatest Cresta rider of all time. He won eight times both the Cresta Grand National, first held in 1885, and the Curzon Cup, first held in 1910. He was also a very genuine amateur. His father had a fruit shop in St Moritz. When asked by the press for his reactions to his son's victory, he answered, 'My son would have done far better to have stayed in the shop. We shan't sell one orange more because he won that race.'

VI Winter Olympic Games, Oslo, Norway 1952

The Olympic Games had come to the homeland of skiing. The Olympic flame was lit, not in Olympia,

but in the Morgedal birthplace of Sondre Norheim. A relay of 94 skiers carried the flame to Oslo. The last of them, the one who lit the brazier in the Stadium for the opening ceremony, was Eigil Nansen, a grandson of Fridtjof Nansen. Thus the Norwegian predominance in the early history of skiing was aptly symbolised and two of the most influential skiers in the history of our sport were commemorated.

Norway had for so long and so strenuously opposed downhill and slalom racing but now once again, they were easily the most popular events of the Winter Olympics. Twenty-seven countries had entered for the downhill and slalom events, 26 for the giant slalom, which was introduced into the Games for the first time. The next most popular event was the 18km cross-country with 18 competing countries; 13 countries had entered for the jumping.

But, despite this, Norwegian interest was centred on the Nordic events of cross-country racing and jumping. The downhill and giant slalom courses, which were at Norefjell, some 100km (62 miles) from Oslo, suffered because there was insufficient money available for their preparation, overriding priority having been given to the Nordic events. As a result, the organisers at Norefjell had to struggle as best they could and succeeded only in the nick of time to remove some dangerous tree stumps from the women's downhill course on the very morning of the race. By then there had been many angry words and ruffled feelings.

Typical of the Nordic bias of those responsible for the overall organisation is that they printed only 11,000 tickets for the slalom, with the result that an estimated 14,000 more watched it without paying for a ticket.

Although popular interest in the slalom had been underestimated, it was the Nordic events which really generated public enthusiasm. And it was the Nordic combination of cross-country racing and jumping which was the true centre of excitement and speculation. In those days it was the all-round Nordic skier and not the specialist in either event who still gained the greatest prestige.

In the first four Winter Olympics, 1924–36, the Norwegians had on each occasion won all three medals for the Nordic combination, a grand slam of 12 medals. But then they had suffered during the war from malnutrition and other factors. In the 1948 Olympics at St Moritz the best Norwegian in the Nordic combination had been only sixth. The winner was Heikki Hasu of Finland who had repeated his success in the 1950 World Championships. Hasu was the strong favourite at Oslo but Norwegian hopes were raised when Simon Slattvik won the jumping for the combined, although it was not really believed that he could win the combined. Hasu was known to be the better cross-country racer, and Slattvik had been so unwell before the Games that he was very nearly dropped from the Norwegian team. But when it came to the cross-country, Slattvik raced the race of his life. He pushed Hasu into second place and won the Nordic combination for Norway. The cross-country gold medal was also won by a Norwegian, Hallgeir Brendan. The same day, Monday 18 February – Norwegian Monday – the Norwegian, Hjalmar Andersen won the second of his three gold medals for speed skating.

The 50km cross-country race was won by a 27-year-old Finn, Veikko Hakulinen, who was destined to become one of the greats in cross-country racing.

The women's Alpine events were dominated by Andrea Mead-Lawrence of the USA. In the downhill race she had a severe fall, but won the giant slalom by over two seconds. On the first run of the slalom she muddled a flag and had to climb back. But on her second run she showed extraordinary fighting spirit; she risked everything and won the gold medal.

Andrea Mead-Lawrence was married to David Lawrence who was in the American men's team. After the Games they had three children in quick succession, the last of them arriving in October 1955. But this did not stop Andrea competing in the 1956 Olympics and finishing 4th equal in the giant slalom.

The men's downhill was won by Zeno Colo, who had had so dramatic a fall in the 1948 Olympics. At

the 1950 World Championships he had won the downhill and giant slalom, and had been second in the slalom. Now he crowned his career with an Olympic gold medal.

Finally the men's slalom events and the paradox of the Games. Norway, the centre of opposition to the slalom, had now produced one of the greatest slalom racers in the history of the sport. Stein Eriksen won the giant slalom at Norefjell. He was the favourite for the slalom, which was held on a steep slope at Rödkleiva near Oslo. On the first run he tied with Hans Senger of Austria. Then, just as the second run was to start, the race was held up over an organisational dispute, and this delay evidently affected the nerves of the two leaders. Senger missed a perfectly easy gate and had to climb back. Stein Eriksen, who normally raced with such elan, skied like a man weighed down by care. His time on the second run was only sixth best. His final place was second, behind Ottmar Schneider of Austria. At the World Championships two years later, Stein Eriksen would win the slalom by over five seconds.

VII Winter Olympic Games
Cortina d'Ampezzo, Italy 1956

These were Toni Sailer's Games. It was not just that this young Austrian won all three Alpine gold medals.

Toni Sailer (AUT) who in 1956 and 1958 won seven World Championships, the record for a man.

Anderl Molterer seems to jump over the Matterhorn,
Zermatt, Switzerland.

It was the sovereign ease with which he did it. What he did excited world interest to an extent that has not been equalled by any other competitor in a Winter Olympics, before or since.

The first of the men's Alpine events was the giant slalom. The 20-year-old Toni Sailer was comparatively unknown, whereas his compatriot, Anderl Molterer had been third in this event at the 1954 World Championships. When at Cortina Molterer clocked 3:06.3, the fastest time so far, press and public gathered round to congratulate. He told them to wait, Toni Sailer was still to come and he could break three minutes. It seemed a fantastic prediction, but Molterer was only out by 0.2 of a second, for Sailer's winning time was 3:00.1. So he had won the giant slalom by 6.2sec.

The second men's Alpine event was the slalom. Toni Sailer won both runs of the slalom and finished four seconds ahead of Chiharu Igaya of Japan, who thus gained Japan's first medal in the Winter Olympics.

After the first run, Toni Sailer had a long wait at the top before the second run started and this can prove very nerve wracking for a leading competitor. 'What did you think about during the long wait?' journalists asked him after his victory. He answered, 'Nothing.'

He certainly had a wonderful ability to keep calm. Just before he was due to start in the downhill race, the long leather strap of his binding broke. There was panic in his entourage. His start in the downhill was jeopardised and thus his chances of a third gold medal. What made it all the more bitter was that the downhill race was his strongest suit. Amid all the turmoil, he borrowed a strap from a companion, calmly threaded it through his ski, put on his crash helmet and got to the starting gate just in time.

It was an intensely cold day – minus 22 °C (−7.6 °F) at the start – which may have had something to do with the leather strap breaking, and there was a strong wind which did nothing to improve morale.

Owing to thin snow cover, the course was very bumpy and uneven. The wind had blown snow from all exposed surfaces so that the tops of bumps and ridges were icy. In hollows the snow was often sticky. As a result of the very difficult conditions, 28 competitors out of 75 failed to complete the course, and this included 10 out of the first 24 to start.

The exit from the shelter of a wood was the point on the course where the worst falls occurred. Here there were a rapid succession of bumps throwing the racer into the air, and the sudden exposure to the wind on coming out of the wood made it all the more difficult to keep balance. It was at this point that Sailer very nearly fell. Those who saw this incident will never forget how he seemed to be thrown completely off balance and his desperate struggle to effect an appar-

Phil Mahre (USA) who won the Alpine overall World Cup three times 1981–3, the giant slalom World Cup twice, 1982–3 and the slalom World Cup 1982.

ently impossible recovery. He went on to win the downhill by 3.5sec.

To such an extent does Toni Sailer dominate our

memory of the Games that it comes as a shock to realise that another skier won more medals than he did. Sixten Jernberg, making his first appearance at an Olympics, won the 50km, was second in the 30km and the 15km, and was a member of the Swedish team that took the bronze medal in the relay race.

The 30km had been introduced into the Olympic programme for the first time. The 18km was at the same time reduced to 15km, this being regarded as something of a 'sprint' distance, as compared to the long distance 50km and the intermediate 30km.

Veikko Hakulinen of Finland, who had won the 50km in 1952, gained one gold medal and two silver at Cortina, winning the 30km, coming second in the 50km and being a member of the Finnish team that came second in the relay race.

Two Finns, Antti Hyvärinen and Aulis Kallakorpi, won the gold and silver medals in the jumping. Harry Glass of Germany was third, this being the first time since 1928 that a non-Scandinavian had been placed in the jumping. More important, it was the first time in the history of the Winter Olympics that the Norwegians had not won the jumping. In the jumping at the six previous Olympics they had won six gold medals, five silver and four bronze: 15 medals for Norway as opposed to three for the rest of the world. At Cortina the best Norwegian was ninth! It would be 1964 before they again won an Olympic medal for jumping.

VIII Winter Olympic Games
Squaw Valley, USA 1960

After his great success in the 1956 Winter Olympics, Toni Sailer became a film star. Under the amateur regulations it was permissible to take money for skiing in a film, provided that one was by profession a film actor. So in order to establish his professional status as a film actor, he first appeared in films that had nothing to do with skiing. It was an enormous tribute to his prestige as a skier that the film company were prepared to go through with the business of starring him in non-skiing roles because his abilities as an actor were certainly unimpressive. But his skiing successes had given him great glamour and there was even a record of him whistling.

His film acting commitments interfered with his training but at the 1958 World Championships he nevertheless managed to win the downhill and the giant slalom, while finishing second in the slalom.

And then he was, after all, debarred from the 1960 Olympics by the amateur regulations. He offered to give up making films. He was prepared to sacrifice money if he might compete. He loved racing and was an amateur in the sense that he was prepared to pay for the pleasure of racing. But in the end it was not the film making that barred him; it was a minor triviality. A firm had produced Toni Sailer ski pants, and in the advertising his Olympic successes had been mentioned. And so the ski events at the 1960 Olympics lost much of their interest. A lot of people are interested to discover at an Olympic Games or a World Championships who is the best skier in the world. But nobody wants to know who is the best skier that hasn't sold his name to a firm manufacturing ski pants.

The vote for Squaw Valley as the site for the 8th Winter Olympics was narrow; 32 as against 30 for Innsbruck. And the choice was an act of faith. At the time of the vote there was one hotel in Squaw Valley and nothing else. The cross-country races were to be held at McKinney Creek, some 30km (18½ miles) from Squaw Valley, which is at an altitude of 2000m (6560ft). Olympic or World Championship competitions in these taxing events had never been held at

such an altitude, although McKinney Creek is not much higher than St Moritz at 1870 (6135ft)). The Scandinavians regarded this as a particular disadvantage for their competitors, who often practise the sport at altitudes close to sea level.

The downhill course was at first criticised as dull, so to make it more interesting the Americans built some artificial bumps into the terrain, contrary to International Ski Federation regulations. Now nobody complained that the course was dull. Instead there were cries about sensation-seeking American organisers, circus athletics and all the rest of it, which grew in volume when it was announced that the opening ceremony was to be designed by Walt Disney.

After all the criticism came bad luck. Immediately preceding the Games it rained 10cm (4in) in two days. Then a bulldozer burst a fire hydrant. Squaw Valley was nicknamed Squaw Puddle. But the rain was followed by heavy snowfalls and the sun came out in time for the opening ceremony.

There is something to be said for having an opening ceremony designed by an artist as opposed to a Lord Mayor. Squaw Valley scored its first success. The teams marched into the stadium and Richard Nixon – then Vice President – declared the Games open. The doves of peace were released, and then eight mortars were fired, one for each of the Winter Olympics, from Chamonix in 1924 to Squaw Valley in 1960. The doves of peace fled for their lives and, in the deafening silence that followed, a moving figure could be seen high up on Papoose Peak. It was the great American racer, Andrea Mead-Lawrence, carrying the Olympic flame, which had as in 1952 been lit at the birthplace of Sondre Norheim in Norway. She skied down to the Stadium, where she handed the torch to the American speed skater Kenneth Henry. He skated slowly round the rink and then climbed the steps to the brazier and lit the flame.

At the Squaw Valley Games there was no-one to step into Toni Sailer's shoes. The most outstanding stars were two cross-country racers, Sixten Jernberg of Sweden and Veikko Hakulinen of Finland. Jernberg was 31 years old and at the height of his powers. It had been thought that he might win all three cross-country races, the 15km, the 30km and the 50km. But he suffered from a cold during the Games and was also affected by the height. He did win the 30km, came second in the 15km and was a member of the Swedish team that came third in the relay race.

Veikko Hakulinen was 35. He was second in the 50km, third in the 15km and a member of the winning team in the relay race. And it was in this relay race that Hakulinen achieved the most dramatic performance of his great career.

Veikko Hakulinen (FIN), the only skier to have won World Championship titles over all three distances, 15km, 30km and 50km. ▶

At the second handover, Norway and Finland were running neck and neck, ahead of all the others. The Norwegian runner, Einar Östby, who had been a last minute selection for the Olympics, raced brilliantly and gave the fourth Norwegian, Haakon Brusven, a lead of 20sec over the fourth Finn, who was Hakulinen.

In the 15km two days before, Brusven had been first and Hakulinen third. How could Hakulinen be expected to gain 20sec on Brusven? The race seemed over, the result a foregone conclusion.

Then came the astounding news that 1km (1092yd) before the finish Hakulinen had caught up with Brusven. After that they raced side by side, sometimes one ahead, sometimes the other. As they came into the long straight stretch leading to the stadium they seemed to be exactly level. Hakulinen tried to increase speed with skating steps. He had not the strength and stumbled. Brusven drew ahead. With the strength of despair, the old Finn threw into his racing everything he had got. He won by a ski length, or 0.8 of a second.

Hakulinen said that never had he been so worn out. He was still feeling the effects when he competed two days later in the 50km. At the 45km (28 mile) mark he was still 48sec behind his fellow countryman, Kalevi Hämäläinen, who had not raced in the relay team. Hakulinen went into his famous final spurt. He gained 28sec on his rival but it was not enough. Hämäläinen's final time was 2.59:16.3, Hakulinen's 2.59:26.7.

During the last few years, interest had concentrated more and more on the specialist as opposed to the combined events. There had been no Olympic medals for the Alpine combination since 1948. There were still Olympic medals for the Nordic combination, but this event had greatly declined in prestige. By 1960 there was much more interest in the separate cross-country and jumping events.

The Nordic combination had remained very much a Norwegian domain. Since the first Winter Olympic in 1924, they had won the gold medal every year except for 1948. Their only rivals had been the other Scandinavian countries. Only once had a non-Scandinavian – F. Gron-Gasienica, a Pole in 1956 – got into the first three for an Olympic Nordic combination.

For the Nordic combination in Squaw Valley, the jumping was won by a German, Georg Thoma, who was known to be a much better jumper than cross-country racer. So, despite this victory, Thoma's hopes were not particularly high. 'If all goes well,' he said, 'I should now get the sixth place.' Thoma is not a

Steve Podborski (CAN) who won the 1982 downhill World Cup. He is here seen in December 1980 breaking the record on the St Moritz course.

chatty individual and the press later said that this was the longest sentence he spoke during the Games.

The favourite for the Nordic combination was a Norwegian Tormod Knutsen, who was known to be an excellent cross-country racer. It was expected that he would easily pick up the minute's lead he needed to beat Thoma for the combined event. At the 5km (3 mile) mark he had gained only 16sec on Thoma, but it was expected that he would pick up more on the later difficult sections of the course, especially the climb between 9 and 11km (5½ and 6¾ miles).

Then came the unexpected. At 10km (6¼ miles) it was announced that over the preceding 5km (3 miles) Thoma had not lost time to Knutsen but had actually gained 13sec on him. Now only three seconds separated them. The race for the Nordic combination was between these two. German spectators feared that Thoma would not be able to maintain his speed. He did so, but only just. He was quite worn out when he arrived in the stadium to become the first non-Scandinavian winner of the Nordic combination.

The special jumping – as opposed to the jumping for the Nordic combined which rates no medals as a separate event – also saw the end of Scandinavian dominance. Again the winner was a German, Helmut Recknagel whose style was so impressive that only one of the four judges did not mark him top. The speed with which he leant right forward after take-off, the calm and stillness of his flight, the steady assurance of his landing, in all these he was the outstanding competitor.

By contrast, the Alpine events produced no stars who could compare with the outstanding Nordic competitors. The most successful Alpine racer was Ernst Hinterseer of Austria, who won the slalom and got third place in the giant slalom.

After the first run of the slalom, the 17-year-old German, Willi Bogner, was leading. He had done the same thing after the first run of the Lauberhorn slalom five weeks earlier. Then he had been too cautious on the second run and had lost. He was determined not to make the same mistake again. From the starting gate he went flat out and had a fall within a few seconds.

In the downhill race three out of the four French racers were using metal skis. In 1948 the British had used metal skis, invented by an Englishman Donald Gomme, but this was the first time that anything other than wood had been used by one of the top teams. These metal skis were believed to be markedly faster than wood and to give their users a distinct advantage. Of the French racers using them, one was first, one was third and one failed to finish. The one who did not finish, Adrien Duvillard, had been the favourite; he had won both the downhill and the slalom at the preceding Hahnenkamm race at Kitzbühel in Austria.

The French team had posted on the course one of

their officials Emile Allais, who had been world champion in 1937 and 1938 and the greatest of the pre-war racers. He had a stopwatch and it was his task to signal progress to the French racers as they flashed past. If a racer was in the lead he was to stand erect, otherwise he was to crouch. As Jean Vuarnet, who had start number 10, came past he was a fraction of a second slower than the German, Hans Peter Lanig. Vuarnet saw Allais crouching; he picked up on the lower part of the course the time he had lost, and won the gold medal.

Adrien Duvillard was immediately behind Vuarnet with start number 11. Waiting for him, Allais crouched so as to get a more accurate sighting. Duvillard came quicker than expected. By the time he came into sight he already had a fantastic lead of two seconds over all the other competitors. Allais shot upright but it was too late, for Duvillard had seen him crouching. He had skied as he had never skied before and could not understand how he could have lost time on anybody. Bewildered, he lost concentration. At a big bump he mistimed his pre-jump and fell. To pre-jump is to jump immediately before a big bump, so that one floats over it and is not thrown into the air by it. If one jumps a fraction of a second too late, instead of floating over the bump, one takes off from it and goes far farther than one would have done had one not jumped at all. The racer who goes into the air, not only risks losing his balance but is also slower than the racer who is able to keep on the surface.

Biathlon was included for the first time at the 1960 Games. During a 20km (12½ mile) cross-country race, competitors had to stop four times and fire at targets with the rifle carried on their back. For each missed target a penalty of two minutes was added to the racer's time. The winner, Klas Lestander of Sweden, had only the 15th best time in the race. But he had shot perfectly and had no penalty minutes to add to his time.

Biathlon is a descendant of the pentathlon which was included in the Ancient Olympic Games from 708 BC. It consisted of running over one stadium (about 200m) (219yd), long jump, throwing the javelin, throwing the discus and wrestling.

The modern pentathlon is the brain child of de Coubertin who was anxious that a similar event should be included in the Modern Olympics. It consists of cross-country running, swimming, pistol shooting, fencing and riding, and was included for the first time in the 1912 Olympics.

A winter pentathlon was included in the 1948 St Moritz Olympics. It consisted of the same events as the summer pentathlon, except that a 10km (6¼ mile) cross-country race took the place of running on foot and a downhill race took the place of swimming. Not all the competitors at St Moritz proved expert in all five fields. In the pistol shooting one competitor missed the target and hit a spectator. My father

Egon Zimmermann (AUT) who won the downhill at the
1964 Olympic Games.

quoted the comment that had been so popular in London during the war-time air attacks, 'We're all in the front line now.'

This winter pentathlon was never repeated in the Games, because hardly any winter sports centres, other than St Moritz, can provide facilities for riding, quite apart from shooting and fencing. But there was a strong feeling in the International Olympic Committee that the Winter Games, like the Summer Games, should include one event that transcended normal sporting divisions. Various winter sports combinations were suggested, until finally the Union Internationale du Pentathlon Moderne came up with the idea of the biathlon.

When the 1960 Games were over, the competitor with the greatest reason for satisfaction was perhaps one who had won only a bronze medal. In the 1958 World Championships Charles Bozon of France had broken his leg so badly that he had been told that he would hardly be able to ski again, never mind race. But at Squaw Valley he had been third in the slalom, an event he would win at the World Championships two years later.

The most disappointed competitor was probably Anderl Molterer of Austria. He had finished 19th in the downhill, 12th in the giant slalom and had failed to make the team for the slalom.

Molterer was a very great ski racer. He had won both the downhill and the slalom at the Lauberhorn in 1953, at the Arlberg-Kandahar in 1956 and at the Hahnenkamm in 1958. The Lauberhorn, the Arlberg-Kandahar and the Hahnenkamm are the three classics of the ski racing season. Very few ski racers in history have won both the downhill and the slalom at any one of these three events, never mind all three. But Anderl Molterer had never managed to win a World Championship or an Olympic gold medal. From Squaw Valley, his thoughts must have gone back over the years to the 1952 Winter Olympics in Norway. He had been 20 then and had shown magnificent form in the training for the downhill. But he had been only reserve for the Austrian team, and the team manager had decided not to make any last minute changes. He did not know if one so young and inexperienced as Molterer could cope with the pressures of a great event. And anyway, he remarked, Molterer would have plenty of later opportunities to win Olympic and World Championship titles.

So Molterer started only as a fore-runner. His time was taken, but was not published. Not many people know that his time was the best, and would have earned him the gold medal if only he had been racing as a member of the team and not as a fore-runner.

IX Winter Olympic Games
Innsbruck, Austria 1964

Even before the opening ceremony, the 1964 Olympics had tragically broken a record. For the first time in the history of the Winter Olympics a competitor was killed. And not just one, but two. Kay Skryzpecki, of Polish descent but racing for Britain, was killed practising for the tobogganing, which was being included in the Olympics for the first time. And Ross Milne, an Australian, was killed practising for the downhill. The course was down the wooded Patscherkofel, as it had been for the downhill 1936 World Championship, in which 17 out of the 54 competitors had been injured. The wood glades had been greatly widened for the 1964 races and snow though scarce in 1964 was much more plentiful than it had been in 1936.

Race training was not as disciplined then as it is now and there were a large number of racers all practising at the same time. Milne came over a blind edge and saw some competitors standing immediately below him. He tried to avoid them and fell. He hit a partially concealed stone and bounced from the stone into a tree. He was not a top class racer; if he had done well he could have hoped to finish in the first half of the field. Some Austrian papers blamed his death on his lack of skill and the fact that there is no qualifying standard for the Winter Olympics; provided a competitor is selected to represent his country he is allowed to enter.

Memories of the Games are very often dominated by one competitor. In 1964 there were two, and they were sisters. Marielle Goitschel, aged 18, was the reigning World Champion in the Alpine combination (downhill, giant slalom and slalom). She won the first run of the slalom, beating her 19-year-old sister, Christine, into second place. But on the second run, Christine more than made up her lost time and won the gold medal. Marielle was placed second. Then, in the giant slalom two days later, the position was reversed, Marielle winning the gold and Christine the silver. Marielle also won the Alpine combination for the best performance in the three events. No Olympic medal was awarded for this, but it did gain her a World Championship title.

Christine and Marielle had sharply contrasting characters. Christine was shy and embarrassed by the sudden attention lavished on her. Marielle, having won a World Championship title two years previously, was not only more used to attention, but positively enjoyed teasing the press. At the press conference after her giant slalom victory she announced her engagement to a then little-known member of the French men's team, Jean-Claude Killy. 'Killy himself,' wrote *The Times*, 'was nowhere around and there lurked the uneasy suspicion that his impending marriage might be news to him.' As it indeed was.

Killy, who was to win three gold medals at the 1968

Sixten Jernberg (SWE) who won nine Olympic medals (4 gold, 3 silver, 2 bronze), 1956–64, a record for the Winter Games.

Olympics, showed in 1964 no promise of such achievement. He finished fifth in the giant slalom and 42nd in the downhill; in the slalom he was disqualified.

The cross-country events provided a fitting climax to Sixten Jernberg's wonderful career. At the age of 35 he was fifth in the 30km, won a bronze in the 15km, a gold in the 50km and another gold as a member of the winning Swedish team in the relay race. In three Olympics, 1956–64, he achieved a total of nine medals (four gold, three silver and two bronze), which is a record for the Winter Games. At World Championships he had won a further four gold medals, making a grand total of eight gold medals, four at 50km, three in the relay race and one at 30km. He had twice been second and once third in the 15km but he had never won over this distance.

His great rival, Veikko Hakulinen of Finland, won seven gold medals in Olympic Games and World Championships. One less than Jernberg, but Hakulinen did have the unique distinction of winning, at one time or another, over all three distances, 15km, 30km and 50km.

In the 1964 Games, Hakulinen was entered only for the biathlon. His shooting was poor and he finished 15th.

In the Nordic combination, Tormod Knutsen of Norway, who had been second to Georg Thoma of Federal Germany in 1960, had his revenge. He won the gold medal, Thoma taking the bronze. But two years later, at the World Championships, Georg Thoma once again took the first prize. In 1963 he had become the first Central European to win the Nordic combination at Holmenkollen, and had gone on to repeat this victory in 1964 and 1965.

A 5km cross-country race for women was included in the Olympics for the first time. It was won by Klawdija Boyarskikh of the Soviet Union, who also won the 10km event and was a member of the Soviet winning relay team.

At the closing ceremony, Avery Brundage, President of the International Olympic Committee, said, 'The Innsbruck Games have shown how much the human will is capable of achieving.' He was referring to the organisers. This had been one of the most snowless winters on record in the Alps. Earlier both the Lauberhorn and Hahnenkamm downhill races had been cancelled for lack of snow. There were no snow-making machines, and the organisers had had to transport nearly 20,000cu m (7290cu yd) of snow to make the events possible.

X Winter Olympic Games
Grenoble, France 1968

Two racers have won all three Olympic gold medals in the Alpine ski events (downhill, giant slalom and slalom), Jean-Claude Killy of France in 1968 and Toni Sailer of Austria in 1956. Nobody at a World Championship has won all three events, though two racers have come very close to doing so, Zeno Colo of Italy in 1950 and Toni Sailer in 1958; in both cases they won the downhill and the giant slalom, and came second in the slalom.

Since 1968 it has become much more difficult to excel in all three events. Karl Schranz, who retired in 1972, was the last racer who regularly won top class events in all three disciplines, downhill, giant slalom and slalom. So with the increasing specialisation, it is very probable that the records of Toni Sailer and Jean-Claude Killy will remain unique. How do they compare with one another?

Toni Sailer very nearly brought off the fantastic feat of winning all three events first at the 1956 Olympic Games and then two years later at the 1958 World Championships. He won his three gold meals in 1956 by far greater margins than Killy did in 1968. He won the downhill by 3.5sec (Killy by 0.08sec); the giant slalom by 6.2sec (Killy by 2.22sec) and the slalom by 4sec (Killy by 0.09sec). So Killy won two of his events by less than a tenth of a second. His greatest margin, 2.22sec was considerably less than Sailer's smallest margin, 3.5sec. Moreover, Karl Schranz was originally declared to be the winner of the 1968 Olympic slalom; the gold medal was only awarded to Killy after a French protest and a fine old row.

All this is not to dispute that Killy was a very great skier. In the 1966 World Championships he won the downhill and the Alpine combination (downhill, giant slalom and slalom). But it was in the 1967 World Cup that Killy achieved his most outstanding success and a dominance over his rivals that can compare very favourably with Sailer's record at the 1956 Olympics.

The World Cup was inaugurated in 1967, the brain child of Serge Lang, a journalist who realised that, with the very small margins often separating racers and with the role that extraneous factors such as wax could play in the result, victory in one race, whether or not it was called a World Championship event, did not in fact prove that the winner was the best in the world. Only consistent success over a number of races throughout the season could prove that.

For certain selected downhill, giant slalom and slalom races during the season racers would be awarded points, 25 for a win, 20 for second place and so on. The World Cup would go to the racer who amassed most points during the season. In order to handicap the supreme specialist as against the all-rounder, no racer was allowed to amass more than 75 points (the equivalent of three victories) in any one discipline, downhill, giant slalom or slalom. (The regulations have been frequently altered in detail since 1967 but the objectives have remained the same.) In addition to the overall World Cup awarded on all three disciplines, separate specialist World Cups were awarded for the racer who amassed most points in the individual disciplines.

Jean-Claude Killy (FRA) on the way to the first of his three
gold medals in the 1968 Olympics.

Harti Weirather (AUT) who won the 1981 downhill World
Cup and the 1982 downhill World Championship.

In 1967 Killy won the World Cup in each one of the three specialist disciplines, a record that stands unique, for no other racer, man or woman, has ever won more than two of the specialist World Cups. Not only that, but he gained in each discipline the maximum of 75 points allowed. In the downhill none of his rivals were able to collect more than 37 points. In the slalom his nearest rival collected 58 points, and in the giant slalom the next best got 60 points. He won the overall World Cup with the permitted maximum of 225 points; second was Heini Messner of Austria who got 114 points.

After the 1968 Olympics Killy went on to win the overall and giant slalom World Cups for that year, but he was defeated in the downhill and slalom World Cups. Then he retired but came back in 1973 to win the Grand Prix on the professional circuit.

Killy was a very great ski racer and it is perhaps wrong that he should be primarily remembered for his success in the 1968 Olympics. That year started badly for him. By the time of the Olympics, he had won only one race, a giant slalom. At the Lauberhorn he had had a slow time in the downhill and fallen in the slalom. He seemed off form and most unlikely to achieve his declared ambition of winning all three gold medals. And the Games did not open auspiciously for him. His first event was the downhill. He had drawn start number 14. This was considered a disadvantage because the snow conditions were soft and the course would not be at its best by the time he descended. Then, shortly before the race was due to begin, he skied over some ice and ruined the wax on his skis. Desperately he hunted around for Michel Arpin, who looked after his equipment. When he found him, it was too late to rewax skis that were wet and cold. Arpin scraped the skis a little and did what he could to give Killy confidence. Privately he knew that the damage could not be righted. He said later that he knew the only hope lay in Killy's fantastic determination to win.

Killy's will to win was symbolised by his explosive start. On one occasion, when he started practising it, he landed out of the start gate into the snow. He had thrown himself forward with such violence that both boots had come out of their bindings. There was much merriment but by the time of the Grenoble Olympics his explosive start was no longer a laughing matter.

Guy Perillat of France had started number one. His time, 1:59.93, was still the best when Killy catapulted himself out of the start gate with such force that it seemed the whole structure would collapse. He took every risk he could on the upper and more difficult part of the course. One big bump he took at maximum speed, something he had never done in training. He was thrown into the air and it seemed to him he would never land. When he did so, after some 40m (131ft) flight, it was on almost flat ground,

and he thought his legs would give way under the impact.

At the end of the top part of the course, he was 1.1sec ahead of Perillat. But his skis were slow on the lower and easier part of the course. His final time 1:59.85, was only 0.08sec faster than Perillat. If the lower, easier section of the course had been a little bit longer, Killy would have lost and Perillat would have won.

The giant slalom was Killy's only easy win. He had a lead of more than 2sec over Willy Favre of Switzerland.

Then and last came the slalom, which was run in a thick fog. On his second run Karl Schranz missed gates 18 and 19 and stopped just below gate 21. He climbed back up the course and claimed that he had been obstructed by a figure who had crossed the course just above gate 21. The British start referee Robert Readhead allowed Schranz a re-run, while warning him that its validity would be subject to later decision by the jury. Schranz did a very fast re-run, and he stood on the victory podium as the winner of the gold medal. Killy stood beside him as the winner of the silver medal.

But before the prize-giving ceremony could take place, the French lodged a protest. It was confirmed that a course policeman had crossed the course just above gate 21, during Schranz's run. The problem was whether his doing so had distracted Schranz and caused him to miss gates 18 and 19. The jury consisted of two Frenchmen, a Swiss, a Norwegian and Robert Readhead, who later told the press that he had abstained from voting because he found it impossible to decide judicially whether Schranz had, or had not, been distracted by the policeman crossing the course. The other four voted 3 to 1 that Schranz should be disqualified. The ballot was secret, but national passions were enflamed and it is not too fanciful to suggest that, if there had been two Austrians instead of two Frenchmen on the jury, the ballot would have gone the other way. So Jean-Claude Killy won his third gold medal by a margin of 0.09sec over Herbert Huber of Austria.

They were Killy's Olympics. When one thinks of Grenoble, 1968, one inevitably thinks of him. But there were other remarkable performances.

Nancy Greene of Canada won the giant slalom by 2.6sec and was second in the slalom. A disappointing 10th place in the downhill – she was said to have been using the wrong wax – was nevertheless good enough for her to win the Alpine combination, which earned her a World Championship title but no Olympic medal.

Second in the Alpine combination was Marielle Goitschel, who had won this event three times running, 1962, 1964 and 1966. And at Grenoble in 1968 she won the gold medal in the slalom, having won the giant slalom at the previous 1964 Olympics. In the

1966 World Championships she also won the giant slalom. Hers was one of the greatest careers in skiing history. During it she won six World Championships (Olympic gold medals counting as World Championships), which is one less than Toni Sailer and one more than Jean-Claude Killy.

History was made in the cross-country events. Franco Nones of Italy won the 30km and became the first non-Scandinavian man to win an Olympic gold medal in a cross-country event.

Soviet women, on the other hand, had won their two individual cross-country races (over 5km and 10km) ever since 1956 when the Soviets started competing in the Winter Olympics. But their record of being undefeated was decisively broken in 1968 when a Swede, Toini Gustafsson, won both the 5km and the 10km races. It must be added that two Soviet stars failed to appear, allegedly because they did not wish to face the femininity test.

It is wrong to assume that this is a problem that only bothers skiers from behind the Iron Curtain. Erika Schinegger won the women's downhill in the 1966 World Championship. About a year later a paragraph appeared in a Swiss paper headed 'Erika and femininity'. It quoted Erika's mother as saying that Erika was in hospital for an operation and would not be well enough to compete in the 1968 Olympics; she hoped however to compete in the World Championships to be held two years later.

From this it was natural to assume that Erika had had an operation to make it easier for her to pass the femininity test. In fact the reverse was the case. The operation had been to make her more masculine. She officially became Eric Schinegger. His/her ambition was, having won the World Championship downhill as a woman, now to do the same as a man. But as a man, Eric Schinegger proved an also ran.

These were the scattered Olympics. The skating events took place in Grenoble itself, the others in five different places in the area. The nearest to Grenoble was St Nizier, which had been chosen for the 90m (295ft) jumping event because it provided comparatively easy access for spectators.

Since 1964 gold medals had been awarded for two different jumping competitions, one on a normal hill and one on a big hill, known as the 70m and 90m (230ft and 295ft) hills, though the actual lengths achieved may considerably exceed these distances. In the 1968 Olympics the longest jump on the 70m hill was 80m (262ft), and the longest jump on the 90m hill was 101m (331ft).

Only the 90m hill was at St Nizier. The 70m jumping and the cross-country events, including biathlon, were at Autrans. The Alpine events were at Chamrousse, on the other side of Grenoble and some 50km away. The tobogganing at Villard-de-Lan and the bobbing at Alpe d'Huez were even further apart.

XI Winter Olympic Games
Sapporo, Japan 1972

Memories of the 1972 Olympics are dominated by an athlete who was not even in Sapporo at the time of the Games, the Austrian, Karl Schranz.

Karl Schranz was 17 when he first drew attention to himself. In the 1956 Arlberg-Kandahar slalom he fell on the first run but did outstandingly the best time on the second. The following year, 1957, was one with neither World Championship or Olympic events. In such years, before the World Cup was started in 1967, the Arlberg-Kandahar was regarded as an unofficial World Championship. And in 1957 Karl Schranz won the downhill by 1.6sec, missed victory in the slalom by 0.3sec, and won the combined. During Karl Schranz's long racing career he won World Championships in downhill, giant slalom and the combined. He won the World Cup twice. But he had never won an Olympic gold medal though there were those who regarded him as the rightful winner of the 1968 Olympic slalom. At the time of the 1972 Olympics, Schranz was 33 and he had been a top class racer for 15 years.

Before the Games opened, rumours circulated that Avery Brundage, the President of the International Olympic Committee, was eager to enforce the amateur regulations against somebody. National teams adopted defensive postures. The Austrians stated categorically that if any Austrian were excluded from the Games other members of the team would withdraw in protest. The French were reported to have made a similar declaration. The Swiss were adopting a policy of unyielding tacitturnity.

In this explosive atmosphere with the Games due to open on 3 February, *The Japan Times* published on 29 January an interview with Karl Schranz. Schranz was quoted as arguing that amateurism was an outmoded concept, dating 'back to the nineteenth century when amateur sportsmen were regarded as gentlemen and everybody else was an outcast'. Brundage, Schranz's argument continued, was a millionaire with no understanding for poor athletes. If his ideas were followed to their logical conclusion, then the Olympics would only be for the very rich.

As a result of this interview, the International Olympic Committee by 28 votes to 14 in secret ballot, banned Karl Schranz from the Games. Marc Hodler, President of the International Ski Federation, commented sadly, 'Karl Schranz was not clever. The interview went against him . . . especially the threats that he would tell all if he alone were singled out.'

Perhaps Avery Brundage had not been clever either. He had to face much hostile questioning from the media as to why one individual should be punished for what all the top racers were known to be doing. And why had Schranz not been allowed to state his case before he was punished? Brundage's answer that the International Olympic Committee dealt with national or international organisations not individuals, failed to convince because it was as an individual that Schranz was singled out for retribution.

After his disqualification, Karl Schranz flew to Vienna where he received a hero's welcome from a crowd estimated at over 100,000 people. But his fellow countrymen in Sapporo had treated him less warmly. The Austrians had announced that, if one member of their team was disqualified, others would return home in protest. And after Schranz's disqualification, Austrian skiers were withdrawn from training. But Schranz's teammates did not see at all why he should deprive them of their chance to compete in the Olympics, and the redoubtable Annemarie Moser-Pröll told him so with some bluntness. Eventually a formula was found. The Austrians went back on their original statement about withdrawing other competitors in protest on the grounds that Schranz had asked them to do so.

These were the first Winter Olympics to be held outside Europe or America. From the summit of Mount Teine, scene of the giant slalom and slalom races, it was possible to see the sea. To the visitors the scenery was strange, even though beautiful, silver birches and bamboo bushes.

More important from the practical aspect of results, the weather and the snow were different to the Alps. Sapporo, in the northernmost Japanese island of Hokkaido, lies some 3° south of the central Alps and the race courses are far lower than in any Alpine centre. The men's and women's downhill ended at a height of only 336m (1102ft) above sea level. But the climate is far from temperate. Snow is brought to Hokkaido by cold winds from Siberia sweeping across the Sea of Japan. Siberia is a high pressure area. On the other side of Hokkaido, the Pacific Ocean is a low pressure area. The weather in Sapporo is subject to violent fluctuations. The snow could change suddenly and was in any case of a consistency different to Alpine conditions. This meant serious problems for the wax experts. Much credit for the great Swiss success in the Alpine events – they won six out of the 18 available medals – must go to their wax experts.

Annemarie Moser-Pröll of Austria was the great favourite for the women's downhill and giant slalom races. In 1971 she had won the overall World Cup as

Karl Schranz (AUT) the last male racer capable of regularly winning top events in downhill, giant slalom and slalom. He retired in 1972.

well as the separate World Cups for downhill and giant slalom. In 1972 she had won all four of the World Cup downhills held prior to the Olympics. But when it came to the Olympic race, she finished second to Marie-Thérèse Nadig of Switzerland. In the giant slalom, she sought her revenge, but again finished second to Marie-Thérèse Nadig.

The men's downhill also went to Switzerland, but here the result was no surprise, the winner being the reigning world champion, Bernhard Russi.

The men's giant slalom was won by Gustavo Thöeni of Italy, who was later to achieve the record of winning the overall World Cup four times, 1971–3 and again in 1975.

But in the slalom Gustavo Thöeni was defeated, coming second to Francisco Fernandez Ochoa of Spain, who had never previously finished higher than seventh in a major event.

XII Winter Olympic Games
Innsbruck, Austria 1976

Those who were at Innsbruck will doubtless remember them as Rosi Mittermaier's Games. Racing for Germany she won gold medals in the downhill and the giant slalom, and the silver medal in the slalom. But it was her charm as well as her athletic ability that impressed all who saw her in Innsbruck. Her modesty was in marked contrast with the self-satisfied arrogance of some sporting stars. At press conferences after her victories she argued that the World Cup, which she had then never won, meant more than the gold medals which she had won. The former proved a consistent superiority based on many events, whereas the latter only proved success on one single occasion. Only after she had failed to win her third gold medal, having taken second place in the giant slalom, did she admit that, yes, there really was something special about the Olympics.

After she had won her second gold medal for Germany, an Austrian paper commented crossly that it was all the fault of Count Metternich, who was the Austrian Foreign Minister from 1809–47. In case the logic of this complaint should not be immediately apparent to the reader, it should be explained that Rosi Mittermaier comes from Reit im Winkl, which was part of Austria till Count Metternich traded what he regarded as a useless snow hole in order to gain an expedient temporary advantage.

Those who were not at Innsbruck and exposed to Rosi Mittermaier's devastating charm, but who watched the events on television, will almost certainly, when they think of the 1976 Olympics, remember first Franz Klammer of Austria and his fantastic performance in the downhill race.

Gustavo Thoeni (ITA) who won the Alpine overall World Cup a record four times, 1971–5.

59

In the 1974 World Championships, he had been second in the downhill, 10th in the giant slalom and 20th in the slalom. This had been good enough to win him the World Championship in the Alpine combination. After that he had concentrated primarily on the downhill. In 1975 he won the World Cup for downhill. By the time of the Olympics he had, in event after event, proved himself the outstanding downhill racer of the time; some were even beginning to argue the greatest downhill racer of all time.

Certainly in the Alpine countries and possibly all over the world, the downhill is the Olympic event attracting most attention. The downhill at Innsbruck was held on the day after the opening ceremony. The hope, indeed the expectation of seeing their great hero, Klammer, win this most prestigious of all events had brought the excitement of the Austrian crowds to fever pitch.

In the 1975 pre-Olympic race down this course, he had had an easy win. In the non-stop training runs during practice he had had the best times. Drama was heightened by the fact that he had drawn number 15, the last of the first group. It was most improbable that he could be beaten by any of the lower seeded racers starting after him. If, as he came through the winning posts he had the best time, then it would be as certain as anything can be that he would have won the gold medal.

But, when it came to the actual race, Klammer did not ski as well as usual on the top part of the course. When his intermediate time was announced, it was only the third best. He evidently knew himself that he had to gain time on the lower part of the course for he seemed at a certain point to throw all discretion to the winds. Lots of racers before him had taken bigger risks and fallen. But of all those who watched the race on television, no-one claimed to have ever seen, before or since, a wilder and more hazardous run that ended in success. Often Klammer was airborne, his limbs flung in different directions by the violence of his speed. Again and again, he seemed to be in a position from which no man could recover his balance. His performance made, as none other has ever done, an indelible impression of the violence and the speed of ski racing, of a man struggling at the very limits of his strength with the forces of an uncompromising velocity. Klammer was already a hero in ski centred Austria, but that performance made him a world hero.

His average speed for the course was 102.8kph (63.9mph), which is fast from a standing start over a difficult course. But other racers were fast too, because the first four all finished within one second of one another. But none of them remains in the memory, so overshadowed were they by the drama of Klammer's downhill rush as he threw everything into the effort to make up for the time he had lost on the top part of the course.

Second to Klammer, and only 0.33sec behind him, was Bernhard Russi of Switzerland, who far from being pleased at getting a silver medal was bitterly disappointed at not winning his third downhill World Championship and his second Olympic gold medal.

Russi had won the World Championship downhill in 1970, and the downhill at the 1972 Olympics. He had wanted to become the first person to win three downhill World Championships in a row, but at the 1974 World Championships he had been only 13th. Then back to a near win in 1976. In the 1978 World Championships he finished 14th, after which he retired.

Klammer had started the great favourite. Not so, Rosi Mittermaier who was comparatively unknown when she got into the starting gate for her first event, the women's downhill. Since 1971 women's racing had been dominated by Annemarie Moser-Pröll of Austria, who had retired at the end of the 1975 season after winning the World Cup five times in succession. (She returned to the racing circuit in 1977, but that is another story.)

In the 1974 World Championships Rosi Mittermaier had not achieved any success. The next year she had been third in the overall World Cup, her best result to date. But just over a minute after leaving the starting gate she had rocketed from obscurity into fame. It was not simply that she had the best time so far (1:46.16), but she had beaten the favourite Brigitte Totschnig of Austria (1:46.68) by 0.52sec. These two times were to remain unbeaten.

Rosi Mittermaier then won the slalom (1:30.54) by 0.33sec. But in the giant slalom she lost by 0.12sec to Kathy Kreiner of Canada (1:29.13). When the press commiserated with her, she said, 'I did not lose a gold. I won a silver.'

There was no man to dominate the men's Alpine events as Rosi Mittermaier had the women's. Gustavo Thöeni of Italy, 26th in the downhill, fourth in the giant slalom and second in the slalom, won the triple Alpine combination, thus gaining his fifth and last World Championship title.

Austrian crowds at ski events have the reputation that, while they are highly nationalistic, they are also very sporting. A really great performance by a foreigner, but it has to be a really great performance, will win their tumultuous applause. At the 1967 Hahnenkamm at Kitzbühel in Austria, Jean-Claude Killy won the downhill. On the first run of the slalom he skied in front of a silent crowd to do the best time. The crowd were equally silent during the first part of his second run. But when he was about half-way down, something about his skiing caught the crowd and they began to yell. When he reached the finish, the board showed that he had again done the best time. A crowd of screaming youths broke through the barriers and rushed towards him. For a moment Killy thought he was going to be lynched. But the youths

Franz Klammer (AUT) who won the downhill World Cup a
record five times, 1975–8 and 1983, as well as the 1976
Olympic downhill.

hoisted him on their shoulders and carried him in triumph to the town.

But something went wrong at the jumping on the big (90m) hill on the last day of the Games. Jumping on the normal (70m) hill, held the week before, had been won by Hans-Georg Aschenbach of East Germany. Another East German had been second and Karl Schnabl of Austria third. In the first eight were the two East Germans, one Czech, one Swiss and the entire Austrian team of four.

The 90m event produced the extraordinary result that the East Germans and the Austrians both got their entire teams of four into the first eight. In this duel between the two nations, nobody could have complained if the Austrians had watched the East Germans in silence. But they booed them loudly. Jumping these distances – the longest jump that day was 102.5m (336ft) – is nerve-wracking, even if concentration is not distracted by a noisy hostile crowd. The Austrians took the first two places, Karl Schnabl giving his country on the last day its second gold medal of the Games.

XIII Winter Olympic Games
Lake Placid, USA 1980

Competing at Lake Placid were a man and a woman, Ingemar Stenmark of Sweden and Annemarie Moser-Pröll of Austria, both of whom could claim to be the outstanding skiers of their generation, but neither of whom had won an Olympic gold medal.

At the 1976 Games, the first in which Stenmark competed, he fell in the slalom and came third in the giant slalom. But that year he won the giant slalom and slalom World Cups, both for the second time. Between then and the opening of the 1980 Olympics he won the slalom World Cup all three times, and the giant slalom World Cup twice, making a total of five slalom wins and four giant slalom. He had won the overall World Cup three times, 1976–8, but then a new points formula had been introduced which made it virtually impossible to win the overall World Cup unless one competed in the downhill as well as in the giant slalom and slalom events. It was dubbed the anti-Stenmark formula, because Stenmark had never

Ingemar Stenmark (SWE) who won the World Cup a record six times for giant slalom and a record eight times for slalom, 1975–83.

Rosi Mittermaier (BRD) who won the downhill and the slalom at the 1976 Olympics.

been a downhill racer. But, determined to regain the overall World Cup, he began to train downhill high up on the glaciers before the opening of the 1980 racing season. Then, in September, he concussed himself in a violent fall and was unable to resume training for several weeks. After that he took the decision to return to exclusive concentration on the giant slalom and the slalom events. But never before had he started serious training for them so late. 'If only I get one Olympic gold medal,' he had said before the Games opened, 'I shall be happy.'

On the first run of the giant slalom, Stenmark leant over so far at the penultimate gate that it seemed he must fall and be out of the event. But, with imperturbable skill, he leant down his hand and pushed himself upright. His place in the event was saved, but he was only lying third at the end of that first run.

Exceptionally the two runs of the giant slalom were being held, not on the same day as had been the practice, but on two succeeding days. Stenmark, normally so calm and unemotional, confessed that he had found the night between the two runs a very great strain. Indeed, afterwards the International Ski Federation announced that great efforts would be made to ensure that in future both runs of the giant slalom were held on the same day.

That Stenmark had not done the best time on the first run was no great surprise. Again and again he had been behind after the first run of a slalom or giant slalom, and had then picked up sufficient time on the second run to win the event. On one occasion he had been only 23rd after the first run but had nevertheless managed to end up the overall winner. In this Olympic giant slalom he ran true to form, picking up sufficient time on the second run to win the gold medal. He repeated this success in the slalom which was run three days later: once again he won the gold medal after being behind on the first run. By the end of the season he had also won the World Cups for slalom and giant slalom.

While these two gold medals went to the outstanding favourite, the men's downhill provided a very different story. The Austrians had such an array of talent that nobody could be certain of a place in the four-man team. First star to be dropped was Franz Klammer, who had won the World Cup for downhill four times, 1975–8, and had won the 1976 Olympic gold medal with such an electrifying performance. But in 1979 and 1980 his results had been mediocre and he was not even selected to accompany the Austrian team to Lake Placid.

For the downhill, the Austrians had a team of four, plus one reserve, Leonhard Stock. In 1979 Stock had ranked sixth in the World Cup downhill. He had never won any of the races counting for the World Cup when he arrived in Lake Placid and suddenly stepped into the limelight. Something about the course there must have suited him, because on both the first and the second days of non-stop timed training, he put up better performances than any of the other competitors. The Austrian officials decided that Stock must be promoted from reserve to full membership of the team and that the three team members who had been least successful in practice should do a trial run to decide which of them should be dropped. This

was done and Josef Walcher, who had won the 1978 World Championship downhill, was dropped from the team. That the reigning World and Olympic champions failed to make the team illustrates how strong the Austrians were in this discipline. And it also highlights the anomaly that great skiers may be excluded from the Olympics, while comparatively indifferent performers from the lesser skiing countries are able to compete.

The decision by the Austrian officials to include Stock, and to submit three of the others to a trial run, caused considerable resentment, and it must have

Peter Müller (SUI) who won the downhill World Cup 1979–80.

Annemarie Moser-Pröll (AUT) who won the Alpine overall
World Cup a record six times, 1971–9.

been a relief to these officials when Stock, who had
done the best training time each day, repeated this
performance in the actual event and won the gold
medal. Second was another Austrian, Peter Wirns-
berger, and third was Peter Müller of Switzerland,
who had won the World Cup for downhill in 1979 and
was to do so again in 1980. He was certainly the best
downhill racer in the world at the time of the
Olympics and he was understandably disappointed at
failing to win the gold medal.

Among the women Alpine racers, Annemarie
Moser-Pröll had a record very similar to that of
Ingemar Stenmark among the men. She had won the
overall World Cup seven times and the giant slalom
World Cup three times. But she had never won an
Olympic gold medal. In 1972 she had surprisingly
twice come second to the comparatively unknown
Marie-Thérèse Nadig of Switzerland. She did not race
in the year of the 1976 Olympics but stayed at home to
nurse her dying father.

When Annemarie Moser-Pröll stood at the start of
the Lake Placid downhill she had been supreme in her
field even longer than Ingemar Stenmark without
ever winning an Olympic gold medal. The cold was
intense and a team assistant used a hair dryer to warm
her boots. On her person she carried a photo of her
father. She was the sixth to start but, quite apart from
her number, her supremely controlled tuck position
made her unmistakable on the course. She won by
0.7sec. Perhaps never has a gold medal been better

deserved and in a sense she fulfilled the hopes of all
who follow ski racing. But afterwards she was more
matter of fact than her fans. 'I figured I had a 99 per
cent chance to win,' she said. 'I never thought I could
lose.'

Second was Hanni Wenzel of Liechtenstein, who
went on to win the giant slalom and slalom events.
With two golds and a silver, her record equalled that
of Rosi Mittermaier in 1976. Moreover, her brother,
Andreas Wenzel, won a silver medal by coming
second to Ingemar Stenmark in the giant slalom. At
the end of the season, Andreas and Hanni put up an
even more remarkable brother and sister feat:
Andreas won the men's overall World Cup, Hanni the
women's. And yet, most people looking back at the
Lake Placid Olympics think of Annemarie Moser-
Pröll's performance in the downhill before they
remember that Hanni Wenzel won two golds and a
silver.

Some remarkable performances in the Nordic ski
events passed virtually unnoticed. First of all, the
greatest cross-country performance of all time.
Nikolai Zimyatov of the Soviet Union won the 30km
and 50km races, while coming fourth in the 15km: he
was also a member of the winning Soviet team in the
relay race. Nobody before has ever won three cross-
country gold medals at an Olympic Games. To do
that, and to come fourth in the only other cross-
country race, was an astonishing feat which deserved,
but did not get, wide recognition.

Ulrich Wehling of East Germany won the Nordic combination for the third time running, and became the first skier to win the gold medal in an individual event at three successive Olympics.

This record is however beaten, if one includes team results. Alexander Tikhonov was in the winning Soviet biathlon team on four successive occasions, 1968, 1972, 1976 and finally 1980 at Lake Placid.

The 1980 Olympics had been preceded by an accident, Ingemar Stenmark's much publicised crash while training for the downhill on the glaciers in September. And they were followed by an accident which received much less newspaper coverage but which was far more tragic. The once great Franz Klammer crossed the Atlantic, determined to restore his shattered prestige in the only World Cup downhill event to be held after the Olympics. At Lake Louise in Canada he had a superb intermediate time in a non-stop training run. Then, for no apparent reason, he crashed. He lay there unconscious, blood pouring from cuts on face and neck. He was flown to a local hospital, and from there back to one in Vienna. The cuts healed quickly enough, but an operation proved necessary on torn ligaments in one of his knees.

Nikolai Zimyatov (SOV) on his way to winning the 30km race at the 1980 Olympics.

9 World Ski Jumping Records

The sport of skiing has many facets. Downhill skiing is a speed sport, akin to motor racing. Cross-country skiing demands economy of effort and endurance; it is akin to cross-country running. Ski jumping involves body control in the air and is akin to diving.

I was reminded of this when, about 1970, I watched Karen Morse, then a child, bouncing up and down on the trampoline at Princes Water Ski Club. Most children doing such a thing are floppy, their limbs all over the place. But Karen always had her feet together, her arms by her side, her body obviously under control. It made me think she would excel as a water ski jumper, and in June 1981 Karen became the first woman in the world to jump more than 40m (131ft) on water.

In 1909 40m (131ft) would have been good enough for the world record, men's or women's on snow. That year the Norwegian, Harald Smith, became the first person to exceed that distance when he jumped 45m (148ft) at Davos, Switzerland. In 1934, 25 years later, another Norwegian, Birger Ruud, generally regarded as the greatest ski jumper of all time, covered just over double that distance, 92m (302ft), at the opening of a new jump at Planica in Yugoslavia. This jump had been designed with the express aim of making possible much longer jumps than hitherto.

The Norwegian skiing authorities, and in particular N. R. Oestgaard, the Norwegian President of the FIS (Fédération Internationale de Ski), strongly disapproved of such monster jumps. At Oestgaard's instigation, the FIS in 1936 passed a rule that start licences would be refused for competitions on hills that had a critical point of more than 80m (262ft). The critical point is where the landing slope begins to flatten. On very long jumps the jumper falls more than 60m (197ft) vertically through the air. It is obvious that if he landed on the flat he would kill himself, and that the more gradual the gradient, the greater the shock of landing. If he lands on the steep ground short of the critical point, the shock to a skilled jumper is slight. The further he lands beyond the critical point, the greater the danger.

The Planica authorities, who had just completed enlarging their jump, decided nevertheless to go ahead with a competition they had scheduled there for

Birger Ruud (NOR) demonstrating what was regarded as the perfect style in the 1930s.

later that year. Jumpers from a number of countries agreed to compete, but the Norwegians, under pressure from their own national authorities, refused. At that time the Norwegians were the leading jumpers in the world, and it seemed that no competition could be an outstanding success without them. But at Planica, on 18 March 1936, an 18-year-old Austrian, Sepp Bradl, made ski jumping history by being the first to clear 100m (328ft); he jumped 101m (331ft). Stanko Bloudek, the engineer who had designed the Planica jump, excitedly shouted, 'That was no longer ski jumping. That was ski flying.'

A new word had been added to skiing and a very apt one. For on these very long jumps the skier has time in the air to experiment with his aerodynamic position till he suddenly gets the feeling that he is gliding. It is this aerodynamic position, rather than the force and timing of the skier's jump as he leaves the platform, which is decisive in achieving distance.

The correct aerodynamic position, while it can only be properly learnt on very large jumps, is also of great importance on jumps of normal size. The Norwegian jumpers were for a long time discouraged from competing on these very large hills, so that jumpers from other countries came to surpass them in acquiring the correct aerodynamic position, and the Norwegians

lost their hegemony even on small hills. In the Olympics 1924–56 the Norwegians won all six gold medals for jumping, five of the silver medals and four of the bronze. In 1956 and 1960 the Norwegians did not win any medals at all for jumping.

In 1948 Fritz Tschannen of Switzerland jumped 120m (394ft) at Planica. Then in 1949 a jump designed to make even longer distances possible was completed at Oberstdorf, Germany. The FIS at first refused its sanction, but in the end agreed that 'exceptionally' a competition could be held there in 1950. The Oberstdorf authorities billed this as an International Ski Flying Week. During it Dan Netzell of Sweden jumped 135m (443ft), 15m (49ft) further than the world record before the week began.

The week was a great success, and when it was repeated the following year, 1951, there were 60,000 spectators. Among the competitors was a 19-year-old Finn, Tauno Luiro, who had never before jumped more than 90.5m (297ft). On the first day of the week he could not compete because his skis had not yet arrived. As he watched the others, he aroused the mirth of the spectators around him by the way he copied the motions of the jumpers, crouching low as they approached the take-off and then jumping into the air as they shot into space.

Above and left: The Planica jump in Yugoslavia was the first to make possible jumps of over 100m (328ft).

The next day Tauno Luiro's skis had arrived and he stood 111m (364ft) on his first jump. He then stood at 119m (390ft), but fell at 131m (430ft). After that he jumped 132m (433ft) as steady as a rock. Dan Netzell's world record of 135m (443ft) was in danger.

The critical point was 120m (394ft), so that 135m (443ft) was already 15m (49ft) beyond this. The top of the tower, where the run down to the take-off started, was 161m (528ft) above the flat at the bottom of the hill. (It has since been considerably raised and the jump redesigned to make even longer jumps possible.) The jumper, gathering speed as he went down the inrun, shot over the take-off at a speed of about 110km (68mph) to drop 60 to 65m (37 to 40mph) vertically through the air to the landing point.

From the top of the tower the jumper could not see the slope on which he was going to land, only the spectators massed around the outrun down on the flat far below. Terrifying, though, when all is said and done, the parachutist has an even greater sense of launching himself into space than the ski jumper. It is real rather than apparent danger that is critical. And the argument that these monster jumps would be

highly dangerous proved quite unfounded. Serious accidents have been extremely rare, rarer it is convincingly argued than in ordinary ski jumping. This was attributed to the engineering skills of those who built the monster jumps. The number of accidents in ski jumping and ski flying very markedly declined as jumps came to be designed by engineers instead of being built without any prior calculations as to the jumper's likely flight path in comparison with the slope of the landing.

It is also true that downhill racing has proved, both where death and injury are concerned, to be a vastly more dangerous sport than ski jumping or ski flying.

Ski flying is uniquely spectacular and especially when a wind is blowing, there can be some very spectacular falls. Because of the danger wind represents, wind speed measurements are carried out during ski flying competitions. In addition there are wind balloons and flags that the jumper can watch before starting down the inrun. But miscalculations can still occur. A sudden gust of wind may not just unbalance a jumper; it can press down on his ski tips causing him to somersault.

At Oberstdorf in 1951, Toni Brutscher was turned upside down and landed head first just short of the 130m (426ft) mark, having fallen 60m (197ft)

▲ Tauno Luiro.

vertically through the air. Nevertheless, because he was landing on a very steep slope, so that the blow to his body was glancing and not direct, he was unhurt. Less fortunate was Bruno da Col of Italy, who fell at the 90m (295ft) mark, 40m (131ft) short of Toni Brutscher. Bruno da Col had made a faulty take-off, and then a gust of wind not only turned him upside down but also twisted him round in the air so that he landed head first and also backwards. The force of his fall caused him to bounce and fly through the air for another 10m (33ft). His spine was severely injured. The spectators who watched this terrifying fall, and then saw him lie still after he had eventually slithered to a stop, could easily imagine he was dead.

Among those who saw the fall was Tauno Luiro; nevertheless that night he seemed unconcerned. But his room companion in the hotel was surprised to see him give himself an injection. The injection was insulin, for he was a diabetic.

Towards the end of the next day Tauno Luiro was standing on top of the tower, his young face strained as he intently watched the wind balloon and flags. They showed hardly any movement. It seemed an ideal moment to jump but still he stood high up there alone, waiting.

◀ The top of the inrun on the Oberstdorf jump in West Germany.

He was watching the balloon and flags for any evidence of an upward wind, which could give him extra distance but which could also endanger him, because an upward wind can turn into a side wind unbalancing the jumper. He waited a quarter of an hour and spectators began to speculate that he had lost his nerve.

Then he saw the evidence of an upward wind and started down the inrun; he crouched low so as to reduce wind resistance to the minimum and achieve maximum speed. After the long delay the spectators watched him fascinated. Later they would say that it seemed he would never land but he can have been in the air for only a fraction of a second longer than the others. They would also say that, when he reached about 125m (410ft), he seemed to gain a new buoyancy which carried him over the extra distance. And here it is possible that he did manage to achieve some last minute improvement of his position, or that he was aided by some sudden air current.

He landed at 139m (456ft), 4m (13ft) further than Dan Netzell's world record, and 19m (62ft) beyond the critical point. He absorbed the shock by the usual method of dropping into the telemark position. So great was the pressure on his legs, that his rear knee nearly touched the ski.

After the long wait and anxiety, the tension for the spectators was suddenly released. Tauno Luiro's

Helmut Recknagel (DDR), who won the 1960 Olympic jumping, gives a superb demonstration of the bird style.

team comrades lifted him into the air as people stormed across the palisades to acclaim the new hero.

The FIS reacted to Tauno Luiro's jump by taking steps to prevent any further record breaking.

On major jumps, the competitors do not have to start down the inrun from the top of the tower. They can also start from a number of platforms lower down, each of which gives access to a different level of the inrun. The lower the platform, and the shorter the inrun, the slower the speed is at which the jumper goes over the take-off, and the shorter the distance that he covers.

The FIS laid down that events must be so organised that competitors did not jump beyond the critical point. If the snow was fast, then they must start down the inrun from one of the lower platforms, so as to keep down their speed and thus the length of their jumps. If in competition any jumper exceeded the critical point by more than 10%, the competition had

to be halted and then resumed from a lower platform.

The FIS also laid down that no jumping would be permitted on hills that had a critical point of more than 120m (394ft). The effect of the new FIS rules was to make it virtually impossible for anybody to exceed Tauno Luiro's record of 139m (456ft). The FIS were seeking, and this is surely something unique in the history of sport, to prevent record breaking by administrative decree.

The next year at Oberstdorf nobody jumped further than 131m (430ft). Tauno Luiro was there but he did not make the longest jump. His diabetes was worse. He was a very sick young man, his exuberance gone. Back at home in Rovaniemi on the borders of the Arctic Circle, he contracted tuberculosis. Two years later he was dead. He is said to have died happy in the belief that, mortal himself, his record was eternal. In fact his record did last ten years, which is itself a record. Since 1900 and the time when jump-

A view of the jump from the top of the inrun, taken at the
1974 World Championships in Falun, Sweden.

ing records were first seriously recorded, none has
lasted as long as that.

In 1936 the FIS had laid down that no jumping hill
should ever have a critical point of more than 80m
(262ft). 15 years later they had accepted 120m (394ft),
which is half as long again as their previous figure.
The record breaking spirit of man is a tide, that can
perhaps be dammed for a time, but which can never
be halted indefinitely. Regulations get circumvented,
then they get broken, and finally they get revised.

In 1961 Tauno Luiro's record was broken. Josef
Slibar of Yugoslavia jumped 141m (463ft) at Oberstdorf. In 1967, 150m (492ft) was jumped there by
Lars Grini, a Norwegian. The Norwegians had come
to accept ski flying and had built a monster jump of
their own at Vikersund. There, later in 1967, an
Austrian, Reinhold Bachler, jumped 154m (505ft).

The Planica jump was enlarged and at a meeting
there in 1969 the record was beaten three times in

rapid succession and a new record established at 165m
(541ft). In its turn, Oberstdorf was enlarged and in
1973 the record returned there, 169m (554ft), jumped
by Heinz Wossipiwo of East Germany.

In 1976 the 170m (558ft) mark was passed. The
Norwegian, Uwe Berg, jumped 173m (567ft) at
Oberstdorf. He had the satisfaction of holding the
record for one hour, and then Toni Innauer of Austria
jumped 174m (571ft). Toni Innauer eventually
pushed the record up to 179m (571ft). And then, in
1981, Armin Kogler of Austria reached the 180m
(590ft) mark.

All this despite the continued efforts of the FIS to
curb record breaking. The FIS failed to prevent
record breaking but they slowed it down. But for
them, larger monster jumps would certainly have
been built. Indeed, as the record approached 200m
(656ft), some people began to argue that if the right
conditions could be provided, there was no limit to

Jumping in the fish style on the Oberstdorf jump in West Germany.

the distances that might be jumped. As long as the jumper held a good aerodynamic position, then even if the jump was so long that he reached terminal velocity, he would still be able to absorb the glancing blow of landing on a steep slope.

The body position of jumpers in the air has changed markedly since ski flying started. Birger Ruud, the outstanding jumper of all time, held the record in 1934 at 92m (302ft). He jumped in what was at that time regarded as the perfect style: the legs comparatively vertical and the top part of the body angled sharply forward from the waist. It was customary then for jumpers to rotate their arms, as it was believed that this helped them to maintain balance and get the body into the ideal position.

From 1950 the position of jumpers in the air began to change radically. They no longer bent the body at the waist; they kept the body straight and angled it more and more sharply forward from the feet. Instead of rotating their arms they kept them still, except for occasional small movements to regulate flight.

For a time there was considerable debate as to whether the arms should be extended in front of the body, the so called bird style, or should be held back alongside the body, the so called fish style. Paradoxically it is the style called after the swimming fish, and not the style called after the flying bird, that has come to be preferred by these flying humans.

Perhaps, after all, it is not such a paradox that the bird style should be rejected. For these men, pushing the record ever further, are doing something that no man and no bird has ever before attempted, flight without wings.

Opposite: Ski tracks in powder snow, Berner Oberland, Switzerland.
Overleaf: Charlie Kahr, Chief Trainer of the Austrian National Alpine Ski Team, photographed on the glacier above Schladming in Austria.

Torchlight skiing in Leutasch, Austria.

Thirteen skiers in Hasliberg, Switzerland.

Above: *Left* Racer in a giant slalom. *Right* Slalom racer at Courmayeur, Italy. **Below**: *Left* Hanni Wenzel (LIE) at the 1980 Olympics where she won two gold medals and one silver. *Right* Steve Mahre (USA) who won the giant slalom in the 1982 World Championships; shown here competing at the 1980 Olympics at Lake Placid, USA.

10 World Ski Speed Records

The desire to know just how fast one skis is obviously very old, and some fantastic claims have been made about speeds timed on manually operated stopwatches. One man, who claimed a world record, stated that his friend timed him on a manual stopwatch 'with uncanny accuracy'. But he had of course no way of knowing whether his friend with the stopwatch was accurate in any sense of the word; all he had was a wish to believe in the accuracy of a timing that credited him with a world record. And obviously, when high speeds are measured over short distances, even a small error in the measurement of time or distance can lead to a very major error in the number of kilometres per hour computed.

The first use of high grade precision instruments for the measurement of time and distance was at St Moritz, Switzerland, in January 1930. It was organised by Walter Amstutz, and he called the event a Flying Kilometre, a name which has stuck, but of course competitors are not timed over a whole kilometre, but normally over a tenth of that distance, 100m (109yd). The winner of the event was the Austrian, Gustav Lantschner, and the speed he achieved, 105kph (65mph), was considerably lower than anticipated. The Flying Kilometre was held at St Moritz annually from 1930 to 1933. The best time achieved there was 136kph (84mph) by the Austrian, Leo Gasperl, in 1932.

In 1947 the Flying Kilometre was held for the first time at Cervinia, which was to become the scene for most of the record breaking over the next years. It was a summer event, for the course was in fact high up on the glaciers above the town. The speed trap was at about 3500m (11,481ft), whereas at St Moritz it was about 1000m (3282ft) lower. Obviously the greater the height, the thinner the air, the less the wind resistance, and consequently the greater the speeds attained.

In 1947 at Cervinia the record was raised from 136kph to 159kph (84 to 99mph) by Zeno Colo, the Italian who had won the world championships in downhill and giant slalom in 1950 and the Olympic gold medal for downhill in 1952. Gustav Lantschner,

who gained the first record in 1930, was downhill world champion in 1932. Leo Gasperl, who held the record from 1932 to 1947, was also a successful downhill racer.

But after 1947 those breaking world speed records ceased to be successful downhill racers; they were flying kilometre specialists. A number of famous downhill racers have visited Cervinia to try the Flying Kilometre, but none of them has achieved really high speeds. Jean Claude Killy went there, but he only did the shorter course, used during the preliminary stages of practice; he never attempted the full run. Another who went there was the Swiss international, Kurt Huggler. He told me that speeds up to 120 or 130kph (74 or 81mph) were very easy for a good downhill racer, but that the difficulties then increased sharply. At over 150kph (93mph)) the skiing became very difficult and frightening.

This is because at very high speeds the skis take off from the snow, so that there is only air beneath their surfaces. The skier is quite literally flying. Because the skis are floating on air, any cross-current will displace the skier to one side or the other. The resultant sense of being out of control is very frightening, particularly for those who are not used to it. Moreover once the skis leave the snow, they must be held in the position which will give maximum aerodynamic stability, something which is beyond the experience of the ordinary downhill racer and can only be learnt by those who specialise in the Flying Kilometre.

The Flying Kilometre was not held again till 1959, when Zeno Colo's record was narrowly beaten; another Italian Edoardo Agreiter achieved 160kph (99mph). The next year at Cervinia, Luigi di Marco again an Italian, did 163kph (101mph), the first record in excess of 100mph.

In 1965 the Flying Kilometre at Cervinia came under the control of the International Ski Federation and the records were officially recognised. The winner was Ludwig Leitner of Germany, who did 172kph (107mph).

That was the year in which the Italian Walter Mussner put his head between his knees in order to achieve a better aerodynamic position. Unable to see where he was going, he crashed into the timing apparatus and died of internal injuries.

In 1973 the record was 184kph (114mph). Then in 1974 an unknown 21-year-old American, Steve McKinney, competed for the first time in the Flying Kilometre. He was destined, not only to break the record in 1974, but also within four years to take the record beyond 200kph (124mph).

Early in 1973 Steve McKinney fell while rock climbing. While leading on a steep pitch, and close to the top, he had suddenly thought 'I can't do it'. Not only was his body severely damaged by the fall, but also his self-confidence. He wrote later in the magazine *Ski*, 'Somehow, thinking back over my climbing accident that day, I knew I had to defeat that thought. ("I can't do it."). It was then that I made the conscious commitment to become the fastest skier in the world.'

The Flying Kilometre had often been in the back of his mind. Now it became his goal. In the summer after his accident, he set off for Cervinia. On the glacier area above the town there are a number of ski lifts that operate throughout the summer, and he did some skiing although his trunk was still encased in plaster. He also watched the 1973 Flying Kilometre.

In 1974 Steve McKinney came back to Cervinia one month before the event and began to practise the course, starting at first from a point low down on the track and then slowly working his way up towards the top.

Zeno Colo (ITA), World Champion 1950, Olympic gold medallist 1952 and holder of the world speed record 1947–59.

The top section of the Cervinia course, the inrun, was gradual, so that the skier gathered speed slowly. But the inrun was long, so that speeds were high by the time the skier reached the top of the very steep slope at the bottom of which was the speed trap. The change of gradient from inrun to steep slope was so abrupt that any skier who had run down from the top was bound to be thrown into the air.

Success in the Flying Kilometre does of course primarily depend on finding and then holding the tuck position that gives least wind resistance. A particular problem at Cervinia was to hold this position when thrown into the air at the top of the steep slope.

Steve McKinney has described how, as he began to achieve really high speeds at the bottom of the steep slope, he suddenly found that he had brought his knees together. At first he was concerned about this. If the knees are together and the feet even a little apart, then the skis are on their inside edges; for maximum speed skis must be held flat on the snow.

Then he realised that, at the speeds he was travelling, his skis had lost contact with the snow and were running on air; he was flying. By keeping his knees together, so that the outer edges of his skis were slightly raised, he had adopted the position that gave maximum aerodynamic stability. This was something he had come to do instinctively, as he practised over the long preceding period, the contact between his skis and the snow becoming less and less as his speeds became ever faster.

At the bottom of the steep slope, shortly after the speed trap, the ground flattened abruptly. The outrun consisted of some 15m (49ft) on the level and then a counter rise. These abrupt changes of gradient, taken at very high speed, could cause tremendous pressure on the skier, if he was not able to absorb them with sufficient elasticity. Steve McKinney has described how, on one occasion, the transition pinned him back and he felt as though iron bands had been strapped across his chest. His worst injury came because as the run out approached he said 'Hold it together'. The compression came on 'together' and he badly bit his tongue.

On three occasions during the final stages of practice, skiers who had started immediately in front of Steve McKinney had accidents. One of them, Jean-Marc Beguelin of Switzerland, did what Walter Mussner had done in 1965. He put his head between his knees and skied blind, sacrificing vision to the reduction of wind resistance. He went off course and killed himself by crashing into some ice blocks at the side. After that the jury took powers to disqualify any racer who looked as though he was unduly reducing his field of vision.

A number of the racers quit after that, including the Italian Alesandro Casse, who had broken the record twice, in 1971 and again in 1973. His wife had seen the accident.

Steve McKinney, who was unsponsored and had very limited financial resources, had had difficulty in getting the best equipment. He asked Alesandro Casse for his skis and Casse gladly gave them to him. They were not the ideal flex for McKinney's weight, but they were better than the ones he had previously been using.

Regulations limited the length of skis to 240cm (7ft 10in) and their weight with bindings to 13kg (29lb). Poles had to be carried and could not be shorter than 100cm (3ft 3½in).

There were 18 racers on the final day, 16 July. It was only on the third and last run that McKinney was the fastest competitor. The record the previous year had been 184kph (114mph); McKinney pushed it up to 189kph (117mph).

In 1977 conditions, including an avalanche, prevented the Flying Kilometre being held at Cervinia. A substitute event was organised at Portillo in Chile.

Flying Kilometres had been organised there in previous years but neither these events nor the one in 1977 were approved by the International Ski Federation because the timing equipment did not meet their standards.

Competitors preferred the Portillo course to the one at Cervinia; it had a shorter inrun, but it was very steep allowing rapid acceleration, and the change of gradient from the bottom of Portillo's steep slope to the outrun was gradual, putting comparatively little pressure on the skier.

At Cervinia in July 1978, Steve McKinney set up a new world record, 198kph (123mph) during practice, and then a snowstorm forced the abandonment of the competition. Later in the year there was again to be a Flying Kilometre event in Portillo, but this time under the full control of the International Ski Federation; it thus became the first official attempt on the world speed record away from Cervinia.

Steve McKinney (USA), the greatest figure in the quest for ultimate speed on skis.

Franz Weber (AUT) setting a new world speed record in 1982 on Storm Peak, now named Velocity Peak, Silverton, USA.

The final day of the Portillo Flying Kilometre was Sunday 1 October 1978. Steve McKinney described in the magazine *Ski* how, as he gathered speed, everything became a blur. He felt the wind pulling one of his arms aside, and he had to fight to hold it straight forward in the ideal aerodynamic stance. One ski hit a slight bump and again it needed total concentration to keep his body in the ideal position. Having passed through the speed trap he raised himself and felt a sudden slamming jolt, which was the force of the wind pressure on his extended body. Finally he reached the finish area, going slightly uphill. After he had stopped, he learnt his time, 200.22kph (124.41mph).

It was not only in pushing the record above 200kph (124mph) that history was made at Portillo. For the first time women were allowed to compete although not over the full course. Two women attempted it, one of whom fell but was uninjured. The other, Catherine Breyton of France, did 165kph (102mph).

At Les Arcs, France, on 22 March 1982, Steve McKinney pushed up his own record to 201.23kph (125.04mph). For three years he was the sole member of the 200kph club. Then, at Silverton, Colorado, USA, on 25 April 1982, Franz Weber (Austria) set up a new speed record, 203.16kph (126.24mph). At the same place and on the same day Marty Kuntz (USA) set up a new women's record, 179.10kph (111.29mph).

Since 1974 the Cervinia organisers had excluded not only women but also all men over 35. This rule was dropped at Portillo, where Kalevi Hakkinen, born 3 December 1928 finished 11th out of 25, clocking 189kph (117mph), his personal best. Hakkinen, who won the Cervinia event in 1968, has been the Flying Kilometre's greatest devotee. He competed 12 times at Cervinia, as well as in unofficial events in France, Japan and Russia. He had a car capable of 150kph (93mph), a friendly driver, and specially designed roof rack, which enabled him to stand aloft practising his tuck.

11 Free Style

Development

Neue Möglichkeiten im Skilauf (New Possibilities in Skiing) by Dr Fritz Reuel was published 1926 in Germany. In this book Fritz Reuel described a number of manoeuvres which, over 40 years later, would come to be accepted as part of a new form of competitive skiing, free style. One of those manoeuvres was waltzing, turning through 360°, when skiing downhill. Another was skiing with the legs crossed over, with the right foot on the left side of the left foot, or vice versa. A third was to turn on the inside ski, the right ski if turning to the right, while the outside ski was held in the air. This is to ski in the manner of a figure skater doing an edge and in his book Reuel juxtaposes photos of a skater doing an edge and of a skier doing this turn. It is now known as a Reuel turn, often misspelt Royal.

At the time the book had no effect. Indeed, it was regarded as a joke. In those days both equipment and technique were primitive. To ski fast and accurately was difficult enough. To invent difficulties, like skiing with the legs crossed, or turning with one ski held in the air, struck people as ludicrous.

In 1958 a 21-year-old Swiss ski teacher, Art Furrer, began to experiment with what he called ski acrobatics. In 1959 he was disciplined for practising ski acrobatics in his spare time. Such things, he was told, were unworthy of a Swiss ski teacher. He emigrated to the United States, where his ski acrobatics became a television attraction, and an American Doug Pfeiffer developed from it a new branch of competitive skiing.

In 1971 Doug Pfeiffer organised at Waterville Valley, New Hampshire, USA, a competition in which entrants were judged by their performance over a three part course. The top section of the course was very steep and mogulled. The second section contained some bumps specially prepared to make possible high flying leaps, now known as aerials. The third section was smooth and comparatively gentle in gradient; here the skier could do acrobatic manoeuvres of his own choice, what is now known as ballet. The following year Doug Pfeiffer organised a similar competition at Vail, Colorado, but this time mogul skiing, aerials and ballet were separated and held as independent events, although the top award was still given to the winner of the combined, that is to the best allround competitor in the three disciplines.

Ballet

The simplest ballet manoeuvres can be practised by ordinary skiers on any smooth slope. Waltzing is something that even skiers who have no interest in ballet have often done to amuse themselves. It is a simple trick. Again a forward crossover is not difficult. The skier picks up one ski, say the right ski, and crossing his right leg in front of his left leg, puts it down on the left side of his left ski. He then picks up his left ski, swings it out behind his right leg and puts it down parallel with the other. The legs are now in the ordinary uncrossed position.

More difficult are turns on one ski. In any turn on two skis the weight is mainly on the outside ski (the right ski if turning to the left) throughout the greater part of the turn. It is therefore easier to start with turns in which the outside ski is on the snow and the inside ski is lifted. Turns on the inside ski with the outside ski lifted are more difficult but if done properly far more graceful.

Waltzing, crossovers and turning on a single ski are basic elements that can be combined in one complex manoeuvre. For instance, a clockwise (left to right) waltz can begin on the right, that is the inside ski. The left ski is then crossed over in front of the right leg. Once the left ski has been put down on the snow in the crossed position, the right ski is picked up and the turn continued on the left ski. As the turn continues, the right ski is uncrossed behind the left leg and then put down on the snow in its proper position parallel with the other.

Rather different in type are manoeuvres done with the skier supported on his poles, for instance pirouettes round the tip or the heel of the ski. More difficult than the pirouette is the somersault forward with the skier supported on his poles. This has been called a Wongbanger after its inventor, Wayne Wong.

In the Wongbanger the skier's head does not touch the snow. But forward and backward somersaults over the snow, as well as headstands and handstands, have also been done in ballet. Such manoeuvres, which involve some part of the skier's body touching the snow, are known as snow contact manoeuvres.

Great imagination has gone into the invention of ballet manoeuvres but most ballet skiers are interested in manoeuvres that are above all graceful and flow smoothly one into the other, rather than in difficult or unusual gymnastic stunts.

Aerials

Aerials can be classified under four headings.
Upright jumps
These are jumps in which the skier neither somersaults nor rotates. An easy jump, and one which any really good skier can practise for himself over a large bump, is the spread eagle. As soon as the jumper is in

the air, he stretches his legs out sideways as far as possible, bringing them together again just before he lands.

A more difficult upright jump is the daffy. Instead of the legs being stretched out sideways, one is thrust forwards and the other backwards, as though the skier were taking a giant step in space. Indeed, when two daffys are done in succession, first one leg being thrust out in front and then the other, it is known as a space walk.

In a mule kick the ends of the skis are kicked up backwards and sideways.

A much more difficult jump is the backscratcher. The skier points his ski tips down and leans back so as to bring the ends of his skis as close to his back as possible. It is dangerous if the skier does not lift up his

The cover of Reuel's book, published 1926, which pointed the way to a whole new domain of competitive skiing.

A line of 30 skiers doing a backward somersault while holding hands at Tschiertschen, Switzerland.

ski tips in time before landing on the snow. Like many other aerials, it is best practised on a jump over water before being attempted on the snow.

Rotational or twisting jumps
In the helicopter the jumper twists through 360°. Double helicopters (720°) and triple helicopters (1080°) have also been performed.

Somersaults
The first person to somersault on skis was probably John Carleton who represented the USA in the Nordic combination at the 1924 Olympics. Somersaults can be forwards or backwards. They can be done in a crouched or tuck position; alternatively they can be done in a stretched or laid out position. The latter are slower and more difficult.

All somersaults are dangerous. In 1973 two American competitors in aerials were paralysed while attempting double back somersaults. Somersaults should first be mastered without skis on a trampoline and then thoroughly practised over water before being attempted over snow.

Combined somersaults and twisting jumps
These are the most difficult of all. The jumper somersaults at the same time as he does a helicopter, thus turning through 360° in both the vertical and horizontal planes.

Moguls

The competitor skis fast through the mogul field, sometimes turning on the moguls and sometimes jumping from them. During the jump he may do one of the aerials described previously, a mule kick, a spread eagle, even a helicopter. To take-off from the top of a mogul is comparatively easy but to land neatly and under control in a mogul field is extremely difficult, especially if one has done an aerial manoeuvre in the course of the jump.

The competitor in the moguls event needs not only technical skill and fast reactions but also a very good eye for the terrain below him.

The Inferno course at Mürren, goes from left to right
along the valley at the top of the picture and then down
this slope, the bottom of which is about half-way to the
finish.

12 Skiing Marathons

The spirit which has led so many thousands to take up marathon running has also found expression in ski racing, in both cross-country and downhill events.

The Vasa Cross-Country Race

There are a number of races which attract a mass entry, but the oldest and most prestigious of these is the Vasa and its history illustrates the explosion of interest in this type of event. It was founded in 1922 to commemorate the 400th anniversary of a journey by two skiers from Mora to Sälen in Sweden (see p. 7).

For practical reasons, the ski race is held in the reverse direction; it is from Sälen to Mora, a distance of 85.8km (53½ miles). In 1922, 50km (31 miles) was regarded as the maximum length for a ski race and only the toughest dared compete in the Vasa. In 1935 there were as few as 47 competitors.

Then in 1959 there were over 1000 competitors, in 1966 over 5000, and in 1973 over 10,000. In 1979, the organisers decided to limit the entry to 12,000, for two reasons. First there were the logistic problems, accommodation, and the supply of food. Secondly, with such great numbers there was the problem of bottlenecks at narrow passages.

The Vasa course was not specially selected to accommodate vast numbers. It was selected for historical reasons, and it was 37 years before the numbers exceeded 1000. It would obviously be possible to find courses more suitable for a mass entry. If such a course were in an area where the logistic problems could more easily be solved, it might be possible to attract an entry which went beyond the limits set at the Vasa. Were this to happen, the Vasa race would lose its position as the ski race with the largest entry.

Already, the Vasa is not the longest cross-country race in the world. It is possible to organise races of any length; but increased length has not come to mean increased prestige. The Vasa continues to be the race with the greatest prestige and the route from Sälen to Mora is still the most famous cross-country race course in the world.

The Inferno Downhill Race

It is far more difficult to find really long downhill courses. The Inferno at Mürren in Switzerland has since 1928 been the longest downhill race in the world. The course from the Schilthorn (2970m) (9744ft) to Lauterbrunnen (826m) (2710ft) includes some uphill sections and is 14km (8¾ miles) in length. It was founded by the British Kandahar Ski Club in 1928 and was at first a purely club event. In 1936 the organisation was taken over by the Mürren Ski Club and it was made an open event. In 1950 the Inferno attracted the enthusiastic attention of Field Marshal Montgomery, who praised the unique character of the race in a letter he wrote to *The Times*. He later arranged for some of the best skiers serving with NATO to compete. In 1968 the cable railway to the summit of the Schilthorn was completed. This meant that competitors no longer had to climb for five hours to reach the start. Nevertheless the number of competitors remained small. In 1972 for the first time there were more than 100. In 1977 there were more than 900. In 1980 for the first time there were more entries than the organisers could accept, the number of starters being limited to 1450. This was a far greater entry than there had ever been in any other downhill race, but it is still tiny in comparison with cross-country races like the Vasa, where all the competitors can be sent off together. This is not possible in a downhill race. Competitors have to be sent off at intervals and this greatly limits the numbers that can be accepted.

Apart from its length and the inclusion of uphill sections, the Inferno differs from other downhill races in two important respects: the course is unprepared and there are hardly any controls. The racer is not confined to a smooth piste. He skis on natural snow and he can choose his own line. The Swiss paper, *Neue Zürcher Zeitung*, in its account of the jubilee Inferno in 1978 said that this was a race in which man-made regulations were reduced to a minimum and which was governed by the natural laws of mountain skiing. It was a race which demanded a complete mastery of skiing, a technique for uphill and downhill, for every type of snow and variety of terrain.

85.8km (53½ miles) to go. The start of the Vasa race in Sweden.

Below and right: Early Swiss postcards.

LE GRAND SAINT-BERNARD

WINTERSPORT IN GRAUBÜNDEN SCHWEIZ

SCHLITTELN
EISLAUF
HOCKEY
CURLING.

13 Ski Mountaineering

Origins

1893 The crossing of the Pragel Pass

It was Fridtjof Nansen's book, *Paa Ski Over Grönland* 1890, which spread enthusiasm for skiing from Scandinavia to the Alpine countries. By then the great Alpine peaks had all been climbed in summer. Interest and ambition had turned to doing these climbs under the harsher and more difficult conditions of winter. The question was whether skis could rival snow shoes as an aid to winter mountaineering.

On 29 January 1893 there was a curious race across the Pragel Pass (1554m) (5098ft) in Switzerland. Three members of the party, led by the Swiss, Christoph Iselin, were on skis; the other, Eduard Naef was on snow shoes, in the use of which he was an expert. Eduard Naef had no difficulty in keeping up with the skiers during the ascent, but on the descent they left him far behind, reaching their destination in the valley more than one hour ahead of him.

The crossing of the Pragel Pass was the most serious Alpine excursion that had so far been undertaken on skis. But it did not entail the sort of mountaineering difficulties which are encountered in the Alps almost anywhere above 3000m (9842ft). Most mountaineers, while conceding that skis could be useful on the lower slopes, argued that they did not allow sufficient control to be anything other than dangerous in the mountains proper.

1897 The crossing of the Bernese Oberland

The first great ski mountaineering expedition was the crossing of the Bernese Oberland in Switzerland by a party of five which was led by the German, Wilhelm Paulcke. On 18 January 1897 they climbed up to the Grimsel Pass (2164m) (7100ft), where they spent the night. During the next two days they crossed the Oberaarjoch (3233m) (10,607ft) and the Grünhornlücke (3305m) (10,843ft); they enjoyed good skiing down long descents which, without skis, would have been a wearisome and far more time consuming slog. On 21 January they made an attempt on the Jungfrau (4166m) (13,668ft) but were defeated by bad weather.

The next day, 22 January, the weather was still bad. From the Concordia Hut, where they had spent the last two nights, they skied down the Aletsch Glacier to Belalp, where they broke into a hotel in order to spend the night. The next day they continued on skis into the Rhone Valley. Their journey had taken six days, four of which were on the glaciers.

On the Aletsch Glacier they had great difficulty in finding their way through a maze of crevasses. Today it seems very odd that Paulcke's party should have skied down the Aletsch Glacier instead of crossing the Lötschenlücke (3204m) (10,512ft), which is now one of the most popular ski tours in the world.

1898 Monte Rosa

Inspired by his success, Paulcke decided on a yet more audacious expedition, Monte Rosa (4634m) (15,203ft). He wanted to prove that skis could be used at over 4000m (13,123ft). He then took a most extraordinary decision. He selected as his companion the Swiss, Robert Helbling, who was a well-known mountaineer, but who had never been on skis.

Paulcke gave Helbling two days of ski instruction. Then on 3 January 1898 they set off for the Bétemps Hut, which is situated at 2795m (9170ft) (1839m (6033ft) below the summit of the mountain). The next day they devoted to reconnaissance.

On 5 January they left the hut at 2.30am. For the first 15 minutes they carried their skis; for the rest of the ascent they wore them. There was in places so much powder snow that, as Robert Helbling wrote later, the ascent would have been absolutely impossible without them. By 2.30pm they had reached 4200m (13,780ft), which was as high as they could go on skis. They did not continue on foot to the summit because Helbling had been attacked by a violent headache. By 4.55pm they were back at the point where they had first put on their skis.

Then and Now

The value of skis for winter mountaineering could not have been proved more decisively than by these two expeditions led by Wilhelm Paulcke. But the ski mountaineering that has developed since is very

W. Paulcke, extreme left, with his four companions on the 1897 ski crossing of the Bernese Oberland, Switzerland.

different from Paulcke's concepts and ideas.

In the first place winter mountaineering has greatly declined in appeal, and winter is now recognised to be the worst season for ski mountaineering. In late spring and early summer, it is far more enjoyable and much safer. In the high mountains wind ruins the powder snow of winter as a skiing surface but has hardly any effect on the hard crust which is formed later in the year by days of sunshine followed by nights of frost. Moreover, in winter the snow covers crevasses making them invisible, but does not bridge them securely. The hard crust which forms later in the year bridges them much more firmly; those that are not securely bridged are normally detectable, the snow over them tending to sag slightly and to be a little darker in colour than the surroundings.

Additionally, the weather later in the year is more clement and the days are longer. The risks of frostbite and of being benighted are far less.

Wilhelm Paulcke's generation saw skis simply as an aid to winter mountaineering. They wanted to repeat the climbs of summer under the conditions of winter. As we have seen, Paulcke followed the ordinary summer route down the Aletsch Glacier, which presented him with dangerous difficulties, instead of using the obvious and comparatively very safe skiing route across the Lötschenlücke. For Paulcke skiing was a means to an end. For a later generation the skiing and the mountaineering would be equal ends. An essential art of ski mountaineering became that of selecting those routes which would provide the most enjoyable skiing.

Robert Helbling's extraordinary performance on Monte Rosa proves that it is mountaineering not skiing skills, that are required for ski mountaineering. On ski mountaineering expeditions, the difficulties have almost invariably arisen when the skis were being carried. The actual skiing has been no more difficult than that carried out at lower levels. That is unless the skier has deliberately sought out slopes so steep that their descent demanded exceptional skills. In this the great pioneer was Sylvain Saudan.

90

Sylvain Saudan

Sylvain Saudan is not the first person to have enjoyed skiing down ultra steep slopes. Others before him have experienced the knowledge that loss of balance would probably prove fatal, have felt towards the end of each turn the sense of dropping through space till the edges once again bit into the snow. But it was Sylvain Saudan who took such performances far beyond what had been dreamed possible and who by the inspiration of his example opened up a new field of skiing endeavour.

He was born on 23 September 1936, and brought up in Combarigny, at that time a small and very remote village above Martigny in the Swiss Valais. If he had been born into a wealthier family, or into a thriving ski centre, the money might have been available to train him as a racer and he might have found his satisfaction in competitive skiing instead of in descending ultra steep slopes.

His first two such descents were not in the high mountains but near famous ski centres. He had always enjoyed difficult skiing away from the piste and in 1967 found himself at the top of an ultra steep gully on the Arosa Rothorn. He had not gone there to ski down it – it was regarded as far too steep for that – but the route he was following happened to pass along at the top of it. Suddenly its challenge attracted him and he started to ski down it. When he got to the bottom he knew what he wanted to do in the world of skiing. Later that year he skied down the north face of the Piz Corvatsch at St Moritz and had his railway season ticket confiscated by the authorities to teach him sense.

Later he moved into the High Alps, where long and very steep slopes are more plentiful. He developed his technique, a rapid succession of sharp turns, to maintain control on very steep and icy slopes. Then on 17 October 1968 he performed what must surely be his most remarkable feat, the ski descent of the Gervasutti Couloir on Mont Blanc. According to the Guide Vallot, Volume 1, the average steepnesses of this gully are as follows: 45° from the bottom at 3465m (11,368ft) to 3761m (12,339ft), 49.5° from 3761m (12,339ft) to 3995m (13,107ft), 55°, and in places even more, from 3995m (13,107ft) to the top at 4200m (13,780ft). There are places at the top around 60° in steepness and Saudan regards this as the limit of what is skiable. It is so steep and icy that it had never been climbed till 1934. At the bottom of the gully there is a large crevasse in which four climbers were killed in 1966. When the guardian of the nearest Alpine hut heard that somebody was about to ski down the Gervasutti Couloir he thought for a moment and then said, 'The Gervasutti hasn't killed anybody this year, but now it will.' After this it is something of an anticlimax to state that Saudan, using the technique he had developed, descended the Gervasutti without

incident, crossing the crevasse at the bottom at a narrow point where he could jump it.

Among Sylvain Saudan's other famous descents are the Marinelli Couloir on the south face of Monte Rosa, the Eiger from the summit down the west face, a steep face of Mount McKinley in Alaska, and from the summit of the 8068m (26,469ft) Hidden Peak in the Himalayas.

The Man Who Skied Down Everest

The first route to be followed up Everest is via the Western Cwm and the South Col. The South Col is at a height of 7879m (25,849ft). The Western Cwm at a point immediately below the South Col is at a height of approximately 6500m (21,325ft). Between the two there is one icy slope with a vertical drop of over 1300m (4265ft). The angle of this slope is not known, but it is so steep that mountaineers do not attempt this direct route, preferring the long detour via the Lhotse Face. On 6 May 1970 Yuichiro Miura of Japan skied from the South Col to the Western Cwm down this face which no mountaineer had ever attempted to climb.

Miura's technique for tackling such a descent could not be more different from that of Saudan and his technique developed from, of all improbable things, the Flying Kilometre, in which he competed in 1964 at Cervinia in Italy. He described the experience in his book, *The Man who skied down Everest* by Yuichiro Miura with Eric Perlmann, 1978. 'I told myself,' he writes 'that to be the fastest skier in the world I would trade my life.'

He achieved 172kph (107mph), which was good enough only for sixth place. What proved important is that he fell three times at speeds around 170kph (105mph) and survived with nothing worse than 'a couple of bruises on my backside'. From the experience he drew self confidence in his own resilience and ability to survive.

At these sort of velocities any turning of the skis triggers a fall. They had only been achieved on slopes that had ample space for deceleration. It struck Yuichiro Miura that the possibilities for such skiing would be enormously increased if, after achieving maximum speed, he could decelerate by releasing a parachute. A number of experiments with parachutes were carried out at the National Air Force Laboratory of Japan. In 1966 Yuichiro Miura successfully used a parachute after skiing down from the summit of the 3776m (12,388ft) high Mount Fuji. In 1969 he tested his parachute technique at a height of just over 6000m (19,685ft) on Mount Everest.

In 1970 he set out for Mount Everest with his team, which included film and cameramen. On their way from Katmandu to the Base Camp they met Sir Edmund Hillary. As Yuichiro Miura says in his book, a number of mountaineers had found the idea of

Perhaps the most daring feat in skiing history. Yuichiro Miura (JPN) skis down from the South Col on Mount Everest.

skiing down Everest to be improper. It is, however, difficult to see why it should be proper to ski in the High Alps but improper to ski on Everest. And even if the slopes of Everest were somehow sacred, they would not be more desecrated by the tracks of skiers than by the imprints of climbers' boots.

Sir Edmund Hillary did not share the woolly thinking of some lesser mountaineers. When asked what he thought of the Japanese ski expedition, he answered, 'It will be the end when people lose heart and stop looking for new and challenging problems. If only I were younger, and a little better skier myself, I would like to join you.'

On 6 May 1970 Yuichiro Miura carried out two quite distinct and separate ski runs on Mount Everest. First he climbed up from their camp on the South Col towards the South Summit of Mount Everest. The wind was very strong, and it was difficult for Miura to hold his skis on his shoulders. At a height of 8082m (26,516ft) he stopped, because above that point the surface was blue ice and unskiable. In the wind and on the slippery slope he had difficulty in putting on his skis. Then he skied down to the South Col in about five wide turns. In the book there is a photograph of him during this descent. He is not wearing an oxygen mask and he is patently in easy control of his skis. Were it not that the background scenery indicates his location, the photograph might have been taken on any enjoyable run.

At the South Col Miura took off his skis, put on his oxygen mask and climbed down to the top of his next run, which was to be right down the icy slope to the Western Cwm. He would not be able to ski to the bottom of the slope because just above the Western Cwm a great crevasse runs right across the slope. Miura's life would depend on coming to a stop before he reached that crevasse. He did not believe that with the aid of his edges alone he would ever be able to get sufficient grip on the ice to bring his skis to a halt. He was relying on his parachute to slow him down to a speed at which he could stop with his edges. But because of the thin air at these altitudes, the parachute would not function properly unless he was going at a considerable speed when it opened. Miura reckoned that the minimum speed needed would be about 175kph (108mph) and that he would achieve such a speed after running straight down the fall line of this awesome slope for about six seconds. Once the parachute had opened it should reduce his speed to between 40 and 80kph (25 and 50mph).

The effectiveness of the parachute would obviously depend on whether the wind was blowing up or down the slope. As he stood at the start, he knew that the wind was being blown into the South Face of Everest and then being deflected both sideways and vertically. He thought it was being blown down rather than up the slope.

Miura schussed in the egg position with the great rock known as the Geneva Spur on his left. When he pulled the rip cord the parachute seemed a long time opening. Just when he despaired of its doing so, he felt, not the familiar jerk pulling him backwards, but a gentle tug. He turned right towards the South Face of Everest, hoping to pick up some of the air being deflected from there. It did not seem to make any difference. He turned left towards the Geneva Spur. Whichever way he turned he could not get enough air into his parachute for it to be an effective brake.

On the lower part of the slope, some unevenness in the surface caused Miura to fall. As he slithered fast downhill, his skis were jerked from his feet and his body thrown from one position into another. Finally he came to a stop 200m (656ft) above the crevasse.

There are those who ask the point of so difficult and dangerous a feat. 'Is it stupid,' Yuichiro Miura asked in his book, 'to test the limits of one's powers, or is that a road to something sacred?'

He himself is in no doubt about the answer to that question and he speaks from experience. In the whole history of skiing has any man shown more courage than he did when he pointed his skis straight down the great icy flank of Everest?

Wilson Bentley photographed over 6000 snow crystals
and thought he had covered only a fraction of the shapes
that can exist.

PART II

SNOWCRAFT

Snow is the medium of our sport. Some understanding of its nature and of the way in which it is affected by wind, thaw, frost and human action, makes skiing more enjoyable, and also safer. More enjoyable because snowcraft enables the skier to differentiate between the various snow types, to know where each is most likely to be found, and to adapt accordingly both his technique and his choice of line. Safer, because some snow surfaces are more likely to cause breaks and sprains, and because a knowledge of snowcraft is essential for any estimation of avalanche danger.

1 Powder Snow

Falling Snow

Snow can fall as grains of ice, or can be so near rain that the crystals are sodden and shapeless before they land. Snow will in fact lie upon the ground as long as the temperature is below 3 °C (37 °F).

Dendrites

Generally snow falls as crystals that retain their independent shape till after they have landed. The commonest form of crystal begins as a flat hexagonal plate, ten times larger in diameter than in thickness. As it falls, rays grow from each point of the hexagon, till a star is formed. Spikes then grow from the rays. The rays are at an angle of 60° to one another, and the spikes tend to be at an angle of 60° to the ray on which they are formed. These star types of crystals are known as dendrites.

Other Snow Crystal Forms

The dendrite is the commonest form of snow crystal, but there are others. The basic plate, instead of growing rays on the horizontal plane, may thicken on the vertical plane, till it forms a needle that is three to five times longer than it is thick. Sometimes the ends of the needle will grow on the horizontal plane, so that the needle becomes a column connecting two horizontal plates.

Wild Snow

The size of flakes is affected by two things. Firstly, the water vapour in the atmosphere which causes the crystals to grow as they descend through the air to the ground. Secondly, wind which can coalesce even cold and simple crystals into larger flakes. Snow that has fallen while a wind is blowing has an inner cohesiveness.

Water vapour in the atmosphere causes the crystals to grow as they descend, so the drier the atmosphere and the shorter the fall, the smaller and simpler the crystals will be. If there has been no wind to coalesce the individual crystals into larger flakes, the snowfall will consist of tiny crystals, without protuberances which can interlock with one another after they have landed, and the crystals will accumulate loosely on the ground. This fallen snow, which is known as wild snow, contains much more air than ordinary powder. It can have a specific gravity as low as 0.01, whereas newly fallen snow normally has a specific gravity of 0.05–0.06.

Wild snow is very light and fluffy, with no internal cohesion. It is very unstable and flows almost like water, and will penetrate the smallest cracks.

The water vapour that causes crystals to grow generally occurs at higher temperatures. So, provided there has been no wind a snowfall is likely to produce wild snow when the accompanying temperature has been low, −15 °C (5 °F) or less.

Interlocking of Dendritic Crystals

Dendritic crystals, which have grown during their fall and developed rays and spikes, do interlock with one another after they have landed, and this does give the snow surface a certain, very temporary, cohesion. As soon as the dendrites have landed, their fine points start to evaporate, so that they no longer interlock with one another. Until this happens, the interlocking dendrites can provide cohesion so that the snow can hang as a canopy from the roof of a house.

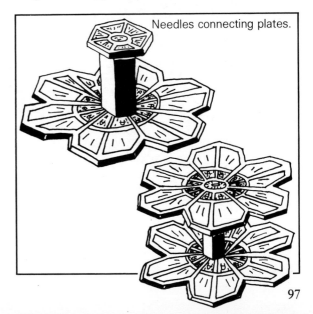

Needles connecting plates.

The Settling of Newly Fallen Snow

Snow settles after it has fallen, losing much of its air content. Normal newly fallen snow has a specific gravity of 0.05–0.06; settled snow has a specific gravity of 0.2–0.3. In settling powder snow loses about half its depth.

Under normal winter conditions it takes newly fallen snow two or three days to settle, longer when the temperature is below normal. Once snow has settled it is far less likely to avalanche.

Size of Snowfalls

The world's heaviest snowfalls are almost certainly those over the Rocky Mountains, which have an average annual snowfall of 7.6 to 10m (300 to 400in). Paradise Ranger Station, on Mount Rainier in the Rockies, claims the heaviest annual snowfall ever recorded: just over 31m between 19 February 1971 and 18 February 1972.

The mountains of the Lebanon, a range swept by wet winds from the neighbouring Mediterranean, also have very heavy snowfalls. But, while the Rockies have a unique reputation for magnificent powder snow skiing, it is very rare in the Lebanon where the snow tends to come down as grains of ice or as wet snowflakes rather than as the individual crystals that make up powder snow.

A steady snowfall produces about 5cm (2in) of snow per hour. The record for the heaviest recorded snowfall in 24 hours again comes from the Rockies; at Silver Lake, Colorado, 1.8m (71in) fell on 14–15 April 1921. This is an average of 7.5cm (2¾in) per hour.

Snow hanging on this tree in Switzerland illustrates the cohesion provided by interlocking dendritic crystals.

The deep powder snow of the Rocky Mountains, USA. Skiing at Alta.

Powder Snow as a Skiing Surface

Powder snow is the best of all skiing surfaces. With correct technique it presents little resistance to the turning ski, and yet provides a soft, resilient surface against which the ski banks as it comes round. The non-skier, who has waded through powder snow, sinking down at every step, may be surprised at my using the word resilient to describe it. But powder snow is like water; it is resilient, not for the static, but only for those in motion. So long as the skier keeps his skis pointed upwards, his tips will rise to the surface of the snow as he gathers speed. And, when he turns at speed, the snow will provide a smooth elastic support against centrifugal force. On hard snow the skier must struggle to maintain precision. But, as he turns on powder, the relationship between him and the element has the gentleness of a caress. Indeed, the Austrians have a saying that there are in life two supreme sensations, and one of them is skiing in powder snow.

2 Beaten Snow

Tracked Snow

Unfortunately powder snow deteriorates as a skiing surface when it becomes tracked, because it no longer provides a true surface against which the turning skier can bank his skis. If as the turn comes round the skis strike another track, they are for that fraction of time unsupported, and the skier must use more effort to maintain his turning arc. The more tracked the snow, the less the skier can rely on its banking effect, the more he must use strength rather than art to bring him round. The ideal obviously is to cut one's first track down a field of virgin powder.

The Piste

A succession of skiers descending a run turns tracked snow into a hard beaten piste. In addition to the natural action of descending skiers, local authorities use tracked vehicles to flatten soft snow and to make pistes as smooth as possible.

Moguls

Under most circumstances, skis are easier to turn if they are unweighted. When skiers turn on a non-icy piste, they cut away the snow during the latter half of their turn, leaving a slight protuberance behind them. Skiers descending a piste will tend to seek out any slight protuberance in the surface and to turn in the instant that they have just gone over it and their skis are unweighted. As each skier does this, he cuts away the snow a little more on the far side of the protuberance.

Where ground is steep, there will tend to be a succession of skiers turning over the same protuberances, though not always approaching them from the same direction. On a popular run the protuberances will get more and more rounded, and they will stand out increasingly from the hill side. Eventually they will come to look like a number of bee hives, all set close together.

These rounded protuberances are called moguls, a corruption from *muggel*, an Austrian colloquial word for a small bump.

In a mogul field, one should try to ski with the moguls, using the instant of weightlessness that each provides, and not to go bumping over them. Mogul fields are more difficult to manage on long skis.

Skiing under control through a mogul field is demanding and enjoyable. Doing it at great speed and with spectacular abandon is one of the three competitions that make up free style skiing.

Skiing on the Piste

A well prepared piste, whether mogulled or not, certainly provides excellent skiing. The surface responds predictably when the skier turns. Unknown hazards are eliminated. He can ski fast with confidence.

That is the appeal of the piste. And when the surrounding snow is windswept, or breakable crust, conditions that will be described later, most people will prefer piste to off-piste skiing.

But on the piste some element of adventure is missing precisely because the unknown is eliminated. And the freedom of choice is restricted. Those who made the piste have chosen its line down the mountainside. The skier is restricted to conditions that others have selected for him.

Skiing off Piste

Many skiers are nervous of venturing from the piste, but those who have had extensive experience of both on and off-piste skiing will provided the snow is good tend to prefer the latter. The skier, able to range anywhere that snow lies, enjoys a far greater variety of terrain and snow conditions. His freedom of choice is greatly extended. He must exercise judgement as to where he will find the best snow conditions. He must think ahead and be prepared for the unexpected. Skiing off piste makes more demands on the mind.

3 Windblown and Windswept Snow

Wind sweeps powder off windward slopes and deposits it on lee slopes. Windswept snow makes a vile skiing surface. Better skiing is likely on the windblown snow that is deposited on lee slopes.

Windblown Snow

Windblown snow forms into three distinct skiing surfaces, windblown powder, windblown crust and windslab. They are distinct but one merges into another; there is no fixed dividing line between them any more than there is between youth, middle age and senility.

Windblown powder

Windblown powder differs from ordinary powder in being more cohesive. My father called it cake powder, a name which is no longer used but which gives a good idea of the snow's quality. Ordinary powder scatters if struck; windblown powder is far more plastic, and tends to break up into soft blocks as one climbs uphill, cutting a ski track across it.

Windblown powder, because it is more cohesive than ordinary powder, presents more resistance to the turning ski and is therefore slightly more difficult as a skiing surface.

Windblown crust

Cohesiveness of the snow increases with the force of the wind and the quantity deposited. Provided the slope is of uniform steepness, there will be more snow deposited near the top than the bottom, and the cohesiveness of the snow will tend to decrease as one descends. On slopes that are not of uniform gradient, the snow will be particularly cohesive below any sudden steepening of the ground. This has great practical importance in assessing avalanche danger. Knowing where windblown snow has been deposited can be a matter of life and death.

Windblown crust is windblown powder with the cohesiveness taken a stage further. On top of the snow a crust is formed, which always breaks under the weight of the skier. Once it ceases to do so, it becomes windslab, which is described below. The difficulty of windblown crust as a skiing surface depends on the thickness of the crust. A thin crust is hardly more difficult than windblown powder; a thick crust presents considerable resistance to the turning ski.

Windblown crust differs from frozen crust, which is formed by thaw and frost, in that it is plastic. Frozen crust is brittle; it breaks into small pieces. Windblown crust is softer, and when it breaks, does so in much larger pieces.

As time passes, windblown crust disintegrates. It loses some of its cohesiveness and reverts to a more powdery character. A thick crust that makes turning very difficult can a few days later provide enjoyable and comparatively easy skiing. So it is as well to remember that a run one had abandoned because the crust was too thick may well be worth another try a few days later.

Windslab

The final stage in cohesiveness is windslab, which is a very hard crust with a sprinkling of powder snow adhering to the surface. In this final stage, windblown snow has become brittle. If the slab snaps under a skier's weight, it breaks into blocks that slide away

Windslab forms on lee slopes and can produce lethal avalanches.

down the hill. Such windslab avalanches have killed many skiers. Because of its lethal quality nobody selects windslab as a skiing surface except by mistake.

Windswept Snow

Ripplemarked snow

If a light wind blows across powder snow, it causes ripple marks on the surface. These marks have their steeper face on the lee side, the wind affecting the powder in the same way as it does water, blowing up the longer side of the wave. Ripplemarked snow has not got the perfect consistency of powder, but it is nevertheless a very good skiing surface.

Windbared snow

It is very rare that the force of the wind is so slight that it causes only ripples on the surface of the powder. If it is at all powerful or prolonged it will sweep the powder off all exposed areas, leaving a hard and bare sometimes icy substratum, on which it is difficult to get any grip with the skis.

Windpressed snow

On most slopes there are depressions in the ground, so shaped that the wind does not sweep them bare of snow. Instead the wind presses down on the snow in the depression, causing it to melt. Windpressed snow is very sticky. To the unhappy skier, who hits it after sliding across the smooth surface of windbared snow, it can seem to have the consistency of glue.

Windpressed crust

If the wind pressure eases, and the temperature is below zero, this damp windpressed snow will freeze and form a frozen crust. Such a crust is hard and brittle. Windpressed crust is normally known simply as windcrust, but I prefer the longer name to differentiate it from windblown crust, from which it is quite different.

Windpressed crust will be thick enough to bear the skier's weight, if a sufficient depth of snow has been melted by the wind and then, after the wind has dropped, the temperaure was at least −3 °C (27 °F): it will then provide a harsh but tolerable skiing surface. But this is unusual. Normally windpressed crust breaks under the skier's weight; it then presents great resistance to the turning ski.

Skavler

Wind has comparatively little effect on the sort of hard frozen crust which forms when a thaw is followed by frost. But there are many degrees of hardness between the light powder snow which the wind sweeps away and the hard crust on which it has very little effect.

Thus, if there has been a general thaw so that the snow is soft and heavy, the wind will not be able to sweep it away. Instead the wind will burrow into the snow, forming waves. These waves, called skavler, a Norwegian word meaning waves of the sea, form in exactly the opposite way to the ripples of ripplemarked snow. Skavler is formed by the wind burrowing into the snow. Skavler have their short face on the windward side, whereas ripplemarks are like waves of water; they have their short face on the lee side.

After a night of strong wind I have seen skavler up to 20cm (8in) high on a piste that had not been beaten hard before the wind blew. I have seen skavler up to 60cm (24in) high on Mount Etna, the upper slopes of which are very windswept, but waves as high as that are very rarely seen in the Alps.

Windswept snow as a skiing surface

Windbared snow on which the skis do not grip, sticky windpressed snow, breakable windpressed crust, they are all, in their different ways, unpleasant skiing surfaces. A combination of them is vile: the skier skidding across windbared snow may suddenly be arrested by breakable crust or skavler.

After wind, excellent skiing may be found on lee slopes. On windward slopes the best skiing is likely to be found on the piste, especially if the piste had been thoroughly hardened before the wind hit it.

Windpressed crust forms on windward slopes and does not avalanche.

4 Wet Snow

Wind and thaw are the two natural factors affecting powder snow.

When thaw is caused by a general rise in temperature, which is normally accompanied by a cloud covered sky, the extent to which a slope will thaw is determined only by its height. Orientation and angle of slope play no role. All slopes at the same height are equally affected.

Temperature as Affected by Altitude

As a rough general rule, for every rise of 100m (328ft) there is a drop in temperature of 0.5 °C (1 °F). Thus, if there is a temperature of plus 2 °C (36 °F) at 1600m (5249ft), the freezing point is likely to be around 2000m (6562ft). So skiing above 2000m (6562ft) should be unaffected by the thaw.

When skiing it is useful to know the temperature each morning, and this can be done by hanging a portable thermometer outside one's bedroom window. It also indicates how warmly one should dress. If one is going to ski on slopes 1000m (3281ft) above one's sleeping quarters, then one must remember that the temperature is likely to be 5 °C (10–11 °F) less up there.

The rule of a 0.5 °C (1 °F) drop for every 100m (328ft) rise in altitude is a rough one, and it is not universally applicable. When a warm wind is blowing – such as the Föhn in the Alps – then the difference may well be less than 0.5 °C (1 °F) per 100m (328ft). And one can sometimes even get inverted temperatures, a trough of cold air in the valleys and warmer air on the heights.

When there is thaw in the sunshine but frost in the shade, then orientation and angle of slope are more important facts than height. Though the general rule of 0.5 °C (1 °F) per 100m (328ft) does remain true for all slopes of identical orientation and angle.

Orientation of Slope

Slopes facing south are the most affected by sunshine. The skier does not need a compass to tell him where south is; it is approximately where the sun is at midday. Only approximately, because it depends partly on the position of the locality within the time zone.

Angle of Slope

Angle of slope is nearly as important as orientation. The more directly the sun shines on to a slope, the greater its power to thaw the snow. South slopes face the sun; because the winter sun is low on the horizon, the steeper a south slope is, the more directly does the sun shine on to it, so that steep south slopes melt before the gradual ones.

Of north slopes the contrary is true. The steeper the slope, the more it is sheltered from the sun's rays. So gradual north slopes melt before steep north slopes.

Wet Snow as a Skiing Surface

As soon as powder snow begins to melt it loses its powdery character and becomes heavy and slow. It provides a firm surface for holding a turn, but the effort necessary to turn is considerable. When running straight, the skis seem to drag unwillingly; if they sink deep into the snow, they tend to stay submerged instead of rising to the surface. On the piste the skiing will be less heavy, though still slow.

Balling

As powder snow thaws, it has a tendency even with modern plastic bindings to ball, that is to adhere in lumps to the surface of the skis. This unpleasant characteristic is unique to new wet snow. Old wet snow, that is snow which has been melted, refrozen, and then melted again, may be slow but it will never ball.

Icing-up

Icing-up, the adherence of ice, as opposed to snow, on the surface of the skis, is different to balling. It occurs when the skier passes from melting snow into cold snow; the water on the surface of the skis freezes on coming into contact with the cold snow and the skis ice-up. This will not happen if the skier keeps moving after running into the cold snow.

Icing-up is most likely to happen when a skier climbs a south slope in order to ski down a north slope and then pauses on the top of the north slope before starting his descent. It can be prevented by immediately skiing down a few feet into the cold snow of the

Powder snow skiing in Austria.

north slope and then, if the skier wishes to pause there, sliding the skis backwards and forwards a few times to make certain that all water is removed from their surfaces.

Accidents in Wet Snow

Snow which, when a skier falls, holds fast one of his skis, can cause a broken leg unless the safety binding functions efficiently.

In wet snow off the piste the skier tends to be skiing slowly and steadily. He has also probably got his weight back, so that his ski tips are riding above the surface. Even if he does fall, it is unlikely that his skis will be trapped beneath the surface.

But if he is on the piste, skiing comparatively fast with his weight forward, and if he then runs off the piste into the soft wet snow at the side, then there is a real danger that a ski may bury itself and throw him in a dangerous fall.

Sometimes there is loose snow beneath the hard beaten surface of the piste. This is most often due to the formation of depth hoar, which will be described in a later chapter. So, when the snow is wet, an apparently firm piste may break under the skier and a ski can get caught in the loose snow beneath. This again can result in a broken leg if the safety binding does not operate.

5 Refrozen Snow

Frozen Crust: Breakable, Unbreakable and Trap

When wet snow has been refrozen, a crust forms on the surface of the snow. The thickness of the crust will depend on the extent of the thaw and the ensuing frost. Skiers call the crust breakable or unbreakable according as to whether it does, or does not, break under the skier's weight.

Unbreakable crust can provide excellent skiing, especially if it has been superficially softened by thaw.

Breakable crust, unless it is very thin, provides considerable resistance to the turning skis. It is a difficult and generally unpopular skiing surface.

Between breakable and unbreakable crust there is an intermediate form, a crust which generally bears the skier's weight, but which sometimes breaks beneath him; such a sudden break will arrest any skidding action and make a fall very difficult to avoid. This sort of crust is aptly named trap crust; it is a trying and difficult skiing surface.

To the skier there is an enormous difference between the various sorts of crust, but scientifically the difference between them is only one of degree, not of kind. Indeed, the classification is subjective and not objective. A heavy man may be skiing on breakable crust, and having the greatest difficulty in turning, while a child on the same slope is turning easily on what to him is unbreakable crust.

Frozen Piste

Beaten snow is less likely to thaw than powder snow, so skiing on the piste may still be good while there is crust on the surrounding terrain. But a piste that has melted and then refrozen makes an unpleasant skiing surface; not only is it icy, but all unevennesses in the surface will have frozen into icy ruts.

Crust Formed After General Thaw

If a general thaw is followed by frost, there will be crust on all off-piste slopes, irrespective of their orientation and gradient. The only determining factor will be height. Above a certain height, the temperature will not have dropped below freezing point and the snow will not have been affected by a thaw. Unless one can ski on slopes this high, the best skiing is likely to be found on the lowest slopes, not on those of intermediate level. This is because the less height, the greater the thaw, and consequently the thicker the crust. So it is on the lower slopes that the crust is most likely to be unbreakable; for that reason one may start down a run on breakable crust and end it on unbreakable.

A substantial general thaw is often accompanied by rain, which is for the skier the most dreaded of all weathers. It diminishes instead of increasing the snow cover. Snow often turns to rain, but if it does not, and is then succeeded by frost, the piste will be icy and the off-piste slopes will be crusted. The crust formed after rain is often scored by lateral indentations where tiny rivulets of water have worn away the surface before it froze solid.

Crust Formed After Sunshine

When the preceding thaw was not general but caused only by sunshine, then the crust will be localised to those slopes that were affected by the sun. The winter sun is not powerful and the crust will at first only be found on steep, south facing slopes.

As the season advances and the power of the sun increases, snow gets melted on slopes that had not previously been affected: first gradual south slopes and steep west slopes. The sun melts west slopes before east slopes. This is because the morning sun has to warm the cold night air before it can affect the snow; the afternoon sun is much more powerful.

North slopes are the opposite to south slopes, in that the flatter the slope the more directly the sun shines on to it. As the year advances, it is steep north slopes that are the last to be affected by the sun.

Spring Snow

Powder snow melts more easily than frozen crust. As the power of the sun increases with the advancing year, its first effect is to spread the area of breakable crust rather than to turn breakable crust into unbreakable.

But, in due course, the sun will begin to melt the crust, until a steadily deeper layer of snow gets thawed during the day and a steadily thicker layer of crust formed by night frost. Eventually a crust will be formed that bears the skier's weight. While it forms first on steep south slopes it will, provided there is continuing night frost, eventually spread to all slopes.

We call it spring snow, because it is the snow we get at spring-time in the Alps and in other areas on approximately the same latitude. But nearer the equator the winter sun is even more powerful than the spring sun we get in the Alps, so that what we call spring snow is normal throughout the winter. South of the equator, spring snow occurs in the autumn.

The Spring Daily Cycle

Provided there is frost at night and sunshine by day, spring snow goes through a daily cycle in six stages.

1 A hard unbreakable crust.

2 An unbreakable crust the top surface of which has been softened by the sun. This is eminently the sort of snow people have in mind when they talk about the delights of spring skiing.

3 A crust which has been so softened by the sun that it breaks under the skier.

4 Wet snow, the crust having been totally melted by the sun.

5 Freezing wet snow which, provided there is a frost, occurs after the sun has left a slope.

6 A hard unbreakable crust, and the cycle is complete.

Variations in the Smoothness of Breakable Crust

The greater the preceding thaw, the more watery the snow that has been refrozen, the smoother the crust will be. In the Alps the crust that follows after rain has saturated the snow normally provides less grip for the skis than does the crust that follows sunshine. Similarly, after a day of strong sunshine in spring, steep slopes facing south will be the most slippery.

As the crust is repeatedly melted and refrozen by days of sunshine and nights of frost, it gets icier and icier, harder and harder. But this does not mean that it gets smoother and smoother; on the contrary, after a certain point, it gets progressively rougher. This is because the sun no longer melts it right through into a sodden mass. It only superficially melts the crust and has greatest effect wherever it is least dense. This uneven melting causes irregularities in the surface which, after the slope has refrozen, provide good grip for the skis.

This sort of rough unbreakable crust tends to occur only at high altitudes where the snow lasts for most of the year. One does however also get it in later winter or spring when the sun, because it has been partly hidden by cloud, has not been strong enough to melt the crust right through.

Once the snow has become very icy, the Alpine sun ceases to have an appreciable effect on it, but in countries where the sun is much more powerful, the superficial melting and then refreezing of the icy crust does cause it to get more and more uneven.

This is because any hollows in the surface concentrate the sun's rays in the same way as does a concave mirror, which causes the snow to melt quicker in the hollow than it does on the surface. As a result the hollows increase in size.

In the Lebanon this got to the point that in some places the surface of the snow resembled plough shares and was quite unskiable. One can occasionally get the very odd result of snow pillars standing in serried ranks on the bare ground. This for some unknown reason is called penitent snow. I never saw it in the Lebanon, but it has been known to occur in Iran.

Summer Snow

It is possible to ski all the year round on the glaciers. After a winter of exceptionally heavy snowfalls, slopes of snow can survive even below glacier level throughout the summer.

It is on east slopes rather than north slopes that snow survives best in summer. This is because, after the equinox, the sun sets to the north of due west, so that north slopes are increasingly subjected to the rays of the afternoon sun, which has the most destructive effect upon snow.

6 Skiing on Refrozen Snow

An understanding of the points outlined in the last chapter is necessary for getting the best out of skiing on refrozen snow.

Breakable Crust

After a day of winter sunshine followed by night frost, powder snow on south slopes will mostly have been turned into breakable crust and the pistes on south slopes are liable to be unpleasantly icy. It is therefore advisable to ski on slopes that face in other directions.

But if one has to ski on a south slope, one should then exploit the fact that slopes are hardly ever uniform in shape. There are gulleys and ridges, as well as less well marked changes of orientation and gradient. By making full use of these a skier can often place his turns in powder snow.

The sides of gulleys and ridges will obviously have been much less affected by the sun than the main south slope, but less obvious changes of orientation can also be exploited. A part of a south slope may be slightly tilted to the east or to the west. Especially if the tilt is to the east, the crust will be thinner and thus present less resistance to the turning ski; it may even be powder snow.

Changes in gradient as well as changes in orientation can be exploited. Anywhere that the gradient eases the crust will be thinner. On many slopes there are bumps or shelves that provide comparatively flat ground, and on the flatter ground the snow is likely to be powder.

So a skier on a slope which might at first seem to consist simply of crusted snow can in fact have an easier, more enjoyable and interesting run, if he watches for all changes of orientation and gradient and then places his turns accordingly.

Sometimes it will be impossible to avoid turning in breakable crust.

Unbreakable Crust

If a slope of hard unbreakable crust has been skied on when it was in a sun-softened condition, there will be tracks on it which after a night of frost are icy ruts. These ruts do mar the smooth flow of one's skiing until the sun has melted the top layer of the snow and softened their harsh contours.

Hard unbreakable crust can also have the disadvantage of being so slippery that the skier can obtain no proper grip with his skis, and the steeper the slope the more difficult this becomes. A slippery slope of unbreakable crust can still provide excellent skiing as long as it is of gentle gradient.

A steep slope of slippery unbreakable crust can be dangerous because a skier who falls is likely to find himself sliding uncontrollably downhill. This can cause a very serious accident, if there are rocks with which one may collide or worse a cliff edge over which one may fall.

Even when one is very aware of this danger, serious misjudgements are possible. One evening in the Lebanon my wife and I were skiing down below the normal runs at the ski centre of Faraya to a point on the road where a car would pick us up and take us back to Beirut. This meant crossing one very steep slope but I assumed the snow on it would, though freezing, still be soft, so that it would provide good grip for our skis.

Once we were on the slope I realised, too late, that it must have been longer in the shade than I had expected. It was already frozen into a hard unbreakable crust. My wife fell and started to slide downhill. I skied below her thinking I should be able to arrest her fall, something I had often done in the past. But this time when she slid into me, I lost my balance and fell over. We slid down the slope side by side. I could see rocks at the bottom. My wife rotated, and must have caught her ski in some obstruction, because she suddenly gave a little yelp of pain. Never have I felt so helpless as sliding down that slope beside her. We missed the rocks at the bottom but a bone in my wife's ankle was broken.

Sun-softened Crust

The spring sun after a time melts the top of the unbreakable crust. This remains firm underneath while having a superficial cover of wet snow which provides admirable purchase for the skis. The skier can let himself go secure in the knowledge that he can turn or stop with the greatest of ease. The superb control he can exercise over his skis gives him a wonderful sense of freedom.

Moreover, as the sun softens the crust it ceases to be harsh and becomes smooth as silk. Only powder snow provides a better skiing surface.

But these idyllic conditions do not last. The sun relentlessly melts and weakens the crust; after a time the skier begins to find it breaking under his weight. At first he will be able to stay on the surface, provided he keeps his weight evenly distributed between his skis and does not jerk his turns. Later whatever he does, it will break under him.

One might expect spring crust to become breakable on steep slopes, into which the sun shines more directly, before gradual slopes but this is not the case. Because a deeper layer of snow is melted on steep slopes, the resulting crust there is thicker and holds up longer even though subjected to more intense sunshine than the thinner crust on more gradual slopes. So the skier will seek to do his turns on the steeper parts of the slope and to run straight when the gradient is gradual. It is when the skis are edged for a turn that the crust is most likely to break under the skier.

Freezing Wet Snow

Once the crust has become breakable the skiing is difficult. When the crust has been melted right through into a soggy mass of wet snow the skiing is laborious. But at the end of the day, provided the shade temperature is low enough, freezing snow is to be found on any slope which the sun has left. And even sometimes on east slopes, before the sun has left them; this is because the sun, sinking in the west, shines very obliquely into any east facing slope. Freezing wet snow makes a good skiing surface. It provides a firm purchase for the skis. Indeed, it presents some resistance to the turning skis which can cause difficulties to the less experienced.

Summer Skiing

I have snow skied all the year round in the Alps and for ten months of the year in the Lebanon where it is easy to swim and ski on the same day, because the snowfields are not far from the sea.

In Switzerland I have snow skied on the Susten Pass and then later the same day water skied without a rubber suit at Gunten on Lake Thun. In fact, so easy is it to ski and swim on the same day that I was surprised when, a few years ago, *The Times* bothered to publish a number of letters from people who had done this, though I was impressed by one hardy person who had done it in Scotland.

Once in the Lebanon when carrying my skis down after skiing on Mount Sannin, I did kill a snake that I found beside my path. Skiing and killing snakes, even more than skiing and swimming, are activities one does not expect to perform on the same day.

The skiing slopes at the Cedars of Lebanon.

Hoar

Hoar is caused by the condensation of water vapour, so that it becomes ice without going through the liquid state.

Surface Hoar

In his *Alpine Skiing at all Heights and Seasons* my father called surface hoar 'leaf snow'. He noted that it was due to the condensation of water vapour and was therefore most likely to be found near stream beds. It is not common but, as my father wrote, one does occasionally 'find large leaf-like formations which rustle under the ski like autumn leaves. Such leaf snow is a dream of paradise.'

The leaf-like formation of surface hoar.

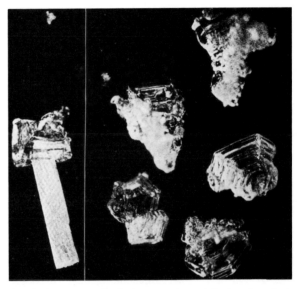

Depth hoar crystals (×4 approximately) showing their smooth shape. Lying loosely together they provide no cohesion.

Depth Hoar

Under frost conditions snow is warmest next to the ground. So evaporation occurs at the lower levels of the snow covering and the moisture-laden vapour rises to condense higher up as depth hoar. A layer of this is particularly probable just beneath a crust through which the rising vapour does not penetrate.

In 1932 the German, Wilhelm Paulcke, wrote an article in *Der Bergsteiger* saying that depth hoar also existed in the Alps. He was the first to make the very important discovery that they were a factor in causing avalanches.

7 Avalanches

Their Power for Destruction

Where there are snow and hills, avalanches may occur. While it is a form of natural disaster from which one feels pretty safe in England, on 27 December 1836 an avalanche in Lewes, Sussex, swept over some houses burying 15 people and killing eight of them. The Snowdrop Inn is now on the site of this very unusual disaster. It is the only case I know of people in the United Kingdom being killed within their homes by an avalanche.

Avalanches can happen in mountainous areas whenever there are exceptional snowfalls. On 11 January 1954 two avalanches came down on the Austrian village of Blons, killing 57 out of the 367 inhabitants. That year the snowfalls were localised but in the winter of 1950–51 the danger was far more widespread. In that year, according to Colin Fraser's *The Avalanche Enigma* avalanches killed 279 people throughout the Alps, and 15,000 acres of woodland were ripped out.

These disasters pale into insignificance compared with the avalanche on Huascaran, which at 6768m (22,200ft), is the second highest mountain in South America. On 10 January 1962 a vast piece of the summit ice cap broke away. The resulting avalanche covered a distance of about 15km (9 miles). The difference in height between the point where the avalanche broke away and the point where it finally came to rest was some 4250m (13,943ft). The avalanche wiped out six villages, partly destroyed three others, and killed more than 4000 people.

That is easily the greatest number of people killed by one avalanche. But even this figure is small compared to the numbers killed on the Alpine front in World War I. The opposing Austrian and Italian armies learnt that it was on occasions far more deadly to fire, not at the enemy, but at the slopes above him. Wilhelm Paulcke, who was a ski instructor with the German army during World War I, has estimated 60 000 deaths caused by avalanches.

Airborne Avalanches

A dry snow avalanche that generates sufficient force and speed may become airborne, great clouds of pul-verised snow flying through the air. The blast of an airborne avalanche can reach speeds of 300kph (186mph) and destroy objects that the snow does not overwhelm. On 22 December 1954 the blast from an airborne avalanche near Langen in Austria threw a bus containing 35 people off a bridge into the river below. Only 11 survived, and they spoke of the tremendous air pressure they had felt. Curiously, vehicles that happened to be just in front of and behind the fatal bus were unharmed.

If an avalanche falls over a cliff, masses of pulverised ice or snow can become airborne without there necessarily being any blast. In the 1952 *British Ski Year Book* James Riddell described how on 28 April 1952 he was in a group who had set out on skis to climb Castor, a 4230m (13,878ft) high mountain above Zermatt in Switzerland. When they were at a height of about 3800m (12,467ft), they saw plunging straight towards them a vast mass of ice and snow which had broken away from the wall of a mountain immediately above them.

At first James Riddell did not take in the enormity of their situation. He was overawed not by horror but by the magnificent beauty of the spectacle. Then came the appreciation of the truth and the thought that death 'was approaching in appalling splendour. This thought brought not fear but rather a strange elation and considerable excitement.'

Only then did the idea of escape occur to him. But looking around he quickly realised that, three to a rope and with climbing skins on their skis, there was absolutely no hope of this.

Approaching them was a wave of snow, which he has described as well over 100ft (30m) high. Now, for the first time, he felt fear. The three of them sat down, their backs to the onrushing avalanche, their skis across the slope. When the wave came over them there was a certain amount of wind but much less than expected. The most surprising thing was the sudden transition from blinding sunlight to darkness. They found themselves choking on snow as they gulped air into their lungs. They waited for the full impact of the avalanche to obliterate them. Nothing happened and there came a great silence. Slowly the billowing snow

High above the clouds in the French Alps.

Down into the powder.

The majesty of mountain scenery, Les Arcs, France.

Cross country skiing at Sils in Switzerland.

The beauty and the devastating power of an airborne avalanche.

clouds subsided and the bright sunshine returned. Nobody in the party had been hurt. The vast avalanche had vanished. Only later did they solve the mystery of its disappearance. Above them was a crevasse, some 4 to 5m (13 to 16ft) wide and several metres long. The snowbridge over this crevasse had collapsed under the weight of the avalanche, and the crevasse had swallowed it up.

Avalanches and the Skier

On 2 January 1899 two men were killed on the Susten Pass (2224m) (7296ft) in Switzerland. They probably have the melancholy distinction of being the first skiers to be killed by an avalanche. They were the first of many. According to *Lawinen* by Melchior Schild, in the 1940s 85 skiers were killed by avalanches, in the 1950s 116, in the 1960s 181, all in Switzerland.

Some skiers are admittedly unlucky, such as the one who, while peacefully queueing for the ski lift, was killed by a snow slide from the roof of the ticket office. But the vast majority of avalanches involving skiers are released by the skiers themselves. A skier who does not venture away from marked runs or ski down those that are posted as closed, takes very little risk indeed of being caught in an avalanche. Those who ski away from pistes obviously run greater risks, but these risks can be reduced by a little knowledge.

The statistics of avalanche deaths, when compared with the millions who go skiing in Switzerland over a decade, shows how minute is the risk, except for those who venture afield. And even for them the risk is very small, provided that some knowledge is possessed and some caution is shown.

Avalanche Dogs

According to Swiss statistics avalanche dogs participated in 305 rescues between 1945 and 1972. They found 45 victims who were still alive, 224 who were dead and in 36 instances they failed to find the victim.

This canine potential for saving human life was in fact discovered quite by accident in Mürren, during a ski tour to the Wasenegg in the late 1930s. One of the party was Godi Michel, who later became President of the Swiss Ski Association. He was accompanied by his dog, which set out happily, little knowing it was that day going to make canine history and inaugurate a development that would save many lives.

An avalanche came down on the Wasenegg and buried a boy. While the rest of the party were searching for him, Godi's dog was seen to scratch in the snow at a particular point. No significance was attached to this, especially when the dog later bounded up the hill to scratch above what was obviously a marmot hole. But later, when the dog returned to scratch in the snow at the original point, the party did try digging there and they found the boy alive, the first case of an avalanche victim's life being saved by a dog. The significance of the incident was not lost and led directly to experiments in training dogs to find persons buried under the snow.

8 Avoiding Avalanches

Avalanches are caused by two interrelated factors: the weight of the snow and the adhesion of that snow to its underlying surface. As neither can be measured accurately, avalanche prognostication is not an exact science.

What the Skier Needs to Know

1 The types of snow cover that are likely to avalanche.
2 Indications that the snow cover may have inadequate adhesion to its underlying surface.

To make it easier for the skier out on the snows to recall at once those indications of danger which should make him pause, I have classified them as the seven deadly signs.

ADHESION

The Shape of the Underlying Terrain

Obviously the steeper the slope, the more likely the snow is to slide away downhill. If the ground is broken and the steep part of the slope very short, then the snow on that steep part is less likely to slide and even if it does it is less likely to gather sufficient momentum to be dangerous. Therefore the steeper, longer, and smoother the slope, the greater the likelihood of a dangerous avalanche.

Many avalanches are triggered by the weight of the skier on the slope. If the slope flattens below the skier it is less likely to avalanche than if it steepens below him. Concave slopes are therefore safer than convex ones. The extreme example of a convex slope is one that ends in a cliff. Any such slope is particularly dangerous because the snow has no support below. **First deadly sign:** steep, long, smooth slopes, especially if they end in a cliff.

The Slipperiness of the Underlying Surface

Sometimes all the snow on the slope comes away, and these are called ground avalanches, because the snow slides from the underlying ground.

Normally avalanches are caused by one layer of snow sliding off another. Very often this is a layer of depth hoar because its loose, smooth crystals provide very little purchase to the snow lying immediately above them. One can discover the existence of depth hoar only by digging a trench in the snow, which is not practical for the skier out on a run.

Sometimes it is obvious that the layer of snow beneath the surface is slippery. This is the case when

AVALANCHE! Cartoon by Samivel.

new snow falls on the top of an icy crust. As one skis across the slope, one notices that the snow tends to slide away downhill. These snow slides are harmless if the slope on which they are sliding is short and they cannot gather sufficient momentum, but on all long smooth slopes, the snow may slide dangerously – even on comparatively gradual slopes.

Particular care must be taken when the underlying surface is not spring crust, which has a certain roughness, but is the smoother crust that forms after a general thaw in winter. If the top layer of snow is thawing, so that the melting water acts as a lubricant, then the conditions are about as dangerous as they can be.

Second deadly sign: new snow resting on an icy crust.

TYPES OF SNOW LIKELY TO AVALANCHE

Powder Snow

Unless powder snow falls on a frozen crust to which it does not adhere, it is unlikely to avalanche unless over 30cm (12in) of snow has fallen. As snow falls at an average rate of 5cm (2in) an hour, 30cm (12in) is about 6 hours of snowfall. An idea as to whether more than 30cm (12in) of snow have fallen can be obtained by finding some spot, such as the edge of the piste, where the snow has fallen on a hard surface, and then measuring the approximate depth with the top end of one's ski stick.

The inner cohesiveness of newly fallen snow
Most snowfalls consist of dendritic crystals, the fine points of which interlock on landing, thus providing a certain inner cohesiveness. But this cohesiveness is very temporary, because the fine points of the crystals start to evaporate as soon as they have landed.

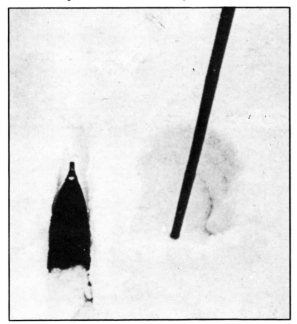

Unsettled snow is light and fluffy.

Powder snow avalanches are therefore most common a few hours after the new snow has fallen. If the snowfall is prolonged, then the inner cohesiveness of the lowest layers will have been weakened by evaporation before the snowfall has ceased. That is why avalanches often come down while it is still snowing.

Moreover, if a snowfall does not consist of dendrites, but of simpler crystals such as needles, then there will be no spikes to interlock and no inner cohesiveness. The only safe rule is to assume that if sufficient snow has fallen for there to be an avalanche danger, then that danger exists from the moment the snow has fallen till it has settled. When skiing for pleasure, it is unwise to rely on the inner cohesiveness of newly fallen snow to protect one from avalanches.

If on the other hand, one awakes in a mountain hut to find that there has been a heavy snowfall in the night, and one cannot wait up there until the snow has settled, then it will certainly be safest to ski down across any avalanche dangerous slopes as soon as possible.

Settled snow is much more compact.

The settling of newly fallen snow
Powder snow settles after it has fallen, losing much of its air content and becoming much more compact. Moreover as it settles, the crystals form bonds with one another. Settled snow is therefore much less likely to avalanche than newly fallen snow. If the temperature after the snowfall remains at 3°–5°C below zero (27°–23°F) then it will take two to three days for newly fallen snow to settle and become safe. If it is colder, it takes longer. If the temperature never rises above 10°C (14°F) below zero, it can take ten days or more for the snow to settle.

To some extent the skier can tell by the feel of the snow if it has settled or not. Unsettled snow is light and fluffy; settled snow is much more compact.

The tip of a saturated snow avalanche.

New wet snow avalanches.

Snowfall accompanied by wind
If the snowfall is accompanied by wind, there will be more snow on lee slopes, which will therefore be the more likely to avalanche. In the Alps, because snowfalls are often accompanied by westerly winds, there are most powder snow avalanches on east facing slopes.

Third deadly sign: more than 30cm of newly fallen snow.

New Wet Snow

Powder snow is much more likely to avalanche if it melts, becoming new wet snow, and this is particularly true if it melts before it has had time to settle. The greater the thaw, the greater the danger. When skiing in powder one must therefore be very alert to any indication of thaw, such as that the snow has started to become heavy and sticky.

Even the slightest thaw followed by frost helps powder snow to settle and makes it more stable. Many people erroneously believe that a thaw by itself makes powder snow safer; it doesn't, it makes it much more dangerous. It is only thaw followed by frost that makes powder snow safer.

A marked thaw followed by frost makes snow completely safe. Frozen crust, whether breakable or unbreakable, will not avalanche.

Fourth deadly sign: thawing powder snow.

Saturated Snow

A frozen crust which has melted, that is old wet snow, is much more stable than melted powder snow, that is new wet snow. But any snow, whether old or new, that has become saturated with water, may avalanche.

Avalanches of saturated snow are rare in winter but common in spring when the heat of the sun can thoroughly thaw the snow. Normally such avalanches slide off an underlying layer of snow, such as a layer of depth hoar, but sometimes they slide off the ground, all the snow on the slope coming away.

So heavy is the snow that slides in a saturated avalanche, that the skier's weight on the slope does not make any appreciable difference. The danger is therefore not so much that the skier will trigger off an avalanche by his weight as that he will be overwhelmed by one falling on him from above. So when the snow is saturated, the skier should avoid, not just crossing, but even going along at the foot of steep, long, smooth slopes. In particular he should avoid being under cliffs which have steep slopes of snow above them.

Fifth deadly sign: saturated snow.

Windslab

Windblown snow can form into a hard and brittle slab. This slab is insecurely anchored to the under-lying surface. When it snaps, the broken blocks slide away down the slope in an avalanche.

Windslab is a hard crust, but it is quite different from frozen crust in appearance. It does not look, or feel, like any form of frozen snow. Adhering to its surface there is a dusting of powdery windblown snow. Windslab has a somewhat chalky appearance but from the top of the ridge it can look like powder snow. If one descends to investigate more closely, it may snap beneath one's weight and avalanche.

Much more deceptive is the windslab which is quite invisible, buried beneath a layer of powder snow. I have seen a slope of apparently safe powder snow which a first skier crossed unharmed; but a second skier broke the underlying windslab and was carried down in an avalanche, from which he was lucky to escape with some nasty bruises and an even nastier fright. Because windslab can be hidden beneath an apparently safe skiing surface, it is of all avalanches the most treacherous. When experienced and careful skiers get killed by an avalanche, it is generally a windslab.

Places where windslab is likely to be found
Windslab lying beneath powder snow cannot be detected by the eye, so the skier can only avoid it by being aware of those places where it is likely to be found, and that is any place where windblown snow may have been deposited in large quantities.

Top of steep lee slopes
Windslab is therefore most often found at the top of steep slopes lee to the prevailing wind. In the Alps, while snowfall is often accompanied by a comparatively gentle west wind, the really powerful winds normally blow from the south. Windslab is therefore most often found at the top of steep north slopes.

Lee slopes below cornices
Cornices projecting over lee slopes are evidence of past wind. Often windslab is to be found beneath cornices. But absence of a cornice does not indicate the absence of windslab. It is the shape of the summit ridge which determines whether a cornice is formed or not. Just as much snow is blown over the ridge in places where there are no cornices as in places where there are, and windslab is often found in areas where there is no cornice above.

Below any sudden steepening of a lee slope
If the top of a lee slope is gradual, then windslab will not be found there, because the wind will tend to sweep the snow off, rather than on to, that part of the slope. But it is likely to be found further down the slope, just below the first point where it markedly steepens. By contrast, if the top of the slope is a cliff, then windslab is likely to be found on the slope at the base of the cliff.

Windward slope below a cliff
Dangerous windslab can also form on the windward slope below a cliff. This is because snow gets blown against the cliff, rather than over it, and then settles

The line of fracture where a windslab avalanche has broken away.

back in quantity at the base of the cliff. The surface on which it settles will be smooth windbared snow. Even if the snow deposited at the base of the cliff has not formed into windslab, but is windblown crust or windblown powder, it will still be dangerous because it will be resting on a very slippery surface and therefore likely to avalanche. Whether one is on the windward or the leeward side, one should beware of steep slopes immediately beneath cliffs.

Hollows and gulleys on windswept slopes

Windslab can form on the snow deposited in hollows on slopes across or down which the wind has blown. Sometimes it can fill the whole hollow, and this is the explanation for small patches of windslab found in the middle of an apparently smooth slope. But the danger of avalanche is minimal.

If wind has swept across a slope, windslab can form on the lee side of any ridge running down the slope. The extent of the danger will depend on the length and the steepness of the lee slope on the other side of the ridge. Sometimes there is a deep gully running down a slope across which the wind has been blowing. On the leeward slope of such a gulley there can certainly be lethal windslab avalanches.

If one has newly arrived in a centre, one can only find out what winds have been blowing before one got there by asking questions or looking out for cornices. The existence of a cornice is evidence of past wind. The formation of the cornice will indicate the direction from which the wind has been blowing. Any projections will be over the lee slope. If the cornice does not project, but has a sheer face, then that face will be lee to the wind that has been blowing.

Sixth deadly sign: steep slopes on which windslab may have formed.

Snow Melted From Below

Sometimes the first snowfalls occur while the ground is still warm. Then the warm ground may melt the snow from below, forming air spaces between the ground and the snow. The snow is then insecurely anchored to the ground, and an avalanche may occur. Such an avalanche will be a ground avalanche, all the snow on the slope being stripped away.

The skier may be able to detect this loose bondage between the snow and the ground in two ways.

First there may be one or more fissures, like very wide crevasses, running across the upper part of the slope. These are caused by the snow slipping downhill for about a couple of metres. This is not an avalanche but a snow creep. There may be the odd wrinkle on the surface of the snow caused by pressure as the snow cover slips but otherwise the surface of the snow remains undisturbed.

Whether there are such fissures or not, the skier on such a slope sometimes gets another indication that the snow is insecurely anchored to the ground: this is a cracking sound from beneath his feet as he skis across the slope. This is caused by the thawed under surface of the snow having frozen to form an icy crust and this crust then cracks beneath the skier's weight.

Seventh deadly sign: snow that has melted from below.

Precautions on Avalanche Dangerous Ground

One has a far better chance of not being buried by an avalanche if one can get rid of one's skis and sticks. Before venturing on to a possibly dangerous slope one should take one's hands out of the wrist straps on one's sticks. If one is wearing safety straps (to prevent loss of skis in the event of the safety binding opening), these must be undone. If one is wearing a rucksack one should be able to jettison this quickly.

One has a better chance of surviving burial by an avalanche if one keeps warm, so wear a windjacket. If the windjacket has a hood, put it up, if possible over a woolly hat, to keep the head as warm as possible. Much of the body's warmth disappears through the head. Doing up the hood also prevents snow working down inside the windjacket.

Summary: the Seven Deadly Signs

1 Steep, long, smooth slopes, especially if they end in a cliff.

2 New snow resting on an icy crust.

3 More than 30cm (12in) of newly fallen snow.

4 Thawing powder snow.

5 Saturated snow.

6 Steep slopes on which windslab may have formed.

7 Snow melted from below.

The end of an airborne avalanche.

9 Responsibility for Avalanches

Assessing Risk

When a well-known ski mountaineer is killed by an avalanche, one hears expressions of amazement that such a thing could have happened to somebody so experienced. But avalanche prediction is not an exact science, especially if one has not got the time or the facilities to dig down and examine the snow layers beneath the surface. Those who like to depart from the beaten piste, and especially those who enjoy powder snow skiing, will forego much pleasure if they ski only on slopes that they are quite certain will not avalanche. Some element of risk-taking is essential to off-piste skiing. When some experienced skier is killed by an avalanche, I assume not that he was blind to the risk but that he took it with his eyes open. He certainly failed to assess the degree of risk correctly but this is bound sometimes to happen. It is illogical to regard somebody who is killed skiing too fast as brave, and somebody who is killed by an avalanche as a fool.

If one is alone then the degree of risk one should take in the pursuit of personal pleasure obviously depends on a number of circumstances, such as whether one has dependents and whether any rescue team might be put at risk.

Setting the First Track

But there is a complicating factor. I have never heard of such a case before the courts, but in some countries a person may be held both morally and legally responsible, if he sets a track down a slope which another skier follows later only to be avalanched.

How much responsibility must one really accept for the folly of others? A slope of powder snow may be safe as long as the snow remains cold, but dangerous later if there is a thaw. Should one really not ski down a safe slope on the grounds that later conditions might render the slope dangerous and that one's track might then be taken as evidence that the slope is safe?

Even a track that has been made immediately beforehand does not prove that the slope is safe. There have been a number of cases where an avalanche has not been released by the first skier but by those following behind him. On one occasion 27 men safely crossed a slope and then an avalanche buried the next three members of the group.

When an experienced skier has gone down a slope ahead of one, this is still not proof that he regarded the slope as safe. He may be willing to take a greater risk than one would oneself.

Certainly a track down a slope, especially if it has just been made, is a factor in assessing avalanche risk. The more tracks there are the greater the argument that the slope is safe. But anyone who skis down the slope must do so on his own responsibility and at his own risk. If he is caught by an avalanche, he has not, in my view, any just grievance against those who went down the slope ahead of him.

Responsibilities of a Party Leader

There have been a number of cases where a party leader has been held legally responsible for an avalanche accident. The most famous of these was the accident in the Val Selin near St Moritz on 12 April 1964. A group of international racers were making a film and had ignored verbal advice and posted notices that the area was dangerous. While 14 of them were skiing down the slope a windslab avalanche broke away. The front skier was able to escape by skiing away to the side. The 13 others were caught by the avalanche. Two of them, both Olympic racers, Bud Werner of the USA and Barbi Henneberger of Germany, were killed.

The film producer, himself an experienced skier, was tried by the Swiss courts and acquitted. The prosecution appealed and the film producer was given a suspended sentence, despite his plea that all members of the group were expert skiers who had with full knowledge accepted the risks they ran.

10 Buried by an Avalanche

Those who get caught in avalanches can be divided into three categories. At one extreme are those who know about avalanche dangers but who decide to accept the risks of skiing down a particular slope. At the other extreme are those who do not know about avalanche dangers and who enter the slope blind to the risks they are running. Then there is the middle and almost certainly the largest category. They know something about avalanche dangers but close their eyes to the risks they run by starting to ski down a particular slope. This is partly because they do not wish to be the one who suggests stopping, and partly because they believe that so ghastly a fate as being buried by an avalanche could not happen to them.

The fate of being buried alive is all the more macabre when it strikes the lighthearted in the midst of enjoying themselves. The most vivid and moving description I have read was by Judy Bland in the February/March 1981 *Ski Survey*. She was skiing with a colleague, Robina, and two young Italians. After a day of magnificent powder snow skiing, the two Italians led them to the top of a steep slope of powder. The men tested the snow and pronounced it safe. Judy had been on an advanced ski course and had studied avalanche dangers. She wrote:

'I should have known the dangers were very real but I simply labelled any doubts as cowardly and blindly accepted the decision of my friends. After all they were mountain lads and had been skiing this mountain all their lives ...'

They paused after a magnificent run down the top part of the slope.

'Suddenly, so very suddenly, our peace was wrenched by an ear-splitting crack, it ripped through the air and immediately a deep ominous rumble followed. The horror of these sounds was totally terrifying. I glanced up towards the noise. There was a definite split from right to left across the top of the gully. The snow beneath the split was sliding slowly down the mountain. I looked at everyone for reassurance. I received none. The two boys had skied out of the path of the snow slide.

Robina was coming down with it; simultaneously, I could feel my skis move involuntarily. Panic raged through me. No longer able to look up the slope, I turned with my skis and began to roll with the snow down the mountain.

'Everything seemed to happen very slowly. I sat back a little and this helped to keep the tips above the heaving mass of snow. I shouted in vain. The rumbling drowned all other sounds. The fear, dread, panic and total uselessness were all-consuming, the snow had such force, such power.

'... I then remembered that I should release my skis and get rid of my sticks. Sticks were easy, skis were far more difficult. If I bent down to release a binding, I would fall into the rumbling sea of whiteness. It did not occur to me that the snow might not have been that deep at this point, and it might have been wise to fall into the snow.

'After what seemed hours, the slide became much slower ... I believed it was coming to a gradual stop. My spirits rose and I leant over and released my left binding. All at once, I went over a ridge. The snow came whirling, swirling, crashing over my head and I stopped dead.

'There was complete silence. No rumblings, roarings. Nothing but complete blackness. Everything buzzed with stillness, darkness and the pounding of my heart. I lost all self control. I just lay there gasping for what little air there was.

'I had fallen with my hands and arms protecting my face, allowing me air space. I screamed and realised my error, what little air I had was worth no more than two screaming lungfuls. I urged my arms to push a way up through the snow. It was futile, I seemed cemented. I couldn't move a muscle.

'My thoughts were of the end – it seemed a logical conclusion. I am still amazed at the ease with which I contemplated my fate. I inhaled the small yet deep breaths of air, grew calm and thoughts of home and family came soothingly to mind. I even remember considering that my one skiing accident had proved fatal! Ironic indeed, I knew there was very little hope. My thoughts became dreamlike and I floated into the land of the unconscious. I thought I was dead . . .

One of the Italians skied off to get help. The other and Robina tried desperately to search the avalanche debris, using their skis as probes. Then snowcats arrived with a rescue team, who worked skilfully and methodically.

'They began to work at the top of the avalanche and slowly moved down. Each man was spaced out and knew the routine. How many other tortuous occasions had they tried to free some neighbour from a burial chamber in the snow?

'They worked slowly, efficiently but they didn't find me! More people arrived – villagers with spades, branches, using their hands. Everyone willing, working as a unit; to find, to find in time and to find alive.

'Poor Robina, how she suffered, fearing the worst and stopping with nausea at the thought of what they might find.

'I was at peace, I lay asleep.

'Thirty long sweaty minutes later, the team found a ski. Forty-five minutes later . . . another shout. An Alpini had contacted something solid with his pole. There were shouts, waves and people hurried, stumbling towards the spot. Shovels began to dig and scrape. People sweated and dug and finally their search was over. For there I lay, face downwards, legs twisted around each other, my face shielded by an arm. Asleep, quiet, silent and horribly blue. I still remember nothing.

'I awoke, I felt a fear so large, a feeling of complete incomprehension. Like a child, I screamed and screamed. Screams filled with horror, relief, panic and the pain of cold. Robina thought I had lost my senses, I had. I was suffering agony. The cold was the ugliest, numbest and most painful imaginable.

'Between my screams, I managed to assure the faces around me that nothing was broken and tried to get up. I glared at those faces, beseeching them for warmth, I was mad with anguish.

'Someone tried to raise me onto the blood wagon. But to be tied down on my back, close to that awful snow, alone and with this searing cold racking my body was too terrifying to consider. I ranted, raged and refused. The snowcat was another means of getting down the mountain. Slower but warmer. I could sit upright and allow my lungs to work, I would feel the comfort and warmth, the reassurance and the strength of Robina.

'The trip in the snowcat was the beginning of reality in my mind. I drifted from consciousness to unconsciousness most of the way. The cold was still terrible, my fears enormous, but I could sense the comfort of an old friend. Finally, we reached the foot of the mountain and my fears began to disappear, blankets swathed me. Warmth crept slowly through my veins but it was hours before my shivering calmed down. Life became life as I sped down the winding mountain roads, the ambulance siren going. I removed my sodden clothes and, wrapped in warmth and security, I began to feel the flow of life flood back into my aching body.'

PART III
PREPARING TO SKI

1 Choosing a Ski Centre

Skiing – a World Wide Sport

Today people go skiing wherever they can get access to snow-covered country, and they do it right around the world. The Winter Olympic Games have been organised in Japan as well as in Europe and America. World Championships in downhill and slalom racing have been organised in the southern hemisphere, at Portillo in Chile, as well as in the northern. At Riksgränsen in northern Sweden there is a comfortable centre, complete with lifts, where it is possible to go skiing by the light of the midnight sun. From Quito, the capital of Ecuador, people go skiing on Cotopaxi, a mountain which is only 75km (46 miles) from the equator.

It would be quite impossible to count the ski centres of the world. In the USA alone there are over 1000. And the number in Europe must be even greater, when one adds together all the centres spread across the continent, in the Alps, Scandinavia, Eastern Europe, the Pyrenees, Scotland and the Apennines. Those with a taste for the unusual can ski in the legendary landscape of Greece or on Mount Etna in Sicily.

The Development of Ski Centres

At first ski centres were summer resorts which saw the possibilities of winter tourism. The village was there. The hotels were there. Nothing was required except some adaptation to winter conditions and the addition of the necessary sporting facilities.

In the second stage, villages which lacked tourist attractions in the summer came to realise that they were sited in, or within reach of, good skiing country. The village was there but the hotels had to be added.

In the third stage centres were created in areas hitherto desolate where there was excellent skiing country. A village had to be built as well as hotels.

A functional development of this third stage was the creation, not of a village with hotels, but of multistory blocks abutting directly on to the ski slopes. Inside the buildings there were arcades with shops and amusement centres as well as living accommodation. The resident need never go out of doors except to ski, and the lifts started immediately outside the doors. These self-sufficient multistory blocks were compared to ocean liners.

At one time this seemed to be the ultimate in efficiency, the final logical development of centres designed to meet the skier's needs. But many people find the efficiency soulless and miss the conviviality of village life.

Factors Involving Choice of Centre

Personal predilections must obviously play a role in the choice of a ski centre, as must inevitably price. It is necessary to read advertising literature carefully in order to establish exactly what is covered by the figures quoted. The most fashionable centres need not be the most expensive. At St Moritz for instance there are very expensive hotels but there are also cheap ones; both share the same skiing facilities.

The skiing factors involving choice are the lift system, the likely snow cover and the terrain.

The Ski Lift System

The extent and the efficiency of the ski lift system is obviously the prime consideration for the downhill skier choosing a centre.

Nowadays it is customary whenever possible to link different centres together by interconnecting lifts into one skiing area, and this obviously greatly increases the range of skiing available to those in any one of the centres concerned. Some of these areas are very extensive, covering two or more separate valleys. It is satisfying to have a day's skiing in which one travels a considerable distance, going from valley to valley, and during which one never skis the same mountainside twice. It is worth checking to see whether one really can ski from the top of one lift to the bottom of the next; sometimes the bottom of an important interconnecting lift can only be reached by walking through a village carrying one's skis. Occasionally a bus service has to be used to make the necessary connections.

It is more important to check the distance from one's living accommodation to the bottom of the nearest interconnecting lift. Does this mean a longish walk or worse, waiting in the cold for a perhaps overcrowded bus?

Wengen, Switzerland. On the right can be seen Mürren on the edge of its precipice.

Queueing for lifts can gravely mar skiing pleasure. Long morning queues are particularly probable in populous centres where the good skiing is all up in the mountains above the living accommodation. There are then rush hour queues every morning and skiers get up earlier and earlier to beat them.

Queues on all lifts, especially at week-ends, are likely in skiing areas which are within easy access from towns, even at small centres with an extensive lift system.

A compact skiing area where it is possible to ski from the top of every lift back into the village, has great advantages for a family. Children enjoying themselves will not admit to being tired until they suddenly start complaining vociferously about being quite exhausted and unbearably cold. It is then very convenient if one can quickly take the child back to the village before returning oneself to the slopes.

Snow Cover

Obviously the higher the skiing the more likely there is to be snow. A low centre, even if it serves a high skiing area, is at a disadvantage because it is obviously far preferable if one can ski right back to one's accommodation.

Sometimes winter snow is very sparse even in high centres. It is then necessary to be in a centre which is linked by cable car, or some other uphill transport that does not depend on snow, to a lift system high up near the summer snow line; which is around 3000m (9842ft) in the Alps. When at a populous centre there is no snow except at one very high lift system, then the queues up there are likely to be appalling.

Height affects snow cover, so does orientation of slopes. North slopes obviously hold snow including powder snow, longer than other slopes. South slopes are not only the least likely to hold snow cover; they have the further disadvantage that one day's sunshine turns powder snow into crust. But south slopes are the first to hold spring snow, which is an advantage later in the season when spring snow is beginning to form.

In the southern hemisphere the reverse is the case: it is south slopes that hold the snow and north slopes that first get spring snow.

Best therefore is a centre which has both north and south facing slopes. The fact that a centre is on a mountain side facing east or west does not mean that it has no north or south slopes. If there are major vertical ridges then one side of the ridge will face north and the other will face south. Mürren in Switzerland, for instance, lies on an east facing mountain side. At Mürren, the Schiltgrat, the Allmendhubel and the Maulerhubel, all of which are served by lifts, are three ridges with descents on both the north and the south side. Above them is the Schilthorn, served by a cable car, the summit of which stands out isolated from its surroundings. The ski descent from this summit is on a north slope. So although Mürren is on an east facing mountain side the majority of the runs are on north or south slopes.

Finally, in assessing a centre's chances of having snow cover, one must take into account the existence of any snow-making machines and try to discover precisely what area is covered by them. Snow machines can never provide the extensive cover nor the variety of natural snow, but they do guarantee some skiing in centres where, in a bad year, there might otherwise be no skiing at all.

The Terrain Served by the Lifts

People are inclined to think that the ideal skiing terrain is wide smooth slopes, unbroken by irregularities or obstacles. Such is the skiing at the Cedars of Lebanon, which takes its name from a small and carefully preserved grove of the cedar trees which must once have covered the mountain side. Now, outside the grove, the mountains are bare of trees.

The Cedars skiing area is a vast semicircular bowl which is open towards the west and the sea. In the centre of the bowl there are lifts which provide a vertical rise of about 600m (1968ft). On either side of the lifts there are wide slopes which are smooth except for occasional outcrops of rock. Though the gradient at the top of the slope is much steeper than at the bottom, there are no sharp variations of gradient and hardly any bumps. Such bumps as do exist are snow covered isolated rocks. Nowhere else have I seen such vast smooth slopes of snow. Only once, when the wind had deposited some sand in the snow, did I see straight tracks from the top of the lifts to the bottom of the slope. That day the snow was gritty and slow; it was easy to schuss the whole slope.

Under normal conditions I would sometimes point my skis straight down the slope from the top of the lifts, but I would always turn off into a traverse before

I was half-way down. The difficulty came not from any sharp variations in gradient, because there were none, nor from the few obstacles which could easily be avoided, but simply from one's own speed. It was possible to let oneself go in almost any direction and then, when the speed became too great, to reduce it by wide and gradual turns. This abandonment to all the speed one can take, this absence of all other difficulties, this sheer delight in fast movement, is intensely exciting, so that one would sometimes find oneself crying aloud in an outburst of exhilaration.

But after a time at the Cedars one begins to long for obstacles, for trees and rocks and bumps and gulleys, for frequent variations of gradient, for all those irregularities of terrain which are common in the Alps. One grows tired of naked speed and wants terrain that will make demands on one. At the Cedars it is brought home to one that irregularities of terrain are not imperfections from which the ideal slope is free.

A featureless and gradual slope, which the skier can schuss without difficulty, can only be made interesting by the setting of a slalom where the skier must abandon all freedom in order to follow one narrow defined track. By enforcing accurate turning it makes demands on the skier's skill. On occasions the artificial can certainly improve upon the natural but only nature can provide that haphazard variety essential to really enjoyable skiing.

Variety is essential for no single problem can test every facet of skiing skill. The best skiing runs are those where the skier must turn accurately but is still left some freedom in choosing his own line. Control of speed on wide open slopes can be achieved by turning almost anywhere; a narrow track presents a problem that is open only to one ordained solution. The most

The first ever drag ski lift, Davos, Switzerland, winter of 1934–5. It was designed by Erich Constam.

satisfactory of skiing problems are those that are open to several solutions, not all equally good, so that the skier must decide for himself how the slope can most effectively be tackled. For it is only then that demands are most rigorously made upon his judgement as well as upon his technique.

So there can be no great skiing terrain without variety. One must not confuse multiplicity of lifts with variety. Some ski centres advertise how many kilometres or miles of downhill skiing are provided by their lift system, but the figure is meaningless if all the lifts serve one monotonous sort of terrain.

Of course, every great ski centre must have some slopes like those at the Cedars, wide open slopes where the skier can let himself go in almost any direction, where he can abandon himself to the heady exhilaration of sheer speed. But there must also be areas where the skiing is restricted, where accurate turning is essential. And there must be abundant terrain that is neither wide and open nor narrow and restricted, terrain that faces the skier with a choice of different problems, many of them open to more than one solution.

Terrain and the Beginner

Ideal for beginners are runs that are gradual and wide so that they can control their speed and also have ample room for the placing of their turns. But an otherwise ideal run can be ruined for beginners if it contains even one steep narrow passage which frightens them, undermines their confidence and destroys their pleasure in skiing. Before taking a beginner to a centre one should therefore check that there are some runs which are gradual and wide throughout their length.

Beginners are particularly frightened of steep and narrow ground if the snow is icy. In spring even the iciest slopes are normally softened by the late morning, so that this is really a preferable season for beginners. In winter icy conditions are most likely on south slopes, so that runs for beginners should be on slopes that face in other directions but there may well be periods, for instance if rain is followed by frost, when there is ice on all slopes.

Couples of widely varying skiing ability should choose a compact ski centre, selecting one which has difficult and easy skiing in close proximity to one another. The more expert of the two can then pack some vigorous and difficult skiing into the first hours of the morning, then collect the less expert partner for skiing over the warmer midday period, eventually returning to the more difficult runs when the other has tired.

Terrain and the Powder Snow Enthusiast

The powder snow enthusiast needs extensive north slopes. It is ideal if some of these slopes can only be reached by a short climb, which deters many people so that the powder does not quickly get trampled flat by descending masses.

Terrain and the Cross-Country Skier

The best cross-country terrain is wide and undulating, making long cross-country tracks in different directions possible. But this, the typical Scandinavian cross-country terrain, provides only minimum possibilities for downhill skiing. A centre such as St Moritz, that lies in a long valley but has high mountains on at least one side can provide good downhill and cross-country skiing.

Exploring New Centres or Sticking to a Favourite

Some people like to visit a different centre every time they go skiing. Unless they are accompanied by somebody who already knows the centre, it may take them a lot of time before they discover the runs that suit them best and this is particularly true if the visibility happens to be bad. On familiar ground it is far easier to make the most of the skiing under whatever weather happens to prevail. Provided a centre has varied terrain one never gets tired of it. Indeed one can come to love a centre so much that one minds very much if one has to leave it for skiing anywhere else. Here I can speak from personal experience. I ski for some eight weeks every year and very much prefer to spend the whole of that time in Mürren, Switzerland, where I first put on skis in 1916.

Opposite: Snow and sunlight, high above Mürren, Switzerland.

Chairlift at Grindelwald, Switzerland. Wetterhorn in the background.

Cross country skiing in Austria.

2 Choosing Equipment

Skis

Length of skis

Cross-Country. Over the years there has been little change in the length of cross-country skis. They are not quite as long as they once were, but they are still well over head height. Most people today use cross-country skis, the tips of which come up to the palm of their upstretched hand: that is about 30cm (12in) above head height. Which means that people of average height use a ski about 210cm (6ft 10½in) in length.

Downhill. Views as to the correct length for downhill skis have fluctuated considerably. So when choosing skis one should not blindly follow the latest fashion, but should try to understand the factors involved and then decide according to individual needs.

The factors are not difficult to appreciate. A short ski is easier to turn; in particular it is much easier to manage in a mogul field. But a long ski holds better on a turn because it has a longer cutting edge. It is also steadier when running straight because it has more fore and aft stability, and is faster because it has a larger bearing surface.

A short ski is easier to manage while a long ski is more exhilarating to use. Therefore use the longest ski that is manageable, bearing in mind the skiing territory. A shorter ski is needed when skiing in mogul fields or very restricted terrain than for skiing in open country.

If the ski is too long it gives you the impression that it is running away, so that you do not feel able to turn suddenly and accurately in the event of some unexpected emergency. This saps self confidence and you ski slower than you would with a ski of the correct length.

Height is far from being the only relevant factor when deciding length of skis. Weight, strength and skill are together much more important. But height happens to be the easier factor to apply. In particular, growing children should not automatically get longer skis to match their increasing height. Children often outgrow their strength and for a time have a bigger body than they can manage. This difficulty is only compounded if they are at the same time given longer skis. At the opposite end of the age scale, a shorter ski is needed by older people as their strength declines.

It is only by trial and error, by hiring skis and testing them out, that you can discover the length which suits you best.

Width of Skis

Cross-country. A narrow ski is obviously lighter than a broad ski, so that cross-country skiers use the narrowest skis that they can manage. Racers use very narrow skis on which less expert skiers would feel unstable. Away from prepared tracks it is necessary to have a broader ski, because a narrow one would sink too deeply into the snow.

Downhill. Skis used for downhill are much broader than those used for cross-country. A broad ski is more stable, but it makes turning more difficult. It is more difficult to hold a broad ski on an edge while the narrower the ski, the easier it is, as long as it is not so narrow that the toe irons project too much and catch in the snow.

Flexibility/stiffness

Skis are arched so that when there is no weight upon them they only touch the ground at the toe and the heel. The stiffness of the ski greatly affects its running qualities.

On Piste. A ski will be faster when running straight if the skier's weight is borne evenly by the whole surface of the ski. If the ski is stiffer than that, the weight is primarily borne by the tips and the heels of the ski; and if it is more flexible the weight is borne primarily by the centre of the ski. In either event the speed is slowed down.

At the end of a sharp turn, when a skier reweights his skis after unweighting them, he comes down hard on the centre of his skis. The tip and the heel will be comparatively unweighted and will not grip properly on icy snow. So to grip well under these conditions a ski must be so stiff that the skier's weight when running straight is primarily on the tips and the heels rather than on the centre. However such a ski needs more effort to start on a turn because the heels and the tips are pressed down hard against the snow whereas a very flexible ski, with the tips and the heels hardly weighted, pivots easily about its centre. Sometimes a new flexible pair of skis seems to hold even better on the ice than an old stiffer pair, but this is simply because the new pair happens to have particularly sharp edges while the edges on the older pair are worn down.

A flexible ski tends to wander when running straight, whereas a stiff ski, holds easily to a straight line on smooth ground but gives a very rough ride over bumps.

In Powder Snow. It is easier to ski in powder snow if the ski tips break the surface of the snow. Because a ski is arched, the tip tends to press downwards through the surface of the snow. The stiffer the ski, the more the tip tends to bury itself. To prevent this happening, the skier can lean back to keep the tips planing on the surface. If his weight momentarily goes forward, there is a likelihood that the tips will bury themselves with disconcerting and possibly dangerous results. That is why it can be alarming as well as difficult to use stiff skis in powder snow.

Ability to ski in powder snow and thoroughly enjoy it has far more to do with the skis used than with the skier using them. I have never known anybody, however untalented, who, provided they had flexible skis, did not find powder snow at least as easy to cope with as hard. So if you find powder snow difficult, hire a really flexible pair of skis and then try again.

With really flexible skis, one can even ski easily, not only in powder snow, but also in powder snow overlying a crust that from time to time breaks underneath one's weight. With ordinary skis, one tends to be thrown whenever the crust breaks, but with ultra flexible skis the tips and the heels stay on the surface so that it is not difficult to maintain one's balance and keep turning.

Some skiers have two pairs of skis, one for hard snow and one for powder. Apart from the expense, this has the disadvantage that only rarely can one ski from the top of a run to the bottom on powder snow. Runs that are a mixture of hard and soft snow tend to be more enjoyable if one has got into the habit of using the same skis for both.

Skis with a flexible front. It is possible to have a ski that is stiff at the back and flexible at the front which has a number of advantages. The flexible front makes for easier skiing in soft snow while the stiffer back makes for increased control on hard snow. Such a ski is also the best for running straight on bumpy ground because the flexible front absorbs the bumps, while the stiff back prevents the ski wandering.

This type of ski makes for steadier skiing in cut up powder. Here the turning skis are sometimes banked against powder, but at other times when they strike old tracks, they have suddenly much less support because they are banked partly against air. A ski that is flexible back and front makes for unsteady skiing, whereas a stiff back to a ski presses down firmly against the snow and makes for a much steadier run.

If the back is too stiff it makes turning very difficult on hard snow as well as soft. On hard snow, if one reweights the skis before the turn is completed, the stiff heels dig into the snow so that they do not skid round but instead force the skis to shoot off at a tangent.

Weight and flexibility. The stiffness of a ski can only be seen in relation to the skier's weight. If a heavy and a light person were to use the same skis, the heavy person would be running more on the centre of the skis while the light person would be running more on the tips and the heels. So with skis of the same length, a heavy person must choose stiffer skis than a light person. An adult who wishes to use short skis cannot simply choose a child's pair, because these would be far too flexible for his weight. He must choose skis from the special range of shorts for adults which will not only be stiffer than children's skis but also broader so as to provide the extra bearing surface that his weight requires.

Assessing flexibility. There are three ways by which one can in a shop seek to assess the flexibility of a pair of skis. The most accurate is by a machine which measures the force required to press a ski down flat in three places, the centre of the ski and the centres of the front and back halves of the ski. Alternatively one can try to measure the flexibility of a ski by feel, pulling the tip and pressing a hand down on the back half of the ski. This is highly inaccurate, even when it is done by a very experienced person. The third way is by make and model. Manufacturers state for what purpose a particular ski of theirs is intended, so that the shop assistant should be able to say for what type of skier and skiing a particular model is suitable, whether for instance it is a ski which an intermediate skier could use in soft snow.

But there is no substitute for trying out a particular pair oneself, because no machine can tell you how stiff a ski you can manage.

Resilience

Resilience is the speed at which a ski reverts to its arched shape after it has been pressed down flat and then unweighted. It is the quality that makes a ski seem lively under one's foot as opposed to the dead feeling of a ski that has no resilience.

In a series of rapid turns, one is weighting the skis at the end of a turn and then unweighting them in order to initiate the next turn. A really resilient ski gives at the end of one turn and then rebounds at the start of the next. This vital response by the ski gives to a series of turns a rhythmic delight, as the effort put into one turn rebounds to make the execution of the next easier.

Side Cut

Skis are broadest at the point of upturn, the shovel, not so broad at the heel, and narrowest at the waist. The degree of side cut, that is the extent to which the skis are narrowest at the waist, depends on the use for which they are intended.

Pronounced side cut slows the ski, so that skis for downhill racing have comparatively little; those for jumping have even less. By contrast a ski designed for turning rather than for running straight has considerable side cut. This is because a pronounced shovel bites the snow and provides a good purchase for the turning ski. But the shovel can only do this if the ski twists about its axis.

Torsion

The ease with which a ski will twist about its be much easier once skis began to be made out of plastic which can be made more resilient than metal. The invention of the plastic ski represented a real breakthrough in ski manufacture.

A ski that is torsionally flexible, so that the entire edge grips the snow, holds better on ice as well as being generally easier to turn. So plastic skis could be made that gripped well on ice even though they did not have the very stiff arch which was previously thought to be essential for this.

Torsional rigidity in a ski makes no appreciable difference in soft snow. It is on hard snow that it makes such a big difference. The degree of torsional rigidity required depends on the skill and strength of the skier. A strong, expert, aggressive skier will at the end of a turn on hard snow put great pressure on his ski ends, thus causing the skis to twist about their axis. If they are not torsionally rigid enough, the ends of the skis will twist too far, and not bite the snow properly and hold as they should. On the other hand, a weak skier with torsionally stiff skis would have great difficulty in putting sufficient pressure on his ski ends to make the skis twist enough to bite properly. A ski that is twisted too little or too much, does not grip properly.

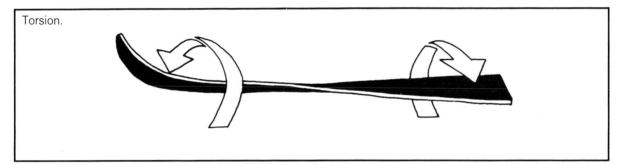

Torsion.

axis – its resistance to torsion – is a most important factor in determining a ski's running qualities.

A ski which is extremely resistant to torsion is very difficult to turn on hard snow. I once had an old pair of metal skis, which had originally been satisfactory, but I later found them very difficult to control on hard snow and virtually impossible to manage among moguls. I had them tested on a machine that could measure resistance to torsion. This is done by clamping the heel of the ski and then using a lever to twist the shovel through an angle of 12°. The force required to do this is measured in metre kilos, that is the weight in kilos which, when applied at the end of a lever one metre long, is required to twist the shovel through 12°. These old metal skis had a resistance to torsion of seven metre kilos, which is about three times what it should have been. The skis had developed metal fatigue and had gone much more torsionally rigid than they had been when new.

It was always difficult to build the required degree of torsional flexibility into metal skis. This proved to

If one makes a mistake when turning on a torsionally flexible ski, it gives easily and it is not difficult to correct one's position, but a torsionally stiff ski does not give and it is far more difficult to keep one's balance. That is why torsionally stiff skis are described as unforgiving.

Torsionally stiff skis are for experts. Getting skis that are torsionally too stiff will make further progress on skis much more difficult as they tend suddenly to throw the skier off balance in a way that can cause a violent fall. Skis that are torsionally too stiff, or too long, sap the skier's confidence and thus cause him to ski slower than he would if he had skis that suited him better.

Bindings

Walking on skis is uncomfortable unless the heel of the foot can rise freely from the ski, but for control in downhill skiing one needs the heel to be clamped rigidly to the surface of the ski. Bindings for cross-country skiing allow maximum freedom for the heel to lift; they are light; lateral rigidity for control in turning is not essential. Bindings for downhill skiing hold the heel rigidly to the ski. The tourer needs a binding which will allow his heel to lift when he is climbing, but which can be clamped down when he is skiing downhill.

For downhill skiing one needs a binding which holds the boot with complete rigidity, allowing no horizontal or lateral play, but which will release the foot in the event of a potentially dangerous fall.

There are plenty of good bindings on the market. Generally, the more one pays the longer the binding should last and the more reliable it should prove.

The shop will fit the skier's own boots to the bindings he has bought. The boot should be absolutely straight on the ski and should be held rigidly by the binding. Sometimes a binding works loose so that there is horizontal or vertical play. If, once the binding is done up, the skier can move the toe of his boot even fractionally from side to side or if he can lift the heel of his boot, then the binding does not fit properly and must be readjusted.

Checking safety bindings

The skier should check frequently to ensure that the binding's safety mechanism is functioning properly.

The safety mechanism should have been correctly set in the shop when the binding was bought, but this is something so important to the skier that he should check for himself. Moreover, even if the binding has been properly adjusted, the release mechanism can subsequently become much too stiff for safety. This is a lesson I learnt by bitter personal experience. The release mechanism of my wife's safety binding had been adjusted on a machine which could measure the pressure required to open it. After this had been done, the release adjustment mechanism was sealed in what was, at that time, indubitably the correct position. As a result I did not think it necessary periodically to check that it was still working properly. Then some time later, my wife had a fall in which she cracked a bone of her ankle. After that I did check the release mechanism and found that it had become much too stiff.

It is important to check, not only that the binding will open under horizontal pressure, that is in a twisting fall, but also that it will if necessary open in a fall straight forward over the ski tips.

The horizontal release can be checked by wearing the ski and then banging the edge of the tip diagonally down against a surface of hard snow; if the binding does not release after a number of vigorous blows, it is too stiff.

The heel release can be checked by wearing one ski at a time on a surface that is not slippery, such as the floor of the ski room, and then stepping vigorously far forward with the free foot; if you cannot open the binding by doing this, it is too stiff.

Properly adjusted safety bindings do greatly reduce the danger of a broken leg but they do not totally eliminate that danger.

Ski stoppers and retaining straps

If a binding opens during a run, there must be something to prevent the released ski running away downhill and possibly getting lost or damaging a skier below. This can be either a retaining strap, which ties the ski to the boot even after it has been released, or a ski stopper, which is a prong that digs into the snow as soon as the pressure of the skier's foot is removed from the ski.

In a high speed fall on hard snow retaining straps can be dangerous. One of my sons still has a scar where a windmilling ski cut his cheek; the damage could have been to his eye. So ski stoppers are safer than retaining straps because the skier falls completely free from the ski that has been released.

In powder snow it is as well to wear retaining straps as well as ski stoppers. In soft snow there is no danger of the skier sliding uncontrollably downhill with the released ski flying around him. But in deeper powder snow it can sometimes be extremely difficult and time consuming to find a ski that has been released well below the surface unless it is attached to the skier by a retaining strap.

Boots

Footwear for cross-country skiing has to be soft and flexible but boots for downhill must be stiff, because it is impossible to hold a ski accurately on its edge if the boot is either soft or ill fitting. The stiffer the boot and the better it fits, the more effectively is the edging movement of the leg transmitted to the ski and the easier the skier finds it to hold on ice.

The skier should try to choose the boot that fits him most perfectly, and which also gives him support at all points. Above all he should make certain that he cannot lift his heel inside the boot. On the other hand, he should be able to move his toes and should not choose a boot which cramps them.

A good skier can manage a more rigid boot than a novice, as he is tranquil on his skis. A novice is shifting about more to keep his balance. A good skier does not have to make nearly so many movements as a novice to complete a turn. A good skier absorbs bumps smoothly while a novice tends to bounce from one to another. A novice is therefore pressing against his boot much more often and the more frequent the instances of pressure, the more likely is a boot to hurt.

A young person can manage a stiffer boot than can an older one, because old people are more sensitive to pressure and take a very great deal longer to form a protective layer of skin at points of pressure.

So unless one knows extremely well what one is doing one should not choose a boot that hurts when one tries it on in the shop. Besides walking up and down in them, one should try standing still and vigorously flexing the knees forward over the toes.

The bones of the leg do not bend. So if boots fitted perfectly, there would be no point in having boots that went above the ankle. But boots do not fit perfectly, so that high boots indubitably give better control. But to take this to its logical conclusion and have stiff boots right up to the knee would be dangerous. Bones encased in modern stiff boots are protected from breaking. So if a leg-breaking fall does occur, then the break will take place above the boot. If a stiff boot went right up to the knee, then, instead of there being a break of the shin bone there would be a dislocation of the knee, which is likely to be a far more serious injury.

After a time boots will cease to hold as well as they did when they were new. A skier will feel for himself that his boots are no longer supporting him properly; a repeated desire to stop and tighten one's boots is a sure sign that they should be replaced by a new pair. If in doubt the skier should try the test of lifting his heels inside the boots when the boots are done up; if he can do so, then the boots should be discarded.

The more expensive the boot one buys, the longer it should last, and the more sophisticated should be the interior padding. This ensures a better fit. By eliminating pressure points, really good padding enables one to wear a more rigid boot, ensuring better control, than one would otherwise be able to endure.

Canting

Most people do not take canting seriously but it is important for the bow legged and to a lesser extent for the knock-kneed.

When traversing and at the end of a turn, a bow-legged person finds it difficult to get his lower ski on to its upper edge. This problem can be solved by canting, that is by fitting wedges between the foot and the ski so that, when he is standing upright on level ground, his skis are flat on the snow and not, as prior to canting, on their outside edges.

The knock-kneed person will also be helped by canting. He tends, when standing upright on level ground, to have his skis on their inside edges. On a traverse and at the end of a turn, it is the upper ski that the knock-kneed finds difficult to edge into the slope. This is not so serious as the problem for the bow-legged because most of the weight should be on the lower ski and it is this ski which has to be edged with particular accuracy.

It is easy to tell whether one is bow-legged or knock-kneed and therefore needs to cant. One stands upright, with bare legs held straight and close together. If the legs touch at the ankles but not at the knees, then one is bow-legged. If the legs touch at the knees but not at the ankles, then one is knock-kneed. If the gap, especially any gap at the knees, is substantial, then one would be helped by canting.

Poles

The cross-country skier needs poles with which he can vigorously propel himself forward. When standing on a hard floor, the poles should come up, at the shortest, to the skier's arm pit, and at the longest, to a point not much above half-way between the skier's arm pit and the top of his shoulder.

Most downhill skiers prefer poles that are much shorter, but views have fluctuated considerably over the years.

Short poles are a disadvantage when going along the level or uphill. So the ski tourer, like the cross-country skier, will probably prefer long poles. Cross-country skiers want poles that are very light, but they may be fragile. The tourer is more concerned with reliability than lightness and should choose a more robust pole of the type used for normal downhill skiing.

Downhill racers use curved poles which fit around their body in the egg position and thus help to reduce wind resistance.

Miscellaneous Equipment

Wide angle goggles are essential when skiing in falling snow. It is worth spending money to buy a good pair; poor goggles that impair one's visibility can ruin the enjoyment of skiing.

If one is going to ski in bright sunlight, one needs dark glasses or dark goggles to protect the eyes from glare. (Goggles have the disadvantage that they are hot if one has to do any walking. With dark glasses, on the other hand, the eyes tend to water if one is skiing at any speed.) I have had snow blindness from failing to protect my eyes from glare. It feels as though there is sand in one's eyes and one cannot open them in any sort of light. I was lucky not to have it at all badly; the condition only lasted about 24 hours and left no after effects.

When there is bright sunlight one also needs to put an effective sunscreen lotion on all exposed surfaces of skin.

Only a couple of minor points need to be made about modern ski clothes. Mitts are clumsy but are considerably warmer than gloves with fingers. Much heat escapes through the top of the head, and therefore a lot can be done to regulate warmth by wearing a thick woollen hat when one is cold and taking it off when hot. A bag on a strap round one's waist is very useful for carrying small items which one does not want to wear all the time. It does not impede one's freedom of movement when skiing downhill.

The delight of long radius turns in powder snow. Aspen,
Colorado, USA.

3 Choosing to be Fit

Pre Skiing Exercise

The following simple exercise, which takes about one minute a day to do, is excellent for strengthening the muscles before a skiing holiday.

STAGE I

1 Stand with your feet about 15cm (6in) apart, heels flat on the ground and your toes pointing straight forward.
2 Your arms must be pointing forwards and downwards at an angle of about 45° to the body.

STAGE II

1 From this position sink till you are squatting on your heels.
2 At the bottom of the movement, your thighs should be in contact with your body; this must be achieved, not by leaning forward from the waist but by sinking right down on to the heels.

STAGE III

Rise again to the upright position described under Stage I.

Throughout the exercise, the heels must remain flat on the ground. (Knee bends done standing on the toes do not strengthen the skiing muscles in anything like the same way.) As you sink down there is a tendency for the toes to twist outwards, and this must be prevented. The exercise is best done with bare feet and the minimum of clothing.

The skier should start by doing ten of these ski ups every morning, and he will probably find that even this small number will lead to stiffness in the legs. He should aim to be doing 35 every day for three to four weeks before the start of his holiday. If one is not going to race, this is the only exercise necessary.

The Danger of Over Exercise

I used to do these ski ups every day when I was not skiing in the belief that I was thereby strengthening my skiing muscles more and more. Then one morning in 1960, I woke up to find that I had a stiff and swollen knee though it had been perfectly alright the evening before. The doctor told me that I had arthritis and said that this normally attacked the most exercised parts of one's body, in my case the knees which I had used so much in skiing. He warned me that the more exercise I took, the worse the arthritis would get. He told me to give up skiing. That winter I skied for some seven weeks, averaging about 5000m (16,404ft) of vertical descent a day. The knee was very painful and I skied atrociously. But the following summer the affliction ceased and it has since bothered me only on rare occasions. So perhaps I did not have arthritis after all, but the incident illustrates the damage we can do to our joints by over exercise. Children when they are growing fast are particularly liable to damage their joints by too much exercise.

World class ski racers have to develop their muscles to the maximum if they are to remain competitive, but this may lead to serious trouble with their joints in later life.

At one time there was much emphasis on weight-lifting to build up muscles for ski racing. It is now realised that the strain of this can damage joints and that the same results can be achieved by exercises which are less intensive but repeated more often.

Isometric exercises, when the muscles are tensed against some strong spring or other device that resists movement, should only be done with great caution, and the same applies to the full knee bends described opposite. However, I have been authoritatively advised that this latter exercise should not cause harm to the knee if it is done in moderation (35 daily for three to four weeks prior to a skiing holiday) by adults who have no previous history of knee trouble.

Other Skiing Exercises

Those who are worried about their knees can achieve the same results as ski ups, though at a far greater expense of time, by walking upstairs no more than one step at a time because then the knee is bent as little as possible. Indeed, walking upstairs is admirable exercise for skiing. The foot should be placed flat on the step above and pointing straight forward.

There are two skiing exercises which can be done without taking any time that might be devoted to other activities. When you have to stand around, stand still, the feet about 15cm (6in) apart and flat on the ground, the toes pointing forwards; in this position gently flex your knees backwards and forwards over the toes. (This is something useful that one can do at cocktail parties.)

Similarly, if one has to sit around one can exercise the skiing muscles by holding one's feet flat on the ground with the toes to the front and then gently pressing one's feet against the floor and then releasing the pressure.

Sports Which Help Skiing

It is noticeable that good oarsmen normally learn skiing very fast, an indication that the same muscles are used in both sports. Rowing is very good exercise for skiing and so is a rowing machine. Walking up and down steep hills is probably even better.

Weight Control

One cannot be fit if one smokes, or drinks too much, or is overweight. The overweight skier is putting an added strain on his muscles as well as running an increased risk of accident. For over 30 years I have been battling with a tendency to put on weight and have regretfully come to conclude that the keen skier is always somewhat hungry.

Diet

Though one will obviously eat less when one is trying to lose weight as opposed to just keeping it down, the diet one chooses to lose weight should end up as one's normal eating habit. That means it must be a balanced diet, which includes on a regular basis, carbohydrates, protein, fats, fresh fruit and vegetables.

Both starch and sugar are carbohydrates, but sugar and anything made from it, can, with benefit, be totally eliminated from one's diet. Sugar puts on fat while providing none of the vitamins and minerals that we need.

I have found that, if one eliminates sugar, one can eat a reasonable amount of starch without putting on weight. I have tried cutting down drastically on starch and eating quantities of protein instead. On such a diet, I did not lose weight and I did not feel well. I have tried hard but have never succeeded in finding any diet which enabled me to eat as much as I wanted and yet not put on weight. Books on diet tend to advance conflicting views, but my own experience has been in line with those stating that there is need for starch as well as protein in one's diet.

It is rare for people to eat too little salt but it can happen, especially if one has lost a lot of salt through sweating. Lack of salt in the body can lead to unnatural tiredness.

Vitamins and minerals
If one is cutting down food it is possible that one may come to lack some of the essential vitamins and minerals that we need. It is therefore a good thing to take daily a pill containing the basic vitamins and minerals, including iron and calcium. Lack of calcium can lead to weak bones, which is something the skier does not want. Milk and most cheeses except those with a low fat content contain plenty of calcium, so do fish like sardines, which are eaten with bones. Calcium absorption however is inhibited by phytic acid, which is found in bran, nuts and pulses, and by oxalic acid, which is found in spinach, rhubarb and strawberries.

Weight watching
It is easy to tell if one is overweight by looking in the mirror or taking between finger and thumb the flesh one is carrying on one's stomach. But, especially as wishful thinking is so powerful, it is as well to have some objective standard by which one measures progress or regress. If one is travelling and cannot use a weighing machine, the regular reading of a tape measure round one's waist is effective.

Adaptation to Altitude

If we go up from the plains to considerable heights and immediately, before the body has had a chance to acclimatise, take a lot of exercise, it puts a strain on the system, which sometimes leads to severe headaches.

This can be alleviated by drinking plenty of liquids before going high and during the acclimatisation period. If the body does not have enough fluid, the blood becomes thick and cannot get oxygen to the brain at the required rate. Drinking alcohol, coffee or tea, makes matters worse, not better, because they are diuretics, which cause one to end up with less liquid in the body than one had before one drank them.

PART IV

TECHNIQUE

The grace of cross-country skiing. Sharon Firth of Canada.

1 Changes in Ski Technique

'The greatest difficulty of the art is going uphill. A good Skilöbner faces the ascent bravely, bending his legs like a frog. Lifting his feet one after the other, he steps boldly up the incline, swinging each leg outward from the hip in turn, and keeping his toes at an angle . . . the strain on the muscles for this performance is tremendous . . . women with their shorter legs and unwieldy skirts cannot accomplish an ascent by this means.'

The quotation is from *The Sport of Skilöbning* by Mrs Alec Tweedie. Though we put things rather differently today, Mrs Tweedie's description of the herring bone method of climbing is still substantially correct. The technique for skiing along the level and uphill, that is for cross-country skiing, has not changed radically over the years.

But with downhill skiing the reverse is true. Ski technique changes constantly, and books on technique have a habit of becoming partly out of date the day they are published.

For instance, when skiing downhill the two skis can be held parallel and rotated by body action. Vivian Caulfeild in *How to Ski*, published 1911, taught that in such a turn the shoulders should be counter rotated. And, as anybody can see for himself, it is easier, when standing on flat ground without skis, to twist the feet in either direction if the shoulders are counter rotated.

Then between the wars it became standard practice to rotate the shoulders with, not against, the turn. The Frenchman, Emile Allais, certainly the greatest of the pre World War II racers and arguably the most beautiful stylist to watch of all time, wrote in his book *Méthode Française de Ski, Technique Emile Allais*, that the rotation of the shoulders seemed to him to be the powerful driving force capable of turning the skis without resource to the legs.

After the sensational victories of the Austrian, Toni Sailer, in the 1956 Olympics the official manual of the Austrian ski teachers laid down that the shoulders should be counter rotated, which, because Caulfeild had been forgotten, was hailed both as revolutionary thinking and the final orthodoxy. At one ski school they taught counter rotating with such vigour that a number of the instructors damaged their spines and had to ski in corsets.

Later it was taught that the shoulders must be neither rotated nor counter rotated, but must be kept still and the turn done by the hips. Then that both the shoulders and the hips must be kept still and the turn done by the knees.

That might seem the logical end of the story, but such was not the case. Counter rotation has made periodic returns to favour, especially as an aid to balance in a series of rapid and tight parallel turns. In 1981 Karl Gamma, President of the International Ski Instructors Association, in *The Handbook of Skiing* laid far more stress on counter rotation as an aid to turning generally, than had been normal before the book appeared.

How does one, in fact, best use the human frame in order to rotate a pair of skis held parallel with one another? This is a problem of anatomics, of the human body in motion over varying terrain. The problem is necessarily very complex, not least because human bodies are far from being all the same which is often overlooked in the drive for a standard orthodoxy.

Another example of cyclic change in ski technique can be used to illustrate this point. I have always skied with my feet apart. Then, in the 1950s, skiers were taught that they should, as far as possible, ski with their feet clamped together. I did not change my own ways and I now find that I am back in the fashion, because it is once again being taught that skiers should keep their feet apart.

A recent ski instruction syllabus lays down that 'skiers still in the habit of holding skis close together should at least not press knees together'.

So in this book should I simply state that the skis should be held apart and leave it at that? Irrespective of the fact that opinion may change yet again, it seems more helpful to state that:

1 A broad base with feet apart makes for greater stability.

2 A narrow base with skis together makes for neater turning.

3 If, when running straight downhill, the knees are together and the feet apart, then the skis are held on their inside edges which helps to stop them wandering.

The aim of such an approach is to help the reader understand those basic principles which must ultimately govern ski technique.

No book can be a substitute for going to a competently run ski school, which is the best method of learning the sport. But a book can certainly help a pupil to understand better the instruction that he is given in the ski school.

Views on ski technique change constantly but not the dogmatism with which they are expressed. The dogmatism is wrong, and not just because views will continue to change, today's orthodoxy becoming tomorrow's heresy or vice versa.

Dogmatism over ski technique will always be wrong, primarily because no two skiers are exactly alike. One individual will find it more natural to use his body in one way to control his skis, while another will find it better a different way. What is right for the one is not necessarily right for the other.

At first the pupil in ski school must try slavishly to follow the instruction he is given. But the great teacher is experience because it is only in actual practice that he can discover the best way to overcome the difficulties involved. Instruction is essential in the early stages but the skier must eventually follow his own instinctive reasoning and develop the style most suited to his individual needs. It is hoped that this book will help him to do so.

2 Skiing Along the Level and Uphill

The Cross-Country and the Downhill Skier

The one is primarily concerned with skiing along the level and uphill, the other with skiing downhill. But the cross-country skier often has to ski downhill, though he is handicapped by equipment that is too loose for good control, and the downhill skier must sometimes ski along the level and uphill, though he is handicapped by equipment that is heavy and rigid. Both will enjoy their skiing more if they learn to master both arts.

Along the Level

The ski step along the level is very similar to walking on foot, except that the skier slides his feet forward instead of lifting them. The arms are swung forward alternately with the feet, just as in ordinary walking. When the arm has been brought forward, the point of the pole is placed in the snow; then the hand is pressed back against it which helps to push the skier forward. Because the arms are used in this way, skiing along the level and uphill is the most superb all round exercise.

The downhill skier wearing bindings that allow no heel lift is handicapped by being able to take only short strides.

After the pole has been brought forward, the point must be placed in the snow so that it is pointing backwards. If the point is too far forward, some of the pressure the skier puts on it will be wasted on lifting him into the air. Placing the pole too far back has the same effect as too short a pole; the propelling power of the backward thrust is curtailed.

The poles must point straight backwards, not slightly outwards, so that all the pressure the skier puts on them goes into propelling him forward. However, the novice on hard snow, who finds it difficult to prevent his skis slithering from side to side, can steady himself by having his hand slightly in front of his chest when the pole is placed in the snow. There is then a slight outward pressure against it and a consequent loss of forward propulsion, but it does help to keep the skis running straight. What the unsteady skier must not do is to put his poles out at the side,

because then they will be pointing almost straight downwards and there will be hardly any forward propulsion.

It also helps to prevent the skis slithering on hard snow if the knees are leant slightly inwards, so that the skis are held on their inside edges. But this does slow one down. Whenever possible the skis should be held flat on the snow and the poles placed in the snow pointing straight backwards so as to provide the maximum forward thrust.

Uphill

When the incline is not too steep, the skier can climb uphill as though he were walking along the level, except that he will have to lean further forward and push harder with his poles. Slopes which are too steep for this can be climbed by the side-step, the herring bone, the traverse or the side-step traverse.

The side-step

This is the easiest method of climbing uphill. It is also the slowest so that it is not used by cross-country skiers. But it is very useful for a novice to climb uphill on a practice slope.

The skier stands facing across the hill with his skis in the horizontal position, so that there is no tendency for them to slide away downhill, either forwards or backwards. It is immaterial which ski is uppermost.

From this position it is easy to side-step up the hill. As the skier steps uphill with the top ski, he presses against the lower pole for support. He then puts his weight on the top ski and brings up the lower one beside it.

The herring bone

This is the fastest method of climbing steep stretches but it is tiring and can therefore only be used over short distances. To start the skier stands in a semi-spread-eagled position, with the tips of his skis pointing outwards and the heels converging at an angle of about 45°. The poles should be in the snow behind the skis. He then climbs uphill in a series of short steps, leaning well forward so as to keep his skis hard on their inside edges. The poles should be moved forward with and behind the skis. As he steps up with the left ski, he brings the left pole forward and presses back against the right pole; and vice versa.

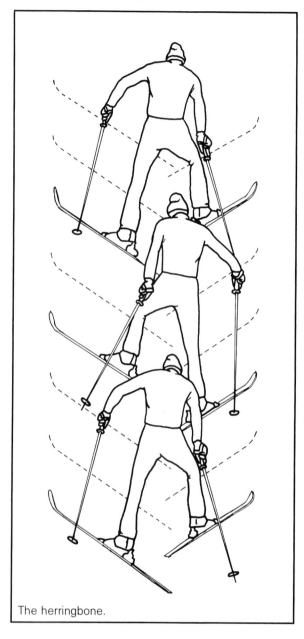
The herringbone.

The traverse
Long slopes are climbed in a series of traverses connected by kickturns. (The kickturn enables the skier to turn round when he is stationary: it is described below.) The skier climbs across the slope at a comfortable angle, using the same technique as he does for skiing along the level, except that he must keep his skis edged into the slope sufficiently to prevent them sliding away down the hill.

At a convenient point the skier kickturns and then traverses back across the slope in the opposite direc-

tion. He should try to make his traverses as long as possible to avoid unnecessary kickturns.

The side-step traverse
This is a quicker method of climbing a long slope, though it is more difficult and more tiring than the normal traverse. The technique is exactly the same except that each time the skier slides a ski forward, he side-steps it uphill at the same time.

The Kickturn

At one time the kickturn was basic to any skier's education. But now that lifts have proliferated and it has become comparatively rare to walk uphill by a series of traverses, some skiers become quite proficient without ever having mastered this simple turn. Which is a pity; not only is the kickturn useful if one does have to climb uphill but it can be almost essential if one has to get out of a tight corner when skiing downhill.

I was on one occasion taking a run off-piste and as conditions were likely to be difficult I had taken the precaution of establishing that all those coming were competent skiers. During the descent one of the skiers got on to an old avalanche track. It was steep and smooth with a drop below. He could not proceed across it because facing him was a cliff. I suggested to him that he kickturn and come back to where I was standing. It then turned out that he had no idea how to kickturn. In the end he had to shuffle backwards off the avalanche track. It was a nasty moment for me and presumably a far nastier one for him. So it is worth mastering the kickturn, especially as it can be practised, even without snow, on any flat piece of ground. You do a kickturn from left to right as follows:

1 Start with the two skis together and parallel. Stretch out your left arm to three-quarters of its length, and place the pole in the snow beside the left ski.

2 Twist your body round to the right without moving your feet. Stretch out your right arm and place your right pole in the snow behind you and beside your left ski. Both poles will thus be on the same side of your skis and you will be able to support yourself by leaning back against them.

3 Lift up your right ski till it is vertical to the ground with its heel in the snow in front of your left foot.

4 Swing the ski round to the right and replace it in the snow parallel with the left one but facing in the opposite direction. Your feet should be fairly close together.

5 Pause for a moment in this spread-eagled position, while you support yourself by leaning back against your poles.

6 Pick up your left ski and swing it round to be parallel with, and facing in the same direction as, the other. To do this you will have to pick your left pole out of the snow and swing it round with the ski while you support yourself on your right pole.

You have thus turned through 180° in two steps. A kickturn in the opposite direction is performed in exactly the same way, except that left must be substituted for right and vice versa.

On a slope it is easier to kickturn away from the hill, that is by starting the turn with the lower ski. But if you are climbing uphill by a series of traverses, you lose height each time you do this. So one should learn to kickturn into the hill, so that one gains height, instead of losing it, every time one does the turn.

The kickturn.

The Roberts of Kandahar downhill race in 1927.

3 Straight Running

Speed

It may seem odd that this should be the first word of the first chapter describing the technique of downhill skiing. Speed, a beginner would naturally think, is something for experts, not for him. But the enjoyment of speed is subjective, and a slow speed is as exciting to the beginner as a high speed is to the expert.

The skier knows the thrill of speed in its purest form. No springs, except his knees, shield him from the roughness of the ground. He exerts his will, not through machinery, but through his own body. He is unprotected from the wind of his own movement. Speed is the excitement of skiing but also its agony, for speed means fear.

Therefore I believe that straight running, not control, is what should be learnt first. Sudden changes of speed can obviously be upsetting but speed in itself presents no real difficulty, though it does require nerve till one gets used to it; the difficulty comes when one tries to control speed. If the beginner can learn as soon as possible to ski fast straight downhill, it will do two things for him. Firstly he will almost certainly be hooked on the sport and enthusiastic to persevere when he begins to encounter difficulties. Secondly, the experience of skiing fast and surviving will do wonderful things for his nerve.

That is provided he does not hurt himself in a nasty fall. So the slope selected for straight running, while it should be long and may even be reasonably steep, must be smooth with no sudden changes of gradient; the transition to the run out must be gradual and the run out itself must be long enough for the skier to be able to stop naturally. The snow must not be so hard and icy that a fall will hurt. For that reason plastic slopes are not good for teaching fast straight running.

Preparing to Schuss

It is easiest if the first schuss can be on a short slope with not only a run out but also a flat space at the top from which one can launch oneself down the slope by a gentle push with the poles.

Once an easy schuss has been done two or three times, the skier needs a longer slope on which he can, as his confidence grows, start from higher and higher up the slope to increase the length of his schuss and the speed at which he will be travelling. At the end of his first day he should have no difficulty in schussing about 100m down a slope of average steepness.

He will have to side-step up the slope. If he is starting on the slope, as opposed to from a flat space at the top, he will have to support himself on his poles while he shuffles round till his skis are pointing straight downhill. He should pause before lifting his poles out of the snow and letting himself go, to make certain that his skis really are pointing straight downhill and that he is relaxed and ready to adopt the schussing position.

The Schussing Position

Knees slightly bent
The knees are the springs which should absorb any unevenesses in the ground. If the legs are rigid, there is no spring in them. That is why the knees should always be slightly bent.

The ordinary schussing position is quite different from the egg position, that low tuck which racers adopt in order to reduce wind resistance. To gain this single advantage the racer accepts a cramped and stiff position.

Weight forward
The skier gets his weight forward, that is on to the balls of his feet, by pressing his knees forward over the toes. Once they are forward, the trunk should adopt whatever position seems most natural, that is best balanced, to him. The stance should be upright. If he is crouched, there is less spring in his legs and his field of vision is restricted. Leaning forward from the waist is wrong because it puts him in a top heavy position.

The position of the hands
The hands perform stabilising movements which help to maintain the skier's balance and they should be in the position where they can best do this. It is a mistake to be dogmatic as to exactly where that is; it is

something which each person can best work out instinctively for himself.

But there are two points. The first is imperative. The poles must be held so that they point backwards with their ends behind one. If they point forwards, one can run on to them and perhaps seriously injure oneself. The second point is psychological: the hands are an index to the skier's morale. As fear increases, the skier tends to lean further and further backwards till he collapses in a fall. His instinct is to shrink away from the danger that seems to be facing him. Normally the skier's hands start to drift back before his weight does so; they are a warning signal that he is getting into a bad backward position. If he can be aware of this and resolutely thrust his hands forward the moment they start to drift back, it should enable him to regain the essential forward stance.

Resolution is the key to success in learning to ski. A skier will make quick progress if he always struggles to stay upright till he is thrown, refuses to collapse when the unexpected happens but fights to maintain his balance. And resolution depends not only on will power but also on enjoyment. The skier who has fallen in love with the sport will have a far deeper motive for persevering against difficulty. That is why it is so important to learn to schuss early on.

The position of the feet

Opinion as to the position of the feet has oscillated. During the 1970s the view that the feet should be kept close together was replaced by the view that they should be kept apart, so that they were directly under the hips. The skier must to some extent do what comes naturally to him. A broad base makes for greater stability and is essential for those who have not got a good natural balance. A narrow base makes for neater skiing. If the skier finds that his skis have a tendency to wander, as they do when the snow is very smooth, he can rectify this by keeping his feet apart and his knees together, so that his skis are running on their inside edges.

Preparing to schuss.

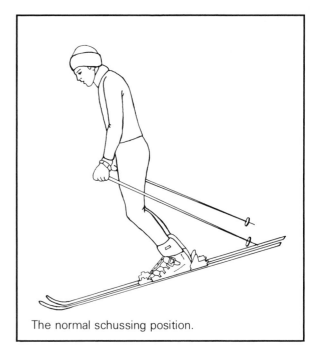

The normal schussing position.

In Search of Speed

Skis that are held on their inside edges run slower than skis that are held flat on the snow. It may seem odd to the novice that he should want his skis to run as fast as possible, and should actively go in search of speed. But all skiers often find themselves on slopes that they can schuss with ease. It is then interesting to try to stand on one's skis so that they run as fast as possible. The skier must not only hold his skis flat on the snow, but also pointing straight to the front, so that there is no side slip. If the skis are held on their inside edges, it is easy to ski with the tips slightly converging without realising it.

The skier must shift his weight backwards and forwards to find the position that is fastest for his skis. They will run fastest if the weight is evenly distributed over the entire running surface of the skis. So if they are stiffer at the back than the front, then the skier's weight should be back, and vice versa. The ability to feel whether one's skis are running their fastest or not and to adjust one's weight accordingly is essential for the downhill racer. But this gliding skill should be cultivated by every skier who wants to ski as well as he can.

One should make certain that one can glide properly before one starts trying to reduce wind resistance by crouching; in the cramped egg position it is far more difficult to experiment in order to make certain that one is standing in the best possible way on one's skis. Once the skier does adopt the egg position, he must thrust his hands forward, and hold them close together to achieve the best possible aerodynamic position. The lower he can go and the more he can tuck his body into a small space, the less the wind resistance.

Where the ground is flattish, one can best increase speed by punting vigorously with one's poles, using both at the same time, leaning forward and then down to get the longest possible backward thrust against the snow. Whenever the skier is not punting, the pole ends must be held clear of the snow so that they do not slow one by unnecessary friction.

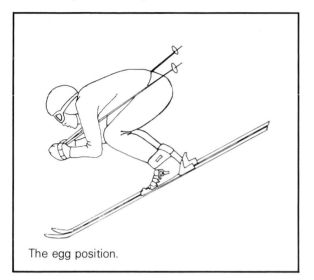
The egg position.

Coping with Unevenesses

Most mountain sides are not smooth, and the skier must learn to cope with unevenesses both in the terrain and in the texture of the snow.

In the terrain
Knees are to the skier what springs are to a car. When he goes over a bump, the knees should bend, so that the bump is absorbed and his head remains at the same distance from the snow. If the bump is followed by a hollow, the legs should straighten so that again the uneveness is absorbed.

If the ground steepens sharply ahead of the skier, there will be a tendency for his weight to be thrown back as he shoots into the air. This is countered by leaning as far forward as possible before the point where the ground steepens.

One might expect the reverse to be the case when approaching a counter rise but this is not so. It also tends to throw the weight back and must therefore be met by an increased forward lean.

In the texture of the snow
If one runs from slow snow on to fast, a stretch of ice for instance, the skis will shoot forward and one will tend to fall over backwards. Leaning forward will counteract this.

If one runs from fast snow on to slow there will be a tendency to be thrown forward as the skis decelerate. This can be countered by pushing one ski about 30cm (12in) forward (it does not matter which ski), so that one has a longer base and thus more fore-and-aft stability. When running from hard snow into soft, the weight should be back so that the tips will ride up over the surface of the snow and the skis will plane in the same way as water skis.

Riding bumps and hollows.

4 Traversing and Side Slipping

Traversing

Angulation

The dynamics of traversing are clear. There are two principles. Firstly, the skis must be edged into the slope and be held on their upper edges because otherwise the skier will side-slip down the slope instead of traversing across it. Secondly, if the skier edges his skis by leaning his whole body towards the slope, he will be in a very unstable position.

So the skier angulates. He presses his knees into the slope to keep his skis on their upper edges, and he leans his shoulders out from the slope to get into a well balanced position. These two principles of dynamics and the consequent need for angulation is something that cannot change.

Weight mainly on the lower ski

The skier should angulate sufficiently for his weight to be mainly on the lower ski. There is no doubt that this makes for the most stable position.

It also helps psychologically to concentrate on weighting the lower ski. There is a tendency when traversing to lean into the slope, and this inevitably causes an inward fall. Especially on a steep slope, the natural inclination is to hug the slope rather than to lean outwards to the fall line. The skier can help himself to overcome slope hugging by making a conscious effort to put most of his weight on the lower ski.

Upper ski ahead

The upper ski on a traverse should be ahead. As the skier can easily establish by experimenting for himself, he is in a more stable position if on a traverse he leads with his upper ski rather than his lower one.

Position of the shoulders

There has been no consistent teaching over the years as to which, if either, shoulder ought to lead.

Before World War II we used to traverse with the lower shoulder ahead. Then Rudolf Rominger, the Swiss who won one downhill and two slalom world championships in the late 1930s, started to traverse

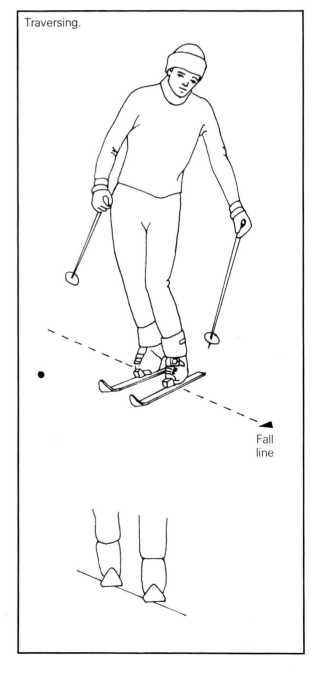

Traversing.

Fall line

with his top shoulder ahead. When he became a ski instructor, he was not allowed to teach that this was the right way to traverse. The Swiss Ski School insisted that he follow the then orthodox doctrine and teach traversing with the lower shoulder ahead. But after the Austrian, Toni Sailer, had won all three gold medals in the 1956 Olympics, his style – which was top shoulder ahead in traversing and counter rotation in turning – became the new orthodoxy and was universally accepted. People used to traverse with the top shoulder so far ahead that the trunk was facing down the slope.

Then there came a reaction against this. Neither shoulder should lead; one should ski with one's shoulder square to the front. Ski teachers took what was regarded as a common sense line. If one traversed a slope on foot one had one's shoulders square to the front. That was the natural thing to do, and that was the way one should ski.

But that view did not last either. It was followed by the teaching that the top shoulder should lead, but only to a moderate extent, not in the exaggerated way that had been taught earlier.

The need to concentrate on fundamentals
The novice, anxious to know which of the many conflicting opinions is correct, is best advised not to worry about his shoulders. Inevitably, as he struggles to keep his balance while learning unfamiliar manoeuvres, he finds it difficult to concentrate. He will not find it difficult to keep his top ski ahead, because this will come naturally to him. But it is not natural to keep most of the weight on the lower ski. He must concentrate on this, and should not be distracted from it by thinking about the position of his shoulders. If he does not think about them, they will probably naturally adopt the position that is best suited to him, and enables him to be best balanced. This will probably be with the shoulders either facing straight to the front or with the top shoulder slightly ahead.

Side-Slipping

Side-slipping is a basic skiing manoeuvre, a mastery of which makes turning easier; it should therefore be learnt early. Moreover, a skier who has learnt to side-slip can get down a slope of hard snow which is too steep for him to be able to turn on.

To side-slip one stands in the traversing position with one's skis horizontally across the slope. The snow must be hard enough, and the slope steep enough, for the skis to slide away sideways as soon as one stops edging them into the hill.

Standing horizontally across the slope, one leans the knees slowly away from the slope till one starts to side-slip down it. The movement can be alarming to a new skier, who reacts by leaning inwards and then

collapsing against the slope. To prevent this and to ensure that he continues to maintain the correct position, he should concentrate on keeping most of his weight on the lower ski.

It also helps if, as soon as the skier starts to side-slip, he presses his knees back into the slope and so brings the movement to a halt. Once he realises that he is thus in control of the situation, he will cease to be nervous.

The knees must not be leant too far out from the hill. Skis side-slip when they are weakly edged, not when they are flat on the snow. If the skis are flat on the snow, the lower edge catches against the snow and may, if suddenly arrested, throw the skier outwards down the hill.

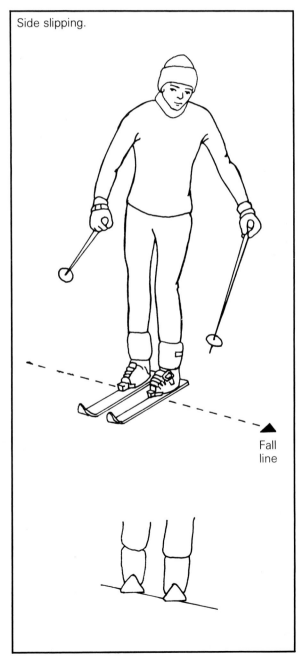

Side slipping.

Fall line

151

5 The Snowplough and the Stem Turn

The Snowplough

Periodically some ski teachers have argued that the snowplough should not be taught on the grounds that it is a 'defensive' technique. What is meant by 'defensive'? Anything other than pointing the skis straight down the fall line can be described as such. And if the skier has not been taught how to snowplough, how is he going to cope with a path or other passage which is too narrow for turning and too fast to be schussed? So the snowplough, though sometimes jeered at as unfashionable, has survived as an essential technique.

In the snowplough position the heels are forced apart, while the tips of the skis converge. The skis are in a V position. Because the heels are forced apart, the skis are inevitably on their inside edges, so that they act as a brake and slow down the skier's pace. When the slope is not too steep, nor the snow too icy, the skier can bring himself to a stop by vigorously thrusting his heels apart. The snowplough is a method of braking on skis.

It should be learnt on a smooth slope of hard snow, which is not so steep that the skier will have difficulty in keeping his speed under control. He should start the descent in the snowplough position and not, until he is more expert, try to adopt it while he is schussing downhill. He can either start from some flat space and ease himself on to the slope having adopted the snowplough position, or he can start on the slope, supporting himself with his poles, while he gets into position.

In either case, he must make certain he is in the correct position before he starts down. The snowplough position is essentially symmetrical. The skier's heels must be so thrust out that each is equidistant from the fall line bisecting his ski tips. And his weight must be equally distributed between the two skis.

A common fault is not to keep the heels forced apart, so that the snowplough angle becomes relaxed and the skis run away with one. One must force the heels outwards, remembering that the more one does so the slower one will go.

A second common fault is not to keep the knees thrust forward over the toes, so that the weight sags backwards till one collapses.

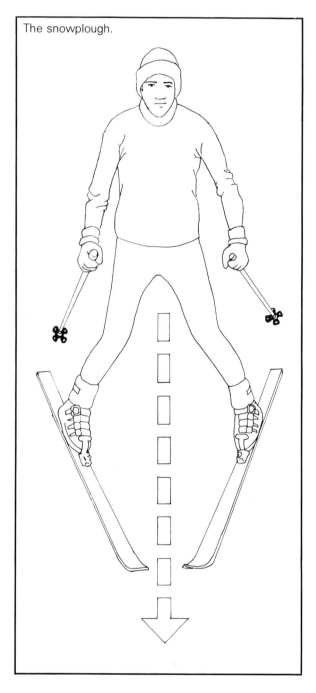

The snowplough.

The Snowplough Turn

When in the snowplough position if the skier weights one ski more than the other, the weighted ski will exert a greater braking effect and the skis will start to turn across the fall line away from that braking effect. One can keep that ski more weighted, thus continuing the braking effect, till one turns right across the fall line and comes to a stop. Or one can weight the other ski, exerting the braking effect on that side, till one turns back into the fall line.

Then one can do one of two things. One can either weight both skis equally and thus go straight down the fall line in the snowplough position. Or one can continue with the weight mainly on the one ski till one turns right across the fall line to the other side.

In this way one can snake backwards and forwards across the fall line, weighting first one ski and then the other. At any time one can bring oneself to a stop by keeping the weight on one ski till one turns right across the slope.

One has in fact discovered one of the four basic methods of turning, which is braking effect: if the two skis are held at an angle to one another, and one ski is brought to exert a greater braking effect, then this will cause the skis to turn.

All turns depend upon one of the four basic methods, or on a combination of them. The first method is stepping the skis round. The kickturn is a stationary step turn in two steps. It is also possible when skiing downhill, if one is not going too fast, to change direction from one traverse to another by a series of steps. The second is braking effect. The third is twisting the skis round by body action, and the fourth is carving.

The Stem Turn

The principles of the snowplough and the stem turn are exactly the same, except the stem turn starts and ends in the traversing position. It is carried through in three stages.

1 If traversing across the slope with the hill on the right, put all the weight on the lower, left, ski. This is done so that one can easily thrust the heel of the upper ski uphill, till it assumes a stemming angle with the other. One has pushed the heel of the upper ski out till it is in a snowplough position.

2 Transfer the weight to the right ski, so that it exerts a braking effect. The skis will turn left away from the braking effect, in exactly the same way as in the snowplough turn.

3 When one has come right round till one is crossing the slope in the opposite direction, with the hill now on the left, one slides the left ski, the inside ski on the turn and now the upper ski, down parallel with the other. One then continues across the slope in the traversing position.

The origin and the value of the stem turn

Mathias Zdarsky discovered the principles of the stem turn for himself and described them in his book published at the end of the last century. Ever since the late 1930s various ski schools have banned the stem turn from their teaching syllabus, arguing that the neatest way to ski is with the skis held parallel and that the skier, especially if he is on very short skis, can be taught the parallel turn from the very start. These schools took pupils straight from schussing, traversing and side-slipping to the parallel turn. They argued that teaching the skier to open his skis for the stem turn, or even for the snowplough, got him into bad habits and must therefore be avoided.

But despite the undoubted authority of some who have argued this case, the stem turn has survived, whereas the telemark, another turn which goes back to the last century, fell into disuse. The simple fact is that the parallel turn, normally known as the parallel christie, in which the skis are held parallel throughout, is more difficult than the stem turn or stem christie. The stem christie starts as a stem turn and ends as a parallel christie.

There are conditions when even good skiers cannot do a turn with the skis held parallel throughout. And there are skiers who, even under easy conditions, can never do the parallel turn. They never get beyond the stem christie. To insist that such skiers must always turn with their skis parallel is to deny them the happiness of skiing.

Indeed, even the stem christie is not absolutely necessary, and it can be said that the novice is able to ski once he has mastered what has so far been described in this book. He can ski straight downhill and control his speed when necessary by the snowplough. He has learnt to traverse and to connect two traverses by the stem turn. If the ground is too steep, or the snow is too difficult, for him to be able to do a stem turn, he can stop and do a kickturn. He can side-slip downhill. He should avoid long steep slopes of icy snow, but otherwise he can ski anywhere he wants.

6 The Uphill Parallel Christie

An uphill turn is a turn into the hill; its purpose is to bring the skier to a stop. It can be done from the fall line, in which case the skier turns through 90° in order to bring his skis horizontal across the slope. Or the turn can be undertaken into the hill from a traverse, in which case the skier turns through something less than 90°, again bringing himself to a stop.

A Question of Nomenclature

The christiania turn, or christie for short, goes back to the last century.

There are three different sorts of christie. One is the parallel christie, which is performed entirely by body action. The other two are the stem christie and the open or scissors christie. These two are performed partly by body action and partly by braking action.

A parallel christie, however, can be performed by carving as well as by body action. Carving is a radically different way of doing the turn.

The word christie, therefore, does not mean any one turn or any one method of doing turns. It is a word lacking in precision and there is a case for dropping it altogether. But if one does there is no universally comprehensible term for the stem christie, which begins as a stem and ends as a parallel turn. I therefore believe it makes for clarity to keep the word christie, and to write about the parallel christie as opposed to just the parallel turn.

The turns described in this chapter are done by body action, by twisting the skis into the desired direction. Twisting is inferior to carving as a method of turning the skis, but carving is only possible under certain circumstances. Twisting must therefore also be learnt as a turning method and, because it is the more universally applicable method, it should be learnt first.

Heel Thrust

The easiest way to learn the parallel christie is from a traverse. One should choose a gradual slope of smooth hard snow and then cross it on a gentle traverse which is nearer to the horizontal than it is to the fall line. At a certain point one twists the skis uphill into the slope so that one comes to a stop.

There has been much debate over the years as to how the twisting action is best performed. But, whatever the rest of the body may or may not do, one thing is quite certain and that is the feet have got to twist. It is best for the beginner to concentrate only on twisting his feet, because, when turning into the hill from a gentle traverse, the skis are rotated through only a few degrees; provided the snow is smooth, this requires very little effort.

One skis across the slope in the correct traversing position, the skis edged into the slope, the body angulated so that the weight is mainly on the lower ski, top ski ahead, the knees thrust forward over the toes. All that is necessary for the uphill christie is to thrust the heels downhill so that the ski tips are twisted uphill into the slope.

Once the skier can do this turn from a gentle traverse, both to the right and to the left, he must do it from progressively steeper traverses, always to both sides, till eventually he is able to do the turn from a direct descent down the fall line.

Steering with the Knees

At some stage as the skier progresses towards the fall line, and is consequently turning through a greater and greater angle, he will find that a simple heel thrust will not bring him round to a stop but will produce a jerky and unsteady movement.

While he will be turning through a greater angle, he will also be doing the turn at greater speed. And speed makes turning easier because its force, if correctly applied, helps the turning motion of the skis. As the skier picks up speed, he learns to turn by steering with his knees. When he wants to turn he presses his knees forward and twists them in the direction of the turn. Because with modern stiff boots there is very little lateral play between the knee and the foot, the skier, by twisting his knees in the direction of the turn, that is into the slope, is at the same time thrusting his heels downhill.

But there is much more to knee steering than that. By concentrating on his knees, by forcing them forward and twisting them into the slope, the skier is making the shovels of his skis bite into the snow. The ski is broadest at the shovel and will twist longitudinally about its axis. If, by knee steering, the shovel is edged into the snow, it will grip and provide a pivot around which the tails of the ski can skid. When the turn is done by heel thrust, the skis simply skid around about their centres. When the turn is done by knee steering, the front of the ski holds its line, while the heel skids around. The result is a far smoother and more satisfying turn than the jerky turn done by heel thrust. Indeed a lot of people steering with the knees think that they are carving the turn, but this is not the case. A carved turn is done by putting the skis into reverse camber and in that position they do the turn on their own. There is no body action required except to weight the skis so that they remain in reverse camber.

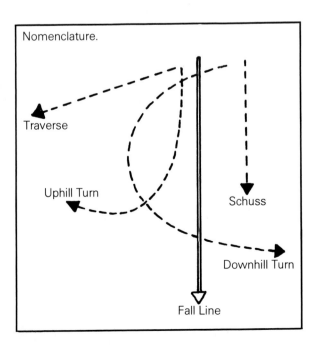

The uphill parallel christie.

Nomenclature.

Traverse

Uphill Turn

Schuss

Downhill Turn

Fall Line

Counter Rotation

Once the skier is attempting the turn direct from the fall line, he will probably find that neither heel thrust nor knee steering are sufficient to bring him round. He must then consider bringing into play the top half of his body.

It is, as anybody can see by experimenting, easier to rotate the feet if the shoulders are counter rotated at the same time. I personally do not use counter rotation as an aid to turning. But it would not keep on reappearing the way it does if it did not make turning easier, at any rate for some people. Let the skier try for himself. If he finds that counter rotation makes turning easier, then let him do it. Even if it does help him, he may find that, as his technique improves, he needs it less and less till finally he prefers to do without it altogether. Counter rotation should not be labelled 'right' or 'wrong'. It is an aid to turning which the skier should be allowed to use if it helps him or to discard if it does not do so.

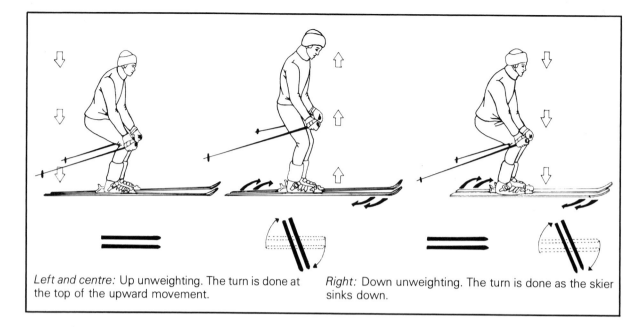

Left and centre: Up unweighting. The turn is done at the top of the upward movement.

Right: Down unweighting. The turn is done as the skier sinks down.

Unweighting the Skis

It is easier to rotate the skis if they are first unweighted by an upward or downward movement of the body, but this requires accurate synchronization of body movements in the vertical and horizontal planes if the turn is to be executed at the actual moment the skis are unweighted. Such synchronization is difficult for the beginner, so he should first learn to do the turn without unweighting.

Up unweighting

It is clear that if you jump up into the air, the skis are totally unweighted once they are off the ground. Except in breakable crust which presents great resistance to the turning skis it is not necessary to jump the skis clear of the snow. It is only necessary to take most of the weight off them by a quick upward movement of the body. It may well be necessary first to go down in order to get sufficient flex in your legs for the upward movement to be effective. So this is really a triple movement in the vertical plane: down to flex the legs, up to unweight the skis, and then down again as one sinks back and the skis are reweighted. But it is called up unweighting, because it is the upward movement which unweights the skis.

Down unweighting

Skis can also be unweighted by a simple downward movement of the body. You can verify this for yourself by standing on a weighing machine and suddenly dropping into a crouch. As you sink down, the scale will swing back to register a very low weight; indeed, if you sink down fast enough, it will register a nil weight.

The uses of up and down unweighting

Those learning to ski have often been confused over up unweighting and down unweighting. Neither is universally right or wrong; it depends on the circumstances because both have their uses.

Up unweighting takes longer to do but also keeps the skis unweighted for a longer period. Down unweighting is quicker but the skis are unweighted for less time. The skier should first learn the simple movement, down unweighting, and should practise this when doing an uphill turn from a traverse. He is only turning through a few degrees, and therefore does not need to unweight the skis for long. As he starts the turn, he should sink rapidly down; he will find that, because the skis are unweighted, the turn will come round more sharply.

Up unweighting is necessary when the skis have to be unweighted for longer. This is the case when the skier is doing a downhill christiania and thus turning through more than 90°. When there is resistance to the turning skis, that is when the turn is not being done on smooth, hard snow, up unweighting will be needed. Also the slower the skier is going, the greater the need for up unweighting, because the momentum of one's own movement helps the skis to turn. Thus, if one was standing still one would have to jump the skis clear of the snow in order to twist them round.

7 The Stem Christie

1

2

3

The stem christie starts as a stem turn and ends as a christie, which means that it begins with braking action and ends with body action. The transition from stem to christie can take place at any point in the turn; the turn can vary from a stem turn with a small christie at the finish to a christie with a small stem at the beginning. The more the christie element predominates, the sharper the turn will be. The ease with which the sharpness of the turn can be varied is one reason why the stem christie is such a very useful turn.

Stages 1 and 2 are the same as they are for the stem turn. In stage 1 the skier traversing across a slope pushes his unweighted upper ski uphill into a stemming angle with the lower ski. In stage 2 he weights this upper ski, so that it exerts a braking effect, which causes his skis to turn away from the braking effect. If the slope were on the skier's left, then the weighted left ski causes him to turn right.

It is the third and last stage that is different. The skier who has already learnt the stem turn and the uphill christie from the fall line will, when practising the stem christie for the first time, be well advised to continue with the stemming action till the turn is more than half-way round. He will then initiate the christie part of the turn, after he has passed the fall line. The christie is done by putting all the weight on to the outside ski of the turn, the left ski if turning to the right, and steering with the knee. At the same time the unweighted inside ski, which becomes the upper ski on the new traverse, is slid parallel with the other. If the surface is rough, it may be easier to lift the inside ski and bring it through the air into its parallel position.

When the stem position is held till well past the fall

line, the christie is really done on one ski and the inner ski on the turn plays no role as it is slid parallel with the other. But if the christie is commenced earlier in the turn, then both skis will be parallel with one another during the final stage and the steering must be done by both knees. This means that some weight must be put back on the inside ski, which had been unweighted so that it could be brought parallel with the other. But most of the weight must be on the outside ski, which not only makes the turn easier to do but also gets the skier into the correct position for the new traverse with most of his weight on what has become now his lower ski.

The skier will find the stem christie easier, and will turn more sharply, if he down unweights (see p. 156) during the christie phase of the turn.

The Step Stem Christie

The ordinary stem christie begins with the unweighted top ski on the traverse being slid uphill into a stemming angle with the other. It makes for a quicker turn if the top ski is not slid, but is lifted and then stepped uphill. The turn can then continue as a stem turn and end as a christie. In that case three forms of action are involved in the one turn, stepping action at the start, braking action in the middle stem stages and body action in the final christie stage.

It is possible to step the top ski out into a stemming angle and then immediately throw all one's weight on to it so that it goes into reverse camber. And once it is in reverse camber, it will start to carve. Carving is the subject of the next chapter.

Powder snow skiing at Park City, Utah, USA.

8   Carving the Turn

A ski will carve if, and only if, it goes into reverse camber. A ski normally has a concave running surface. When it is forced into reverse camber, it has a convex running surface.

If a moving object with a convex running surface is edged, then it will immediately start to turn. If it is edged to the right, it will turn to the right; if it is edged to the left, it will turn to the left. The more convex the running surface, the more it has the appearance of a U, the more sharply it will turn. The turning is effected simply and solely by the shape of the running surface. So a ski will turn of its own accord as long as it is held in reverse camber and is edged. The more the skis are edged, the more sharply they will turn.

This has led to a belief that one can turn a ski simply by putting it on its edge, which is not so. An edged ski will only turn if it is in reverse camber. This is something that can perhaps more easily be appreciated by somebody who has grass skied as well as snow skied. A grass ski has a convex running surface. If, when traversing across the slope on grass skis, one presses one's knees into the slope and so edges one's grass skis more sharply, they will immediately turn into the hill and one will come to a stop. This is not true when traversing across a slope on snow skis. One cannot make the skis turn uphill simply by pressing one's knees into the slope and putting the skis on a sharper edge. One can only force the skis to turn uphill by putting them, or one of them, into reverse camber. When traversing there is no centrifugal force, as there is when one is turning, to help press the skis into reverse camber. One has only one's weight to do this. Unless a ski is much more weakly arched than it should be, one cannot force it into reverse camber simply by putting all one's weight on it.

Learning to Carve

One needs the assistance of centrifugal force to press the skis into reverse camber, so one can only learn to carve when actually turning, and the turns have to be done at a certain speed. The stiffer the skis worn, the greater the speed required.

The stem or the snowplough turn is the easiest way to learn carving. When doing the turn, one suddenly throws all one's weight on to the outside ski, forcing it into reverse camber. The skier will immediately feel for himself that the ski is no longer skidding round but is turning in a groove and of its own accord. It is carving. The skier who wishes to practise carving should, as soon as he feels that one ski is carving,

Carving the turn. Note skis in reverse camber.

throw all his weight on to the other ski, forcing that into reverse camber so that it carves. By throwing all his weight first on to one ski and then on to the other, he will quickly get the feel of carving.

Some speed is necessary for carving, and so is resilient snow. If the snow is so hard and icy that the centre of the ski cannot be pressed down into it, then the skier can do no more than flatten his ski on the snow; however hard he presses he will not force it into reverse camber. Equally, if the snow is so soft that it cannot support the fronts and the backs of the skis, forcing them upwards, the ski cannot be forced into reverse camber.

Step Carving

The skier on a traverse lifts his top ski uphill into a stemming angle, and then puts his weight on to it so that the ski exerts braking action and effects the stem

159

phase of the stem christie turn. If the skier is going fast enough, and immediately throws all his weight on to the ski which he has just stepped out into a stemming position, that ski, instead of exerting a braking action, will be forced into reverse camber and will start to carve. This is a very fast way of turning.

Carving: General Considerations

Skidding, whether it is effected by braking or body action, slows the skier because, depending on the extent of the skidding, the skis are going sideways as well as forwards. In a carved turn the skis are going only forwards and therefore it is the fastest turn.

It is possible, as Karl Gamma has stated in his *The Handbook of Skiing*, that there may be no such thing as a pure carved turn. When watching skiers one notices that unless conditions are icy, in which case carving is impossible anyway, there always seems to be some snow thrown up by the turning skier, which is an indication of skidding. The less snow there is thrown up, the less the skier will be skidding, the more he will be carving, and the faster he will be going. So the amount of snow thrown up by the different competitors is something to look out for when watching races.

The extent to which short radius, that is sharp, turns can be done by carving depends partly on the

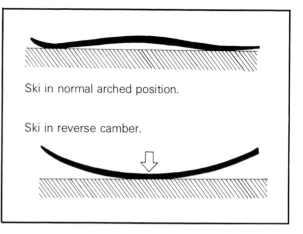

Ski in normal arched position.

Ski in reverse camber.

skier's speed and the resultant centrifugal force and partly on the snow conditions. On ice the skis cannot be thrown into reverse camber and carving is impossible; the skis must be turned by some other method. If the snow is very hard, the skis can be forced only into very slight reverse camber; their running surface is then only slightly convex. A running surface that is only slightly convex will certainly carve, but it will do so only in a gradual long radius arc. So on very hard snow it will be impossible to do very sharp turns by carving.

Carving with the skis parallel will be discussed in the next chapter.

9 The Downhill Parallel Christie

A downhill turn is one used to connect traverses. A skier who has learnt the uphill parallel christie and the stem christie is in a position to learn the more difficult downhill parallel christie.

Difficulties of the Downhill Parallel Christie

There are three main reasons why the turn is more difficult.

Firstly, the skier is turning with his skis parallel through a far greater angle, not just from the fall line or from a traverse into the hill, but right round from one traverse to another.

Secondly, the edging of the skis has got to be changed during the turn. Thus, if the skier is traversing with the hill on his right, his skis will be on their right edges, that is their upper edges. At the end of the turn, when the skier is traversing across the hill in the opposite direction, his skis have once again got to be on their upper edges, which will now be their left edges.

Thirdly, to initiate the turn, the backs of the skis have got to be rotated up the hill.

Aids to Turning

Up unweighting
First of all there is up unweighting. As it is the backs of the skis that have to be rotated up the hill, it is particularly important to unweight them; one does this by leaning forward as one rises upwards.

In the moment that the skis are unweighted they must be rotated into the new direction. The skier has already learnt rotation by body action in the uphill parallel christie and the stem christie. The difficulty now is to synchronize the rotation with the up unweighting. This is made much easier if one does not try to complete the turn in the moment of weightlessness or try to jump the skis round. One is trying only to get the skis pointed towards the fall line; the rest of the turn can be completed by knee steering.

As well as rotating the skis one has to change over their edges from one side to the other. If the skier concentrates on the fact that he is going to knee steer

in the second half of the turn, he will find that he naturally moves his knees across from one side to the other; if the turn begins with the hill on his right and ends with the hill on his left, he will be moving his knees from right to left. By moving his knees thus he automatically changes the skis over from their right edges to their left edges.

Pole plant
Up unweighting can be aided by a pole plant. The skier, traversing across the slope prior to the turn, plants his lower pole so that it will support him as he rises upwards. The fact that the pole is below him so that he leans out on to it means that he has taken some of the weight off his skis even before he has up unweighted.

Anticipation
Twisting the body round in the anticipated direction of the turn is a way of building up turning pressure on the skis, which takes effect the moment the skis are unweighted.

The body exerts pressure on the skis to rotate in the direction of the turn while at the same time the skis are prevented from rotating by the skier's weight upon them. The moment the skis are unweighted, the pressure that has been built up by anticipation causes the skis to follow the body round into the new direction.

Terrain
A sudden steepening of the surface, including that on the lower side of any protuberance in the snow, has the effect of momentarily unweighting the skis. So the skier who wishes to turn can watch out for any protuberance or any minor steepening of the slope and then go over it so that he uses the moment of weightlessness to rotate his skis.

Carving the Parallel Christie

Once the skier has rotated the skis, and his weight sinks back on to them, there will be centrifugal force tending to throw him outwards. To prevent this he

must lean his knees hard into the turn so that his skis are sharply on their edges. Moreover in this position the centrifugal force is brought down directly against the tops of the skis as they are tilted inwards and edged into the snow. Then if the snow conditions are right the centrifugal force will force the skis into reverse camber and thus cause them to carve.

The faster and sharper the turn, the greater the centrifugal force and, so long as the knees are pressed sufficiently hard inwards, the more the skis are forced into reverse camber. It is steadier and altogether better if both skis can be pressed into reverse camber, but there may not be sufficient centrifugal force to do this. In which case, the skier should throw all his weight against the outer ski, so that it will be forced into reverse camber and will by itself provide the carving action for the turn.

Downhill Parallel Christie.

10 The Open or Scissors Christie

The open christie is done by knee steering, that is by body action, helped out by braking action.

The open christie is only of value in soft snow when it is easier to ski if the weight is back so that the ski tips are kept planing on the surface of the snow, like water skiing on two skis.

To do a downhill open christie to connect two traverses, the skier twists the tip of the lower ski downhill, so that it diverges from its partner while the heels of the two skis remain close together. It is normal to keep the skis in this position till the turn is completed, the divergent ski becoming the inside ski on the turn and eventually the upper ski when the skier comes right round into the new traverse.

Throughout the skier steers with his knees, and this is the main factor in effecting the turn, because pressure of the soft snow against the divergent tip exerts only a slight braking action. While it would be possible to do the whole turn simply by this braking action, without any knee steering, it would be a very long drawn out turn. In the open christie, braking action facilitates turning which is primarily effected by knee steering.

Skiing at Alta, Rocky Mountains, USA.

Uses of the Open Christie

For over 50 years, ski teachers and writers on ski technique have ignored or denigrated the open christie. But, it has not fallen into disuse, and I have seen young skiers, who have never heard of it and who most certainly could not explain its principles, using it in powder snow. Its survival despite a hostile silence from teachers and writers does prove that it has value.

One reason for denigrating the open christie is the belief that keeping the skis parallel throughout the turn is an end in itself. The parallel christie in soft snow is difficult because of the resistance presented to the turning skis. To help do the turn, the skier can either use up unweighting with a pole plant or he can start the turn with braking action by doing a stem or open christie. In the latter case, no up unweighting and pole plant is necessary.

Using a pole plant to aid the turn makes for neat skiing and sharp turns. But the skier, bobbing up and down and planting his pole first to one side and then to the other, has a jerky movement compared with the skier who is relying on braking action. The stem and open christies mean turns which though not so sharp are smoother and faster.

Whichever method one uses to help out the turn is a question of taste, not of ethics; there is no right or wrong way about it. The reason for insisting on freedom of technique for skiers is that many people are quite unnecessarily worried in powder snow because they are told to keep their skis parallel and cannot do so. So powder snow gives them a sense of inadequacy and they consequently tend to avoid it, which is sad for them because of all snow surfaces it is the richest in delight for the skier.

The skier should not worry about technique when he starts to ski in powder snow. If he lets himself go naturally, he will find that he automatically adapts his technique to the new skiing surface.

The lower skier is using a pole plant to do a short radius turn in powder snow.

164

11 The Jump Turn

The jump turn is the turn for breakable crust. With modern piste machines flattening the runs into hard snow, the downhill skier need never ski on breakable crust unless he wants to, which is unlikely as the piste provides a more enjoyable skiing surface. But the ski tourer may have to ski on breakable crust.

When touring I once had to descend some 900m (2950ft) vertically entirely on breakable crust, which was far too thick for me to do a stem turn or any sort of christie. I came down the whole run in a series of jump turns. Though I was wearing a substantial rucksack I found the run very enjoyable. If I had not been able to do a jump turn, I would have had to do an uphill turn to a stop at the end of every traverse and then do a kick-turn. I should have had to ski much slower, and would have found the run more tiring.

Technique

The jump turn is performed by body action with the skis parallel throughout. The entire turn is done with the skis in the air, the skier coming to a brief stop the moment that he lands.

The jump turn is easiest if the poles are long enough to reach the arm pits or just above, when the point of the pole is resting on a hard floor. For downhill skiing shorter poles are generally preferred but longer ones make climbing uphill much easier and less tiring. It is the person who climbs uphill on skis, the ski tourer and the ski mountaineer, who is likely to need the jump turn.

There are two sorts of jump turn: the two pole and the one pole.

The Two Pole Jump Turn

The two pole jump turn is not so stylish, nor so much fun, as the one pole turn, but it is much easier, which is why it should be learnt first. It relies for its ease of execution on anticipation. The body is twisted round in the anticipated direction of the turn before the skis are jumped clear of the snow.

Traversing across the slope, the skier plants both poles upright (that is pointing straight down) in the snow just below his skis, as far forward as he can without altering his normal upright position or putting himself to any sort of strain.

Holding his poles planted in the snow, he continues traversing forward for the fraction of a second necessary for him to ski past his poles. His body will then be twisted right round in the anticipated direction of the turn. He then gives a slight jump – it is not necessary to leap into the air – and his skis, as soon as they are clear of the snow, will automatically follow his body round into the new direction. When he lands, he comes briefly to a halt and then skies off in the new direction.

Beginners have a tendency to take off more from one ski than the other, but this is a fault which is soon cured by practice.

The One Pole Jump Turn

The one pole jump turn is much more fun and can be done faster; indeed it is very difficult unless the skier is going at a certain speed.

When traversing across the slope, the skier crouches slightly and plants his lower pole, pointing forward as well as downward, into the snow. The point must go into the snow just below the skis and as far forward as is comfortable.

Because the pole is not planted vertically, but is at an angle to the surface of the snow, the skier presses against it as he runs forward. He must jump as soon as he feels that he can put all his weight on to it. Because his body is not twisted round in the direction of the turn, he has to make a substantial leap and rotate his skis in the air. Provided the skier's speed is right, this is not nearly as difficult as it sounds.

12 Problems of Downhill Skiing

Downhill skiing is a speed sport and there are problems in all speed sports. It is also a mountain sport and there are problems in the mountains that one does not encounter on the plains.

The Skier's Rule of the Road

The International Ski Federation has laid down certain basic principles to govern the conduct of skiers. In most countries these principles play an important role in settling any legal dispute between two skiers who have collided with one another.

1 A faster skier can pass a slower skier on either side, but must allow the slower person room for any manoeuvre he might undertake. In this sense, the slower moving skier has right of way, but in the interests of his own safety he is well advised to glance over his shoulder before making a wide turn in either direction.

2 The skier who has been stationary and who has just started down again must before moving make certain that he is not going to inconvenience skiers coming from behind. Equally, a skier who enters a piste from the side must first make certain that he is not going to inconvenience those who are already on it. The principle that the slower moving person has the right of way does not apply in these two instances.

3 A skier who wishes to stop on a piste must first draw to the side. He must not stop in some narrow passage or just below a blind edge where he would be invisible to those descending from above.

4 A skier who wishes to climb up a piste must do so at the side.

A skier who causes an injury to another can be sued for damages and this may happen even when the collision occurred through circumstances apparently beyond the skier's control. For instance, a skier who falls on an icy slope and slides into another might be sued. One must therefore make certain that one's insurance does cover one against such third party claims.

Catching Edges

Catching an edge can be the cause of a sudden and sometimes violent fall. It can happen when side-slipping, traversing or turning.

Side-slipping

If one is side-slipping and then, instead of keeping the skis weakly edged, flattens them completely, there is an obvious danger that the lower edge may catch against some unevenness in the snow and throw one downhill.

Beginners do sometimes trip over their lower edge in this way but it is very rare for experienced skiers to catch an edge when side-slipping. But even the most experienced skiers sometimes catch an edge when traversing or turning.

Traversing

If the slope is steep, one's knees will be pressed into it so as to hold the skis firmly on their upper edges; so it is most improbable that anybody would catch an edge on a steep slope. But if the slope is gradual, so that one does not feel there is any tendency to side-slip down, it is easy to forget one should lean one's knees towards the hill with the result that the skis will be flat on the snow. Then if there is some side-slip, and this is very likely if conditions are icy, a lower edge is likely to catch – it is normally the lower edge of the lower ski – with the result that one is thrown down the hill.

This can easily happen on a path, or ski way, running across a hillside when the path is tilted slightly sideways. Especially when conditions are fast and icy, the skier tends to have his skis flat on the snow in the search for greater stability. It is then possible that a lower edge will catch and throw one. The remedy is to make certain that the knees are tilted, even if only slightly, towards the hill, so that both skis are on their upper edges.

Turning

If the turn is sharp or the slope is steep, the knees will certainly be pressed into the turn and they will be held firmly on their inner edges, that is the left if turning to

Skiing on the First above Grindelwald, Switzerland.

the left. But if the turn is gradual and is on the flat, then at some point one may well have one's skis flat on the snow. If at that moment one is skidding outwards, the outer edge of the outer ski on the turn may well catch and throw one in an outward fall. Again this is most likely to happen when conditions are fast and icy. The remedy is to ensure that the knees are tilted inwards throughout the turn, that is to the left if turning to the left.

Skiing Away from the Piste

Powder snow

When skiing in powder snow there is a danger that one's skis may strike some hard object such as a rock that lies hidden beneath the snow. If this does happen one is most likely to fall over the rock into the snow on the far side, which will only be serious if there happens to be a second rock waiting for one there. This is very improbable on pasture land where rocks are comparatively rare. But on higher slopes, that is above about 2500m (8200ft) in the Alps, rocks tend to be far more common and a skier should be correspondingly more careful.

On lower slopes a greater danger than rocks is a line of fence posts. A skier who strikes one fence post with his ski may well be unlucky enough to fall on to one of the other posts in the line. But when these fence posts are just below the surface, there is normally a small snow protruberance above each one. A skier who sees a row of such protruberances should recognise them for what they are.

It is just possible for a powder snow skier to get his ski tips caught under the top bar of a fence. I have once seen this happen; it was without serious result. Such accidents are very rare because most skiers in powder snow have their weight back and their ski tips planing on the surface of the snow.

Blind edges

Lift companies have a responsibility for the safety of skiers on their pistes, and may in some circumstances be sued for negligence by a skier who has an accident. So they put up warning signs near particular dangers and they close runs that have become generally dangerous. But away from the piste there are no warning signs against dangers; the skier must assess them for himself.

A person who is accustomed to skiing away from the piste will never go fast over a blind edge, unless he is on a familiar run and knows what is on the other side. This is as instinctive to him as it is to the townsman that he should look before stepping off the pavement. But the skier whose experience is limited to the piste may – and I have seen this happen – run over a blind edge, fall head first into a gulley on the other side, and then pick himself up with a feeling that hazards like that should not be allowed. And of course on a piste they wouldn't be; any blind edge with a gulley on the other side would be roped off.

Cornices

The wind blowing snow over a mountain edge can form a cornice of hard but brittle crust, which projects out over the lee side. It is easy to step on a cornice without realising till too late that there is no ground beneath the snow, only air.

One should therefore be cautious when approaching the edge of a ridge or summit. In the Alps, where the prevailing wind blows from the south, one should be particularly careful when approaching an edge at the top of a north facing slope.

Accidents

Avalanches are the most serious hazard to the skier away from the piste. Sprained and broken legs are caused not so much by skiing in deep snow as by accidentally running out of the piste into deep snow at the side. Nowadays, when safety bindings normally operate and when snow machines usually beat a wide swathe of piste, such accidents to the leg are getting rarer. On the other hand, today people ski faster, there are more people skiing, and because pistes are beaten so smooth skiers tend to slide further if they fall. As a result there are an increasing number of collisions, either with other skiers or with inanimate objects. In the old days most accidents were to the body below the waist; now they tend to be to the body above the waist. People who ski fast would be well advised to wear crash helmets but as they are uncomfortable and can be appallingly hot, this advice is not likely to be taken.

Collisions can occur away from the piste but they are less likely. If an accident does occur off piste, it may take much longer to get help in transporting the injured skier. This need not be tragic provided that the accident does not occur so late in the day that help cannot reach the injured skier before nightfall and he can be kept warm. Off piste, and sometimes on piste as well, a helicopter may be necessary to transport the injured skier. This is an expensive service and it is important to check that one's insurance does cover transport from the scene of accident.

The solitary off-piste skier who has an accident may be unable to summon help and may die of cold before he is found. This risk is so obvious that many people regard skiing alone off-piste as culpably irresponsible. In fact, the risk involved though real is small; in many other sports people take far greater risks without being accused of foolhardiness.

Skiing in Bad Visibility

Skiing in a mist is much easier and pleasanter if there are dark objects, such as trees, to break up the whiteness of the foreground. Snowfall is often accompanied by bad visibility and, if there is already a layer of powder snow, this is just the time when the skier wants to let himself go. The ideal slope then is one studded with trees. When skiing above the tree line, it is a help if one can follow downhill the line of a chair or drag lift, and occasionally focus on the pylons. In between the pylons the line of the lift cable does greatly help one's sense of direction.

It is very easy to lose a sense of direction on snow slopes that are bare of all distinguishing marks. Around there is nothing except whiteness. As one skis forward, the sense of movement is diminished because there is no sense of passing anything. On stopping there is often an uncanny sensation of continuing movement. One thinks one knows where one is and then, looming out of the mist there is an unfamiliar object. This can happen even on well-known terrain, even on the piste. In theory one should be able to follow the track of the piste, even when it is impossible to see from one direction pole to the next, but in a real white out this is often very difficult to do. Away from the piste it is even more difficult to find the way.

If there are no cliffs around, it is possible simply to ski downhill until a familiar object appears, or a path that one can follow, or in the last resort the valley. But if there are cliffs around, this is dangerous. In a real white out, it is possible to ski unexpectedly over a sheer drop. I know it is possible because I have done it; luckily for me the drop was not a long one and I landed on a smooth slope of hard crust down which I slithered harmlessly.

No skier, unless he is extremely foolish, is likely to start in thick fog down a run over bare slopes where there are cliffs around, or when it is late in the evening. But, especially when the run is from a high altitude, it is possible to start down in clear visibility and then run into a band of cloud at some potentially dangerous section of the descent. Skiers have sometimes got themselves into alarming trouble from doing just that. So, before starting down a run that might prove dangerous in bad visibility, one should make certain that there are no bands of mist at dangerous places on the mountain below one.

Skiing above Oberstdorf, West Germany.

13 Skiing Without Snow

Artificial Slopes

Those who are going to ski for the first time are well advised to take some lessons on an artificial slope before they go on holiday. They will then be able to go on ski runs from the first day instead of being stuck on the practice slope while they master basic techniques. Advanced skiers can also profit from a course of instruction on an artificial slope.

Even if one takes no instruction, these slopes can provide enjoyable skiing. A few of them are long and steep so that it is really stimulating just to ski on them. Indeed some skiers have achieved a very high standard on such slopes before they ever skied on snow. Obviously a long and steep slope can only be laid on a substantial hill. Where the country is flatter, they tend to be short and gradual in gradient. Skiing on them is much more interesting if there is something to test the skier's skill, some focus for his endeavour such as moguls or slalom gates.

The technique for skiing on artificial slopes is basically the same as for skiing on snow; however, the skier must keep his thumbs held over the tops of his poles and not in their usual position round the handles. This minimises the risk of a thumb being caught in the weave of the artificial slope and then being bent backwards, when the skier falls. The great majority of accidents on these slopes are to the thumb. A much less important hazard is that they are rough and can scratch the hands; so it is as well to wear gloves at all times.

Grass Skiing

Grass skis are radically different from snow skis. The binding on a grass ski is mounted on a framework above a caterpillar track. A snow ski slides forward on a slippery surface. A grass ski runs forward on a revolving belt with a series of 'feet', studded plastic attachments, which provide the actual running surface. Grass skis vary in length. They are much shorter than snow skis, the average performer using a ski between 60 and 70cm (24 and 28in) in length. The longer skis are steadier while shorter ones are easier to turn.

Grass skis run forward like snow skis but any sort of side-slipping on them is impossible. They will not skid, which means that no turns that depend on skidding can be done on them. They cannot be turned by braking action as in the snowplough and stem turns, nor by body action as in the uphill parallel christie. But the grass ski has a convex running surface so that it will turn the moment it is edged. It is like a snow ski that is permanently in reverse camber, which is why every turn on a grass ski is carved.

The technique for grass skiing is much simpler than for snow skiing because, unless grass skis are lifted from the ground and stepped round, there is only one way in which they can be turned. If the knees are pressed over to the right, the skis will turn to the right and vice versa. The shorter the skis, the more convex is the running surface and they turn more readily.

The first turn to learn on grass skis is the uphill turn from a traverse into the slope. The skier traverses across the slope and at a certain moment he presses his knees into the hill. His skis will then turn uphill and come to a stop. Just as on snow skis, the skier should master this from an ever steeper traverse till he can eventually do it from a direct descent down the fall line. He is then in a position to learn the downhill turn to connect two traverses. He should first try this where the gradient is gentle and as near to the bottom of the slope as possible so that, if he finds it difficult to complete the turn, he will simply run without harm on to flat ground.

The skier on a traverse presses his knees away from the hill, to the right if he has the hill on his left. He will then start to turn downhill. When the skis are running straight downhill, the beginner often has a feeling that the turn is taking a long time to come round and that his skis are running away with him. As a result he tends to stop pressing his knees over into the turn and to stand straight on his skis, because he then feels more secure; but if he does that, the skis will certainly just run straight down the hill. So he must concentrate throughout on pressing his knees into the turn.

Once the skier has learnt the downhill turn to connect two traverses, he should learn to do a succession of snaking turns down the slope. If he is turning to the right, then, as soon as he starts to come into the new traverse with the hill on his right, he presses his knees over from right to left so that he starts to turn back to the left. When he starts to come into a new traverse with the hill on his left, he presses his knees over to the right so as to repeat the process. In this way he snakes down the hill with his skis never departing far from the fall line.

The snow skier is at a certain disadvantage when he starts to learn grass skiing, because he inevitably tries to skid his grass skis round in the same way as he would his snow skis. When doing his first downhill turn he is particularly apt to feel that the turn is not coming round properly and he automatically tries to rotate his skis by body action; because grass skis will not skid, any attempt to rotate them in this way is likely to end in a fall. It takes the snow skier about two hours to adapt his technique to grass skiing. Once he has done this, and appreciates instinctively as well as rationally that he can only turn his skis by edging them, he will find his snow skiing experience a great help, in particular the way in which he uses his upper body to maintain balance while he is turning.

Because a grass ski will not skid, one cannot use bumps the way one does snow skiing, that is to unweight the skis so they can the more easily be skidded round. Grass skis are not enjoyable on rough or broken ground. They are best on a smooth slope but this tends to lack interest because it does not make sufficient demands on the skier's judgement and ability. So once the grass skier has achieved a certain basic skill, he will almost certainly find that he enjoys grass skiing most when there is a slalom course down which he can practise. For the great majority, advanced grass skiing is essentially slaloming, and

The thrill of slalom racing on grass.

slalom races are the most natural form of grass ski competition.

Water Skiing

Water skiing is much the oldest form of skiing without snow. There have been many inaccurate statements about its origins, so it is worth recording here that the first person known to have done it was Ralph Samuelson in 1922 on Lake Pepin, Minnesota, USA. He is also the first person to have jumped over a ramp on water skis and the first person to have been towed on water skis behind an aeroplane.

Water skiing on two skis is exactly the same as skiing on snow; the first time that a snow skier does it, he is amazed to find that he can manage his skis on water in exactly the same way that he does on snow. But water skiing on a mono ski, that is a single ski with two bindings set one behind the other, demands a quite different technique to snow skiing. Most water skiers graduate quickly from two skis to a mono, because owing to the resilience of the water it is possible to turn far more sharply and gracefully on a mono ski than on two skis.

The only competitive form of water skiing that is done on two skis is jumping, and it is therefore the one that comes easiest to snow skiers.

Roller Skiing

Cross-country skiing can be practised on roller skis, which are short skis on wheels. They are used with the same bindings, footwear and poles as for cross-country skiing on snow.

Roller skis need a reasonably smooth surface, but are excellent for cross-country skiing along roads, preferably country roads. They are easy to use, even for somebody who has never done any cross-country skiing on snow. Provided one does not aim for speed at first, one can quickly acquire a good rhythmic motion which is very satisfying. Because one is using, not only the legs, but also the arms and poles to push one along, it is excellent all round exercise as well as pleasurable.

There is a ratchet on roller skis to prevent them slipping backwards when going uphill, but, because they cannot be turned except by stepping them round, there is no way of slowing speed when the road goes downhill; they are then dangerous unless there is space to slow down before one might hit anything.

Appendices

Winter Olympic Games and World Championships

World Championship titles are awarded on Olympic events except for the Alpine events in 1936, when there were Alpine World Championships as well as the Winter Olympic Games.

Olympic medals for the Alpine combination have been awarded only in 1936, when no medals were awarded for the downhill and slalom events, and in 1948. In other years there have been no Olympic medals for the Alpine combined, but World Championship titles have been awarded.

1931–48 the Alpine combined was awarded on the downhill and the slalom. 1950–52 no Alpine combined was awarded. 1952–80 it was awarded on the downhill, the giant slalom and the slalom. 1982 the Alpine combined was awarded on a downhill and a slalom, which were specially organised for the combined and were in addition to the downhill and the slalom organised for World Championship titles in these disciplines.

In 1931 the weather forced the postponement of the men's slalom till after the date advertised as the end of the meeting; it was therefore unofficial, did not count as a World Championship and no Alpine combined was awarded.

The Nordic combination has always been awarded on a cross-country race (now over 15km, previously over 18km) and a jumping competition (on the smaller hill when two available).

Olympic events are shown in bold type. 1956–68 competitors from East and West Germany competed together in a single German team.

1940–47 there were no World Championships or Olympic events.

Results

OLYMPIC AND WORLD CHAMPIONSHIPS – NORDIC EVENTS

MEN

18km CROSS-COUNTRY	15km CROSS-COUNTRY	30km CROSS-COUNTRY	50km CROSS-COUNTRY
1924 T. Haug (NOR)			**1924 T. Haug (NOR)**
1925 O. Nemecky (TCH)			1925 F. Donth (TCH)
1926 J. Grøttumsbraaten (NOR)		1926 M. Raivio (FIN)	1926 M. Raivio (FIN)
1927 J. Lindgren (SWE)		1927–52 Not held	1927 J. Lindgren (SWE)
1928 J. Grøttumsbraaten (NOR)			**1928 P. Hedlund (SWE)**
1929 V. Saarinen (FIN)			1929 A. Knuttila (FIN)
1930 A. Rudstadstuen (NOR)			1930 S. Utterström (SWE)
1931 J. Grøttumsbraaten (NOR)			1931 O. Stenen (NOR)
1932 S. Utterström (SWE)			**1932 V. Saarinen (FIN)**
1933 N. Englund (SWE)			1933 V. Saarinen (FIN)
1934 S. Nurmela (FIN)			1934 E. Wiklund (SWE)
1935 K. Karppinen (FIN)			1935 N. Englund (SWE)
1936 E. Larsson (SWE)			**1936 E. Wiklund (SWE)**
1937 L. Bergendahl (NOR)			1937 P. Niemi (FIN)
1938 P. Pitkänen (FIN)			1938 K. Jalkanen (FIN)
1939 J. Kurikkala (FIN)			1939 L. Bergendahl (NOR)´
1948 M. Lundström (SWE)			**1948 N. Karlsson (SWE)**
1950 K. Åström (SWE)			1950 G. Eriksson (SWE)
1952 H. Brenden (NOR)			**1952 V. Hakulinen (FIN)**
	1954 V. Hakulinen (FIN)	1954 V. Kusin (SOV)	1954 V. Kusin (SOV)
	1956 H. Brenden (NOR)	**1956 V. Hakulinen (FIN)**	**1956 S. Jernberg (SWE)**
	1958 V. Hakulinen (FIN)	1958 K. Hämäläinen (FIN)	1958 S. Jernberg (SWE)
	1960 H. Brusveen (NOR)	**1960 S. Jernberg (SWE)**	**1960 K. Hämäläinen (FIN)**
	1962 A. Rönnlund (SWE)	1962 E. Mäntyranta (FIN)	1962 S. Jernberg (SWE)
	1964 E. Mäntyranta (FIN)	**1964 E. Mäntyranta (FIN)**	**1964 S. Jernberg (SWE)**
	1966 G. Eggen (NOR)	1966 E. Mäntyranta (FIN)	1966 G. Eggen (NOR)
	1968 H. Grönningen (NOR)	**1968 F. Nones (ITA)**	**1968 O. Ellefsaeter (NOR)**
	1970 L. Aslund (SWE)	1970 V. Vedenin (SOV)	1970 K. Oikarainen (FIN)
	1972 S. Lundbäck (SWE)	**1972 V. Vedenin (SOV)**	**1972 P. Tyldum (NOR)**
	1974 M. Myrmo (NOR)	1974 T. Magnuson (SWE)	1974 G. Grimmer (DDR)
	1976 N. Bazhukov (SOV)	**1976 S. Saveliev (SOV)**	**1976 I. Formo (NOR)**
	1978 J. Luszczek (POL)	1978 S. Saveliev (SOV)	1978 S. Lundbäck (SWE)
	1980 T. Wassberg (SWE)	**1980 N. Zimyatov (SOV)**	**1980 N. Zimyatov (SOV)**
	1982 O. Brå (NOR)	1982 T. Eriksson (SWE)	1982 T. Wassberg (SWE)

| NORDIC COMBINED | 4 × 10km RELAY | JUMPING (1924–60 held on one hill) |

1924 **T. Haug (NOR)**		1924 **J. Tullin-Thams (NOR)**
1925 O. Nemecky (TCH)		1925 W. Dick (TCH)
1926 J. Grøttumsbraaten (NOR)		1926 J. Tullin-Thams (NOR)
1927 R. Purkert (TCH)		1927 T. Edman (SWE)
1928 **J. Grøttumsbraaten (NOR)**		1928 **A. Andersen (NOR)**
1929 H. Vinjarengen (NOR)		1929 S. Ruud (NOR)
1930 H. Vinjarengen (NOR)		1930 G. Andersen (NOR)
1931 J. Grøttumsbraaten (NOR)		1931 B. Ruud (NOR)
1932 **J. Grøttumsbraaten (NOR)**		1932 **B. Ruud (NOR)**
1933 S. Eriksson (SWE)	1933 Sweden	1933 M. Reymond (SUI)
1934 O. Hagen (NOR)	1934 Finland	1934 K. Johansson (NOR)
1935 O. Hagen (NOR)	1935 Finland	1935 B. Ruud (NOR)
1936 **O. Hagen (NOR)**	1936 **Finland**	1936 **B. Ruud (NOR)**
1937 S. Roen (NOR)	1937 Norway	1937 B. Ruud (NOR)
1938 O. Hoffsbakken (NOR)	1938 Finland	1938 A. Ruud (NOR)
1939 G. Berauer (GER)	1939 Finland	1939 J. Bradl (GER)

1948 **H. Hasu (FIN)**	1948 **Sweden**	1948 **P. Hugsted (NOR)**
1950 H. Hasu (FIN)	1950 Sweden	1950 H. Bjørnstad (NOR)
1952 **S. Slåttvik (NOR)**	1952 **Finland**	1952 **A. Bergmann (NOR)**
1954 S. Stenersen (NOR)	1954 Finland	1954 M. Pietikäinen (FIN)
1956 **S. Stenersen (NOR)**	1956 **Soviet Union**	1956 **A. Hyvärinen (FIN)**
1958 P. Korhonen (FIN)	1958 Sweden	1958 J. Kärkinen (FIN)
1960 **G. Thoma (GER)**	1960 **Finland**	1960 **H. Recknagel (GER)**
1962 A. Larsen (NOR)	1962 Sweden	
1964 **T. Knutsen (NOR)**	1964 **Sweden**	
1966 G. Thoma (BRD)	1966 Norway	
1968 **F. Keller (GER)**	1968 **Norway**	

		JUMPING ON 70m HILL	JUMPING ON 90m HILL
1970 L. Rygl (TCH)	1970 Soviet Union		
1972 **U. Wehling (DDR)**	1972 **Soviet Union**		
1974 U. Wehling (DDR)	1974 East Germany	1962 T. Engan (NOR)	1962 H. Recknagel (DDR)
1976 **U. Wehling (DDR)**	1976 **Finland**	1964 **V. Kankkonen (FIN)**	1964 **T. Engan (NOR)**
1978 K. Sinkler (DDR)	1978 Sweden	1966 B. Wirkola (NOR)	1966 B. Wirkola (NOR)
1980 **U. Wehling (DDR)**	1980 **Soviet Union**	1968 **J. Raska (TCH)**	1968 **V. Belussov (SOV)**
1982 T. Sandberg (NOR)	1982 { Norway, Soviet Union	1970 G. Napalkov (SOV)	1970 G. Napalkov (SOV)
		1972 **Y. Kasaya (JAP)**	1972 **W. Fortuna (POL)**
		1974 H. Aschenbach (DDR)	1974 H. Aschenbach (DDR)
		1976 **H. Aschenbach (DDR)**	1976 **K. Schnabl (AUT)**
		1978 M. Buse (DDR)	1978 T. Räisänen (FIN)
		1980 **A. Innauer (AUT)**	1980 **J. Törmänen (FIN)**
		1982 A. Kogler (AUT)	1982 M. Nykänen (FIN)

OLYMPIC AND WORLD CHAMPIONSHIPS – NORDIC EVENTS
WOMEN

5km CROSS-COUNTRY	10km CROSS-COUNTRY	20km CROSS-COUNTRY	3 × 5km RELAY	4 × 5km RELAY
	1952 **L. Wideman (FIN)**			
	1954 L. Kozyreva (SOV)		1954 Soviet Union	
	1956 **L. Kozyreva (SOV)**		1956 **Finland**	
	1958 A. Kolchina (SOV)		1958 Soviet Union	
	1960 **M. Gusakova (SOV)**		1960 **Sweden**	
1962 A. Kolchina (SOV)	1962 A. Kolchina (SOV)		1962 Soviet Union	
1964 **K. Boyarskikh (SOV)**	1964 **K. Boyarskikh (SOV)**		1964 **Soviet Union**	
1966 A. Kolchina (SOV)	1966 K. Boyarskikh (SOV)		1966 Soviet Union	
1968 **T. Gustafsson (SWE)**	1968 **T. Gustafsson (SWE)**		1968 **Norway**	
1970 G. Kulakova (SOV)	1970 A. Olunina (SOV)		1970 Soviet Union	
1972 **G. Kulakova (SOV)**	1972 **G. Kulakova (SOV)**		1972 **Soviet Union**	
1974 G. Kulakova (SOV)	1974 G. Kulakova (SOV)			1974 Soviet Union
1976 **H. Takalo (FIN)**	1976 **R. Smetanina (SOV)**			1976 **Soviet Union**
1978 H. Takalo (FIN)	1978 Z. Amosova (SOV)	1978 Z. Amosova (SOV)		1978 Finland
1980 **R. Smetanina (SOV)**	1980 **B. Petzold (DDR)**	1980 V. Hesse (DDR)		1980 **East Germany**
1982 B. Aunli (NOR)	1982 B. Aunli (NOR)	1982 R. Smetanina (SOV)		1982 Norway

OLYMPIC AND WORLD CHAMPIONSHIPS – ALPINE EVENTS
MEN

DOWNHILL	GIANT SLALOM	SLALOM	ALPINE COMBINED
1931 W. Prager (SUI)		1931 D. Zogg (SUI)	
1932 G. Lantschner (AUT)		1932 F. Däuber (GER)	1932 O. Furrer (SUI)
1933 W. Prager (SUI)		1933 A. Seelos (AUT)	1933 A. Seelos (AUT)
1934 D. Zogg (SUI)		1934 F. Pfnür (GER)	1934 D. Zogg (SUI)
1935 F. Zingerle (AUT)		1935 A. Seelos (AUT)	1935 A. Seelos (AUT)
1936 R. Rominger (SUI)		1936 R. Matt (AUT)	1936 R. Rominger (AUT)
1936 **B. Ruud (NOR)**		1936 **F. Pfnür (GER)**	1936 **F. Pfnür (GER)**
1937 E. Allais (FRA)		1937 E. Allais (FRA)	1937 E. Allais (FRA)
1938 J. Couttet (FRA)		1938 R. Rominger (SUI)	1938 E. Allais (FRA)
1939 H. Lantschner (GER)		1939 R. Rominger (SUI)	1939 J. Jennewein (GER)
1948 **H. Oreiller (FRA)**		1948 **E. Reinalter (SUI)**	1948 **H. Oreiller (FRA)**
1950 Z. Colo (ITA)	1950 Z. Colo (ITA)	1950 G. Schneider (SUI)	1950–52 Not held
1952 **Z. Colo (ITA)**	1952 **S. Eriksen (NOR)**	1952 **O. Schneider (AUT)**	
1954 C. Pravda (AUT)	1954 S. Eriksen (NOR)	1954 S. Eriksen (NOR)	1954 S. Eriksen (NOR)
1956 **A. Sailer (AUT)**	1956 **A. Sailer (AUT)**	1956 **A. Sailer (AUT)**	1956 A. Sailer (AUT)
1958 A. Sailer (AUT)	1958 A. Sailer (AUT)	1958 J. Rieder (AUT)	1958 A. Sailer (AUT)
1960 **J. Vuarnet (FRA)**	1960 **R. Staub (SUI)**	1960 **E. Hinterseer (AUT)**	1960 G. Périllat (FRA)
1962 K. Schranz (AUT)	1962 E. Zimmermann (AUT)	1962 C. Bozon (FRA)	1962 K. Schranz (AUT)
1964 **E. Zimmermann (AUT)**	1964 **F. Bonlieu (FRA)**	1964 **J. Stiegler (AUT)**	1964 L. Leitner (GER)
1966 J. Killy (FRA)	1966 G. Périllat (FRA)	1966 G. Senoner (ITA)	1966 J. Killy (FRA)
1968 **J. Killy (FRA)**	1968 **J. Killy (FRA)**	1968 **J. Killy (FRA)**	1968 J. Killy (FRA)
1970 B. Russi (SUI)	1970 K. Schranz (AUT)	1970 J. Augert (FRA)	1970 W. Kidd (USA)
1972 **B. Russi (SUI)**	1972 **G. Thoeni (ITA)**	1972 **F. Ochoa (SPA)**	1972 G. Thoeni (ITA)
1974 S. Zwilling (AUT)	1974 G. Thoeni (ITA)	1974 G. Thoeni (ITA)	1974 F. Klammer (AUT)
1976 **F. Klammer (AUT)**	1976 **H. Hemmi (SUI)**	1976 **P. Gros (ITA)**	1976 G. Thoeni (ITA)
1978 J. Walcher (AUT)	1978 I. Stenmark (SWE)	1978 I. Stenmark (SWE)	1978 A. Wenzel (LIE)
1980 **L. Stock (AUT)**	1980 **I. Stenmark (SWE)**	1980 **I. Stenmark (SWE)**	1980 P. Mahre (USA)
1982 H. Weirather (AUT)	1982 S. Mahre (USA)	1982 I. Stenmark (SWE)	1982 M. Vion (FRA)

BEST ALLROUND PERFORMANCES

Downhill, Slalom, Jumping, Cross-Country

In the 1933 World Championships Ernst Feuz (SUI) was fifth in the Nordic combination (jumping and cross-country) and eighth in the Alpine combination (downhill and slalom).

Downhill, Slalom, Jumping

In the 1936 Olympic Games Birger Ruud (NOR) was first in the downhill, sixth in the slalom, (fourth on the combined result) and first in the jumping. He did not compete in the cross-country. He only won one gold medal, that for the jumping. In 1936 medals were not awarded for the downhill and slalom races but only for the Alpine combination.

SKI FLYING WORLD CHAMPIONSHIPS

Ski flying is jumping on hills that allow distances much longer than those possible on the 70m and 90m hills which are used for the Olympic Games and for World Championships in ordinary jumping.

1972 W. Steiner (SUI)
1973 H. Aschenbach (DDR)
1975 K. Kodejska (TCH)
1977 W. Steiner (SUI)
1979 A. Kogler (AUT)
1981 J. Puikkonen (FIN)
1983 K. Ostwald (DDR)

OLYMPIC AND WORLD CHAMPIONSHIPS – ALPINE EVENTS
WOMEN

DOWNHILL	GIANT SLALOM	SLALOM	ALPINE COMBINED
1931 E. Mackinnon (GBR)		1931 E. Mackinnon (GBR)	1931 E. Mackinnon (GBR)
1932 P. Wiesinger (ITA)		1932 R. Streiff (SUI)	1932 R. Streiff (SUI)
1933 I. Lantschner (AUT)		1933 I. Lantschner (AUT)	1933 I. Lantschner (AUT)
1934 A. Ruegg (SUI)		1934 C. Cranz (GER)	1934 C. Cranz (GER)
1935 C. Cranz (GER)		1935 A. Rüegg (SUI)	1935 C. Cranz (GER)
1936 E. Pinching (GBR)		1936 G. Paumgarten (AUT)	1936 E. Pinching (GBR)
1936 L. Schou-Nilsen (NOR)		**1936 C. Cranz (GER)**	**1936 C. Cranz (GER)**
1937 C. Cranz (GER)		1937 C. Cranz (GER)	1937 C. Cranz (GER)
1938 L. Resch (GER)		1938 C. Cranz (GER)	1938 C. Cranz (GER)
1939 C. Cranz (GER)		1939 C. Cranz (GER)	1939 C. Cranz (GER)
1948 H. Schlunegger (SUI)		**1948 G. Frazer (USA)**	**1948 T. Beiser-Jochum (AUT)**
1950 T. Beiser-Jochum (AUT)	1950 D. Rom (AUT)	1950 D. Rom (AUT)	1950–52 Not held
1952 T. Beiser-Jochum (AUT)	**1952 A. Mead-Lawrence (USA)**	**1952 A. Mead-Lawrence (USA)**	
1954 I. Schöpfer (SUI)	1954 L. Schmith (FRA)	1954 T. Klecker (AUT)	1954 I. Schöpfer (SUI)
1956 M. Berthod (SUI)	**1956 O. Reichert (GER)**	**1956 R. Colliard (SUI)**	1956 M. Berthod (SUI)
1958 L. Wheeler (CAN)	1958 L. Wheeler (CAN)	1958 J. Björnbakken (NOR)	1958 F. Dänzer (SUI)
1960 H. Biebl (GER)	**1960 Y. Rüegg (SUI)**	**1960 A. Heggtveit (CAN)**	1960 A. Heggtveit (CAN)
1962 C. Haas (AUT)	1962 M. Jahn (AUT)	1962 M. Jahn (AUT)	1962 M. Goitschel (FRA)
1964 C. Haas (AUT)	**1964 M. Goitschel (FRA)**	**1964 C. Goitschel (FRA)**	1964 M. Goitschel (FRA)
1966 E. Schinegger (AUT)	1966 M. Goitschel (FRA)	1966 A. Famose (FRA)	1966 M. Goitschel (FRA)
1968 O. Pall (AUT)	**1968 N. Greene (CAN)**	**1968 M. Goitschel (FRA)**	1968 N. Greene (CAN)
1970 A. Zyrd (SUI)	1970 B. Clifford (CAN)	1970 I. Lafforgue (FRA)	1970 M. Jacot (CAN)
1972 M. Nadig (SUI)	**1972 M. Nadig (SUI)**	**1972 B. Cochran (USA)**	1972 A. Moser-Pröll (AUT)
1974 A. Moser-Pröll (AUT)	1974 F. Serrat (FRA)	1974 H. Wenzel (LIE)	1974 F. Serrat (FRA)
1976 R. Mittermaier (BRD)	**1976 K. Kreiner (CAN)**	**1976 R. Mittermaier (BRD)**	1976 R. Mittermaier (GER)
1978 A. Moser-Pröll (AUT)	1978 M. Epple (BRD)	1978 L. Sölkner (AUT)	1978 A. Moser-Pröll (AUT)
1980 A. Moser-Pröll (AUT)	**1980 H. Wenzel (LIE)**	**1980 H. Wenzel (LIE)**	1980 H. Wenzel (LIE)
1982 G. Sorensen (CAN)	1982 E. Hess (SUI)	1982 E. Hess (SUI)	1982 E. Hess (SUI)

WORLD CUP – ALPINE
MEN

OVERALL	DOWNHILL	GIANT SLALOM	SLALOM
1967 J. Killy (FRA)	1967 J. Killy (FRA)	1967 J. Killy (FRA)	1967 J. Killy (FRA)
1968 J. Killy (FRA)	1968 G. Nenning (AUT)	1968 J. Killy (FRA)	1968 D. Giovanoli (SUI)
1969 K. Schranz (AUT)	1969 K. Schranz (AUT)	1969 K. Schranz (AUT)	1969 J. Augert (FRA) / A. Matt (AUT) / A. Penz (FRA) / P. Russel (FRA)
1970 K. Schranz (AUT)	1970 K. Schranz (AUT)	1970 G. Thoeni (ITA)	1970 A. Penz (FRA) / P. Russel (FRA)
1971 G. Thoeni (ITA)	1971 B. Russi (SUI)	1971 P. Russel (FRA)	1971 J. Augert (FRA)
1972 G. Thoeni (ITA)	1972 B. Russi (SUI)	1972 G. Thoeni (ITA)	1972 J. Augert (FRA)
1973 G. Thoeni (ITA)	1973 R. Collombin (SUI)	1973 H. Hinterseer (AUT)	1973 G. Thoeni (ITA)
1974 P. Gros (ITA)	1974 R. Collombin (SUI)	1974 P. Gros (ITA)	1974 G. Thoeni (ITA)
1975 G. Thoeni (ITA)	1975 F. Klammer (AUT)	1975 I. Stenmark (SWE)	1975 I. Stenmark (SWE)
1976 I. Stenmark (SWE)	1976 F. Klammer (AUT)	1976 I. Stenmark (SWE)	1976 I. Stenmark (SWE)
1977 I. Stenmark (SWE)	1977 F. Klammer (AUT)	1977 H. Hemmi (SUI)	1977 I. Stenmark (SWE)
1978 I. Stenmark (SWE)	1978 F. Klammer (AUT)	1978 I. Stenmark (SWE)	1978 I. Stenmark (SWE)
1979 P. Lüscher (SUI)	1979 P. Müller (SUI)	1979 I. Stenmark (SWE)	1979 I. Stenmark (SWE)
1980 A. Wenzel (LIE)	1980 P. Müller (SUI)	1980 I. Stenmark (SWE)	1980 I. Stenmark (SWE)
1981 P. Mahre (USA)	1981 H. Weirather (AUT)	1981 I. Stenmark (SWE)	1981 I. Stenmark (SWE)
1982 P. Mahre (USA)	1982 S. Podborski (CAN)	1982 P. Mahre (USA)	1982 P. Mahre (USA)
1983 P. Mahre (USA)	1983 F. Klammer (AUT)	1983 P. Mahre (USA)	1983 I. Stenmark (SWE)

WORLD CUP – NORDIC

MEN	WOMEN
CROSS-COUNTRY	*CROSS-COUNTRY*
1979 O. Brå (NOR)	1979 G. Kulakova (SOV)
1980 Not held	1980 Not held
1981 A. Zavialov (SOV)	1981 R. Smetanina (SOV)
1982 B. Koch (USA)	1982 B. Aunli (NOR)
1983 A. Zavialov (SOV)	1983 M. Hamalainen (FIN)

The World Cup for cross-country was made official in 1982.

JUMPING	
1980 H. Neupert (AUT)	The World Cup for jumping was official from the start. There is no women's event.
1981 A. Kogler (AUT)	
1982 A. Kogler (AUT)	
1983 M. Nykaenen (FIN)	

GRASS SKIING
WORLD CHAMPIONSHIPS

MEN	WOMEN
GIANT SLALOM	*GIANT SLALOM*
1979 V. Riewe (BRD)	1979 B. Single (BRD)
1981 E. Gansner (SUI)	1981 I. Hirschhofer (AUT)
SLALOM	*SLALOM*
1979 V. Riewe (BRD)	1979 I. Hirschhofer (AUT)
1981 R. Christen (SUI)	1981 C. Petitjean (FRA)
COMBINED	*COMBINED*
1979 V. Riewe (BRD)	1979 I. Hirschhofer (AUT)
1981 E. Gansner (SUI)	1981 C. Petitjean (FRA)

The first grass skis were produced in 1963 by a German knitting machine manufacturer, Kurt Kaiser.

WORLD CUP – ALPINE
WOMEN

OVERALL	DOWNHILL	GIANT SLALOM	SLALOM
1967 N. Greene (CAN)	1967 M. Goitschel (FRA)	1967 N. Greene (CAN)	1967 A. Famose (FRA) ⎫ M. Goitschel (FRA) ⎭
1968 N. Greene (CAN)	1968 I. Mir (FRA) ⎫ O. Pall (AUT) ⎭	1968 N. Greene (CAN)	1968 M. Goitschel (FRA)
1969 G. Gabl (AUT)	1969 W. Drexel (AUT)	1969 B. Cochran (USA)	1969 G. Gabl (AUT)
1970 M. Jacot (FRA)	1970 I. Mir (FRA)	1970 M. Jacot (FRA) ⎫ F. Macchi (FRA) ⎭	1970 I. Lafforgue (FRA)
1971 A. Moser-Pröll (AUT)	1971 A. Moser-Pröll (AUT)	1971 A. Moser-Pröll (AUT)	1971 B. Clifford (CAN) ⎫ B. Lafforgue (FRA) ⎭
1972 A. Moser-Pröll (AUT)	1972 A. Moser-Pröll (AUT)	1972 A. Moser-Pröll (AUT)	1972 B. Lafforgue (FRA)
1973 A. Moser-Pröll (AUT)	1973 A. Moser-Pröll (AUT)	1973 M. Kaserer (AUT)	1973 P. Emonet (FRA)
1974 A. Moser-Pröll (AUT)	1974 A. Moser-Pröll (AUT)	1974 H. Wenzel (LIE)	1974 C. Zechmeister (BRD)
1975 A. Moser-Pröll (AUT)	1975 A. Moser-Pröll (AUT)	1975 A. Moser-Pröll (AUT)	1975 L. Morerod (SUI)
1976 R. Mittermaier (BRD)	1976 B. Habersatter-Totschnig (AUT)	1976 L. Morerod (SUI)	1976 R. Mittermaier (BRD)
1977 L. Morerod (SUI)	1977 B. Habersatter-Totschnig (AUT)	1977 L. Morerod (SUI)	1977 L. Morerod (SUI)
1978 H. Wenzel (LIE)	1978 A. Moser-Pröll (AUT)	1978 L. Morerod (SUI)	1978 H. Wenzel (LIE)
1979 A. Moser-Pröll (AUT)	1979 A. Moser-Pröll (AUT)	1979 C. Kinshofer (BRD)	1979 R. Sackl (AUT)
1980 H. Wenzel (LIE)	1980 M. Nadig (SUI)	1980 H. Wenzel (LIE)	1980 P. Pelen (FRA)
1981 M. Nadig (SUI)	1981 M. Nadig (SUI)	1981 T. McKinney (USA)	1981 E. Hess (SUI)
1982 E. Hess (SUI)	1982 M. Gros-Gaudenier (FRA)	1982 I. Epple (BRD)	1982 E. Hess (SUI)
1983 T. McKinney (USA)	1983 D. de Agostini (SUI)	1983 T. McKinney (USA)	1983 E. Hess (SUI)

WORLD RECORDS
SPEED

MEN	WOMEN
SNOW Franz Weber (AUT) 203.16kmh (126.24mph) Silverton, Colorado, USA 25 April 1982.	*SNOW* Marti Kuntz (USA) 190.375kmh (118.29mph) Les Arcs, France 25 March 1983
WATER Grant Torrens (AUS) 219.44kmh (136.36mph) Windsor, New South Wales, Australia 7 March 1982.	*WATER* Donna Brice (USA) 178.81kmh (111.11mph) Long Beach, California, USA 21 August 1977.
GRASS Erwin Gansner (SUI) 86.88kmh (53.99mph) Owen, West Germany 5 September 1982.	

WORLD RECORDS
JUMPING

MEN	WOMEN
SNOW Pavel Ploc (TCH) 181m (593ft 10in) Harrachov, Czechoslovakia 19 March 1983	*SNOW* Anita Wold (NOR) 98m (321ft 6in) Sapporo, Japan 14 January 1975.
WATER Michael Hazelwood (GBR) 60.20m (196ft 10in) Kirtons Farm, Reading, England 2 August 1981.	*WATER* Kathy Hulme (GBR) 45.30m (148ft 6in) Kirtons Farm, Reading, England 1 August 1982.

Glossary

This glossary covers only general skiing words, used in the historical chapters. For an explanation of technical terms, such as the names of the various skiing turns, please consult the index, where the page on which the explanation occurs is depicted in bold type. Words in italics indicate a cross-reference to another entry in the glossary.

Aerials: *Freestyle* manoeuvres, such as somersaults and twists, performed in mid air in the course of a jump.

Alpine combination: A competition based on performance in a *downhill race* and a *slalom*; or a *downhill race*, a *giant slalom* and a *slalom*.

Ballet: Performance on a smooth slope of various *freestyle* manoeuvres, such as turning on one ski with the other held in the air.

Combined event: e.g. combined *slalom* or jumping competition: An event on which no championship titles are awarded but which counts towards the combined Alpine or Nordic title.

Cross-country race: Race for a considerable distance over undulating terrain.

Cross-country skiing: Skiing along the level and uphill as well as downhill.

Downhill race: An Alpine skiing timed speed contest in which the controls are set further apart than in a *giant slalom*. It is the fastest of all the ski races.

Egg (or tuck) position: Crouch adopted by the skier to reduce wind resistance, when skiing downhill.

Fall line: The steepest, shortest and fastest route down a slope, i.e. the line which most closely approximates to the gravitational pull.

Flying kilometre: A *downhill* speed contest, designed so that competitors achieve maximum speed. The speed is measured as the competitor passes through a short 'time-trap'.

Free-style: Acrobatic and trick skiing, which incorporates *aerials*, *ballet* and *moguls*, the three free style events.

Giant slalom: An Alpine race over a longer course than a *slalom* and with the gates set further apart, but not as far apart as in a *downhill* race.

Intermediate time: Time of competitor at an intermediate point on the course; it is of interest to those following the event but has no effect on the result.

Langlauf: German word for *cross-country skiing*.

Loipe: Track followed by a cross-country skier.

Moguls: Bumps caused by a succession of skiers turning repeatedly on the same spot. A heavily mogulled or bump slope, looks as though it is covered by a series of bee hives all set close together. Moguls is also the name for a *free-style* event, which consists in skiing fast and accurately with some jumps, down a mogul slope.

Nordic combination: A competition based on performance in a *cross-country race* and a jumping competition.

Off-piste: Away from the *piste* or *trail*, that is natural snow as opposed to beaten snow.

Piste (or trail): Downhill run on which the snow has been artificially flattened.

Pole (or stick): For most forms of skiing other than jumping a skier carries a pole in either hand.

Safety binding: Binding designed to release the boot from the ski in the event of a dangerous fall.

Schuss: A straight run down a slope. A skier schusses when he follows such a line. It is pronounced like puss in pussycat.

Slalom: A speed race down a course defined by gates (pairs of poles) set close together.

Special event: e.g. special slalom or jumping competition; an event on which championship titles are awarded but which does not count towards the combined Alpine or Nordic title.

Stick: See *pole*.

Stick-riding: Putting the two *poles* (sticks) together, and either sitting on them, or leaning back against them, so as to use them as a brake.

Trail: See *piste*.

Traverse: To ski across the slope at an angle to the *fall* line.

Tuck position: See *egg* position.

Wax: Substance applied to surface of skis in order to improve their performance.

Bibliography

Allais, Emile *Méthode Française de Ski, Technique Emile Allais* Flèche, Paris 1947.

Austrian Association of Professional Ski Teachers *Oesterreichischer Schi-Lehrplan* Otto Müller Verlag, Salzburg 1957.

W. A. Bentley and W. J. Humphreys *Snow Crystals* Dover Publications Inc., New York 1962.

Caulfield, Vivian *How to Ski* James Nisbet Ltd., London 1911.

Dreyfus, Paul *Sylvain Saudan, skieur de l'impossible*. B. Arthaud, France 1970.

Evans, Harold; Jackman, Brian; and Ottaway, Mark *We Learned to Ski* Collins, London 1974.

Fanck, Arnold; and Schneider, Hannes *Wunder des Schneeschuhs* Gebrüder Enoch Verlag, Hamburg 1925. (English translation *The Wonders of Skiing* Allen & Unwin, London 1933.)

Fraser, Colin *Avalanches and Snow Safety* John Murray, London 1978.

Fraser, Colin *The Avalanche Enigma* John Murray, London 1966.

Furrer, Art; and Renggli, Sepp *Skiakrobatik für jedermann* Benteli Verlag, Bern 1970.

Gamma, Karl *The Handbook of Skiing* Pelham Books, London 1981.

Huntford, Roland *Scott and Amundsen* Hodder and Stoughton, London 1979.

Lundqvist, Magnus *Finds of Skis from Prehistoric Times in Swedish Bogs and Marshes* Generalstabens Litografiska Anstalts Förlag, Stockholm 1950.

Lunn, Arnold *A History of Skiing* Oxford University Press, London 1927.

Lunn, Arnold *Alpine Skiing at all Heights and Seasons* Methuen, London 1921.

Lunn, Arnold *Skiing* Eveleigh Nash, London 1913.

Lunn, Arnold *The Story of Skiing* Eyre and Spottiswoode, London 1952.

Luther, Carl *Geschichte des Eis- und Schneesports*, contribution to *Der Sport aller Völker und Zeiten*, Leipzig 1926.

Mehl, Erwin *Grundriss der Weltgeschichte des Schifahrens* Karl Hofmann, Schorndorf bei Stuttgart 1964.

Mehl, Erwin ed. *Zdarsky* Deutscher Verlag für Jugend und Sport, Vienna 1936.

Miura, Yuichiro with Perlman, Eric *The Man who skied down Everest* Harper and Row Inc., New York 1978.

Nansen, Fridtjof *Paa Ski Over Grönland* Christiania (Oslo) 1890. (English translation *The First Crossing of Greenland* Longmans Green Ltd., London 1890.)

Palmedo, Roland ed. *Skiing: the International Sport* Derrydale Press Inc., New York 1937.

Polednik, Heinz *Welt Wunder Ski Sport* Verlag Welsermühl, Wels 1969.

Raudonikas, W. J. *Les gravures rupestres des bords du lac Onega et de la Mer Blanche*. (2 Vols.) Moscow 1936 and 1938.

Reuel, Fritz *Neue Möglichkeiten im Skilauf* Dieck, Stuttgart 1926.

Ritchie, David *Ski the Canadian Way* Prentice Hall Ltd., Ontario 1979.

Schild, Melchior *Lawinen* Lehrmittelverlag des Kantons, Zürich 1972.

Seligman, Gerald *Snow Structure and Ski Fields* Macmillan, London 1936.

Tweedie, Mrs Alec *The Sport of Skilöbning* contribution to *Ice Sports*. Isthmian Library, London 1901.

Valvasor, Johann *Die Ehre des Herzogtums Krain* Laibach (Llubljana) 1689.

Wechsberg, Josef *Avalanche* Weidenfeld and Nicolson Ltd., London 1958.

Zdarsky, Mathias *Alpine (Lilienfelder) Skifahr-Technik* Hamburg 1908. Originally published as *Lilienfelder Skilauftechnik* Hamburg 1897.

Index

Few skiers realise the great beauty and vast variety of
dendrites photographed by Wilson Bentley.